THE GREAT AMERICAN TAX DODGE

THE GREAT AMERICAN TAX DODGE

How Spiraling Fraud and Avoidance Are Killing Fairness, Destroying the Income Tax, and Costing You

BY DONALD L. BARLETT
AND JAMES B. STEELE

Little, Brown and Company
Boston   New York   London

FIRST EDITION

Library of Congress Cataloging-in-Publication Data

Barlett, Donald L.

The great American tax dodge : how spiraling fraud and avoidance are killing fairness, destroying the income tax, and costing you / by Donald L. Barlett and James B. Steele.

p. cm.

Includes bibliographical references and index.

ISBN 0-316-81135-1

1. Income tax — United States. 2. Tax evasion — United States. I. Steele, James B. II. Title.

HJ4652.B27 2000

336.24'16'0973 — dc21

00-036536

10 9 8 7 6 5 4 3 2 1

Q-FF

Designed by Interrobang Design Studio

Printed in the United States of America

For Eileen Reynolds and Nancy Steele,
whose contributions and support were so critical

CONTENTS

ACKNOWLEDGMENTS

---

*I*n the thirty years that we have worked together, we have developed an ever-widening circle of sources who are invaluable to us in a project such as this — university professors, lawyers, government workers, foundation staffers, and others knowledgeable in their fields. They are all public-spirited individuals who believe, as we do, that in a democracy all citizens should be treated the same. We owe a special debt of gratitude to these people, who are too numerous to mention. But they know us all too well, because we tend to descend on them when they are busiest with their own lives and work. Yet they give freely of their time. For generously sharing their expertise, observations, and impressions, and for their willingness to be sounding boards, we can only say thanks.

We would like to express our appreciation to many employees of federal, state, and local agencies who were most helpful in locating and retrieving government documents and reports. In particular, we would like to thank employees of U.S. Tax Court in Washington, D.C.; the Internal Revenue Service; the Department of Justice; the General Accounting Office (GAO); the U.S. Securities and Exchange Commission (SEC); the Washington office of the Organization for Economic Cooperation and Development (OECD); the County Clerk's Office of Bergen County, New Jersey; and the Assessor's Office for Santa Barbara (California) County. Numerous foreign offices aided us, including the Office of Land Registry in Antigua, whose staff helped us navigate the island's complicated land-ownership system.

We are indebted to employees of federal and state courts and offices throughout the country, including the Los Angeles County Superior Court; the U.S. Bankruptcy Court in Philadelphia; the U.S. District Court in Detroit; the Essex County (New Jersey) Superior Court; the U.S. Attorney's Office in Sacramento, California; the State Supreme Court in New York County; and the U.S. District Court in Tulsa, Oklahoma.

As always, we benefited from the specialized knowledge of librarians from New York to Philadelphia to Los Angeles. The archivists at *Tax Notes,* the nation's foremost publication on tax matters, were most helpful in locating documents.

We are deeply appreciative of the wise counsel of our longtime agent, Andrew Wylie, in both editorial and publishing matters. He believed in this book and, more important, has been a strong supporter and advocate of our work for many years.

At Time Inc., we have the good fortune to be associated with one of the world's premier news-gathering and research organizations. We owe very special thanks to Lany McDonald, director of the Time Inc. Research Center, and members of her staff, particularly Joan Levinstein, who has been a great boon to us from the day we came to work at Time Inc.; as well as to our diligent research assistant, Laura Karmatz.

At Time, we have also been able to work once again with our longtime editor, Steve Lovelady, who has been so instrumental in shaping and enhancing our work for a quarter-century, and from whom we have learned so much.

Norman Pearlstine, the extraordinary Editor in Chief of Time Inc., who invited us to join Time, has given us unwavering support, in addition to encouragement and guidance. To work for such an editor is every reporter-writer's dream.

Finally, we would like to express our deepest appreciation to everyone at Little, Brown, but especially Sarah Crichton, whose early interest and creative input shaped critical pages in this book; and to our editor, Bill Phillips, whose good humor and patience are exceeded only by his keen editorial judgments and insight, and whose vision improved this work immeasurably; and to Ryan Harbage, for all his help and many courtesies.

As always, whatever errors there may be, and we hope there are few, are ours alone.

To that end, a cautionary word is in order. Sections of the book draw on material from Internet Web sites. The Web addresses are listed in footnotes or in the text. However, because the World Wide Web is constantly changing, by the time you read this some of these addresses may have disappeared, changed, or been replaced by new ones.

THE GREAT
AMERICAN
TAX DODGE

AN AMERICAN ORIGINAL

N ext time you do your taxes, take a look at Line 56 on Form 1040, the amount of tax you owe.

At least $3,000 of that goes to cover taxes that other people should pay — but don't. If you earn less than $40,000 a year, like most people, that's just about every dollar you pay in federal income tax. But whatever your earnings, the chances are you're probably picking up part of the tab that others should be paying, especially if your sole source of income is a paycheck subject to withholding.

To put it bluntly, the people in Washington are taking advantage of you, squeezing from you every dollar while ignoring the tens of millions who are cheating.

For the first time in American history, there is massive tax fraud. The U.S. income tax, once a model to other nations, is widely avoided and ignored. In a way, Leona Helmsley, the hotelier by marriage who earned the title "The Queen of Mean," was right when she said, "Only the little people pay taxes."[1] Now even they have found a way to beat the system.

How much more in taxes do honest people pay because their neighbors don't? At a minimum, $300 billion dollars, enough money to provide health care for the 44 million Americans who are uninsured. And prescription drugs for senior citizens. Or cut everyone's taxes.

The IRS, Congress, and the White House play down the scope of tax evasion and avoidance because it's in their interest to do so. After all, the entire tax structure depends on maintaining the public's confidence that it is fair and that everyone pays his share. For years, most everyone did. But gradually, as other taxes on the middle class increased, as evidence of favorable tax treatment by Congress for special interests became more apparent, and as Congress scaled back the IRS's already limited auditing capability, voluntary compliance plunged.

Evidence abounds, as you soon will see. But for now, consider this: From 1990 to 1997, the number of returns for individuals showing tax paid edged up 4 percent, from 90 million to 94 million. During the same period, the number of individuals and families who filed returns but paid no tax soared five times as fast, from 24 million to 29 million.

This represents a dramatic change from the decades when Americans were most likely to pay their taxes, the 1940s to the 1960s. From 1950 to 1969, for example, the number of returns reporting taxes paid shot up 68 percent, from 38 million to 64 million. In those same years, the number of returns reporting no tax owed actually fell 20 percent, from 15 million to 12 million.

This means that in the 1950s and 1960s, the annual growth rate of tax return filers who paid taxes was six times that of the 1990s — the decade that is being called the biggest economic boom of its century. To be sure, some of the difference may be attributable to changes in the tax law. But mostly it's because people voluntarily paid their taxes in the past; today, more and more do not.

What accounts for this change in behavior? The reasons are varied: Growing economic pressures on families struggling to make ends meet under a crushing and unfair load of combined local, state, and federal taxes, especially Social Security and Medicare. A growing contempt for government. The influx of large numbers of immigrants from countries where tax cheating is a way of life. A society whose people have become ever more obsessed with self rather than neighborhood, community, and country. Declining moral and ethical standards. Disgust with Washington's spending priorities. And most of all, a series of Congresses and presidents, Democratic and Republican, who have emasculated the IRS and rewritten the tax laws to favor the privileged and the powerful.

Over the last three decades, America's elected officials have turned a reasonably fair tax code into one crafted for the benefit of those who give the largest campaign contributions, enjoy the greatest access, hire the most influential lobbyists, or otherwise exercise power beyond that enjoyed by average citizens. Congress and the White House have auctioned off the tax code to the highest bidders at the expense of ordinary individuals and families.

As the number of individuals and corporations paying little or no tax has escalated, as pressures have mounted on middle-income working people whose earnings trail those of their parents and grandparents, and as the once widely accepted moral obligation to pay one's taxes is increasingly scoffed at, tax dodging has become a way of life for one-third to one-half of all Americans. If the guy next door has found a way not to pay and goes unpunished, why shouldn't you?

The income tax observed its eighty-seventh birthday in the year 2000. But even as growing numbers of hardy folks are living to celebrate their hundredth birthdays, the income tax probably won't make it to that milestone.

Like a terminally ill hospital patient kept alive by machines, the income tax is all but dead. The only event that remains to be recorded is the actual hour of its passing. Barring a miraculous recovery, sometime early in this century Congress will pull the plug and pronounce it officially dead. Depending on who occupies the White House then, the president either will make no serious effort to save it or will cheer its demise.

But isn't that good? What could be better than no income tax?

No one likes paying income taxes, of course, or any other taxes, for that matter. But as long as there is a federal government there will be taxes. The only question is what type. On that score, the income tax, for all its imperfections and shortcomings, remains the fairest for the greatest number of citizens.

To understand why, let's revisit the age of the robber barons in the late 1800s and early 1900s, when the tax system was decidedly different.

It was a time when more than half the wages of a New York City tenement dweller went to pay the rent on his foul and dilapidated living space, leaving but 25 cents a day to feed and clothe his family.

It was a time when children were forced to work to contribute a needed $2 a week to family income — a boy from four to six years old "can sew on buttons and pull basting threads" and a girl "from eight to twelve can finish trousers as well as her mother."[2]

It was a time when young women worked in a bindery from eight in the morning until ten at night, with a half-hour for dinner and a half-hour for supper, six days a week, for $1 a day.

And it was a time when the concept of upward mobility and a broad-based middle class was unknown; when a few people accumulated huge fortunes, creating the greatest concentration of wealth in the nation's history — while most everyone else lived in varying degrees of squalor.

Those at the bottom were almost guaranteed a lifetime of poverty thanks, in part, to a tax system that fell hardest on those least able to pay. In 1912, the government derived 45 percent of its revenue from duties imposed on imported goods, and another 42 percent from excise taxes on alcohol and tobacco. There was no income tax. So tariffs and these two excise taxes accounted for 87 percent of government receipts. They were a kind of national sales tax, though no one called them that.

For the great mass of people, the consequences were crushing. Any man who bought a cheap pair of work shoes and any woman who purchased an inexpensive dress contributed a far larger percentage of their income to the government than did Mr. and Mrs. John D. Rockefeller. The tax system was rooted in the idea that those with the smallest incomes should pay the largest share.

The Populist and Progressive movements of the day believed this arrangement was upside down, that the rich should contribute a larger portion of their income than the poor to support government. Against this background, the income tax was born in 1913.

Within a decade, by 1922, it provided 21 percent of the government's revenue. The tariff's contribution had plunged to 9 percent, and excise taxes on alcohol and tobacco to 8 percent. In contrast, the corporate income tax generated 19 percent. All the rest came from a series of new taxes, such as manufacturing excise levies and pipeline transportation taxes, and expanded miscellaneous taxes. The system was working as envisioned: The burden was shifting from the poor to include the rich and corporations as well.

In the beginning, the income tax was imposed only on the more affluent. The first year, in 1913, just 358,000 returns were filed by a population of 97 million. That was 1 return for every 271 persons. Not until World War II, with the introduction of withholding, did the income tax become the mass tax we know today. Since then, the top tax rate has gone up and down, fluctuating from a high of 91 percent on taxable incomes over $400,000 in the 1950s to a low of 28 percent on taxable incomes over $29,750 in the late 1980s. The 1999 maximum rate, 39.6 percent on taxable incomes over $283,150, was low by historic standards, but even so assured that the very wealthy paid at least a portion of their vast income to maintain the government.

If the income tax is killed or allowed to die, the nation will return by one means or another to the tax system that prevailed in the early 1900s — one that penalized those least able to pay and rewarded the wealthy with token tax bills. If this happens, the widening wealth gap in America between those at the top and everyone else will become a chasm. That does not bode well for the future of a democratic society.

In the meantime, growing numbers of Americans are arbitrarily setting their own tax rates. Estimates of the tax fraud found herein cover only individual taxpayers, not corporations, a subject worthy of its own book. Also, the obvious needs to be underscored at the outset. Not everyone cheats. There are millions of thoroughly honest taxpayers across all classes. Some high-income individuals and families decline to claim legitimate deductions and instead pay taxes at the top rate. Millions of middle- and lower-income wage earners pay the maximum through weekly withholding from their paychecks. Still others sincerely believe that taxes are the price paid to maintain a civilized society — and who accept that price as a fair one.

But this is a book about those who dodge their taxes. On that score, two points should be made. Income tax *evasion* is a crime. *Avoidance* is perfectly legal. But the line between the two is often blurred, a murkiness fostered by Congress. For example, establishing bank accounts under multiple names to disguise income is a criminal act. Moving money into offshore tax havens might be legal — or might not. A magazine for tax professionals summed up the subtle line between the two more than seventy years ago in a definition that rings even truer today: "Certain acts of tax escaping are clearly evasion; others are clearly avoidance; between the two is a twilight zone in which it is extremely difficult to determine whether a given act falls on one side of the line or the other."[3]

With a far more complex tax code in place in this new century, that twilight zone has become a black hole in space. Hence, some of what you will read in the following pages represents tax evasion, and some falls into the twilight zone.

As for the individuals and businesses that provide the many and varied services that allow people to escape taxes, it is not illegal in and of itself to make available the tools for tax cheating. What's illegal is failing to report income from the schemes. While there are legitimate individuals and entities mentioned in this book, it would be naïve to believe that the entrepreneurs offering these services are not aware that U.S. citizens can use them to evade taxes.

In this book, you will meet people who brag that they have not paid any income tax in years. You will meet multimillionaires who don't even bother to file tax returns. You will explore the money trails that course through the Internet and into the world's tax havens. You will discover how the federal government applies a double standard when it comes to enforcing the tax laws: one for the rich and well connected, another for everyone else. You will see how the new economy enables the largest companies in America to hire workers who pay no income tax. You will see how members of Congress have undermined tax fairness. You will find out what the lawmakers, and the powerful interests who support them, have in store for you. And you will learn how they plan to turn back the clock.

CHAPTER 1

THE TAX CHEAT NEXT DOOR

$1 MILLION A MONTH AND NO TAX RETURN

*S*cenes from the new America:

• A woman forms a company to conduct "research" for the benefit of her minor children and writes a monthly "rent" check to her husband to cover use of the space in their home occupied by her new "business." Coincidentally, the "rent" equals the mortgage payments on their home. She writes another check to lease a car — the family car, as it happens — and then deducts both expenditures as "business expenses" on the couple's joint tax return.

• A fast-food-franchise owner whose family enjoys a typical middle-class lifestyle instructs his accountant to prepare a tax return showing that he owes no income tax. The accountant obliges. He shaves income, inflates expenses, and creates mythical deductions.

• A young man shows up at a designated street corner in Phoenix, Arizona, where illegal immigrants line up to wait for curbside interviews by affluent individuals and contractors seeking hired help. The jobs range from lawn care to housekeeping to construction. The workers are all paid in cash. No taxes deducted. No questions asked.

- A Fortune 500 company hires a computer programmer from India to work on a specific task for a fixed period of time. The programmer is employed by a consulting firm that specializes in placement of foreign workers. The programmer receives a tax-free paycheck — no withholding for U.S. income tax, Social Security or Medicare taxes, state or local taxes.

What are all these people doing? Cheating on their taxes, of course.

Tax fraud is exploding in the United States. In ways large and small, Americans are cheating like never before. One of every three people, perhaps as many as one of every two, is doing it. It's one of Washington's dirty little secrets, a ticking time bomb with the potential to destroy the country's tax system and to undermine essential government programs like Social Security. Disguised by a robust economy and record tax collections, fraud is growing at an exponential pace among all groups, with more and more income concealed from the IRS each year.

How bad is it? No one can put a precise number on lost tax revenue. But it's bad, and getting worse. Even the IRS, which doesn't like to acknowledge this problem for fear it will only encourage more taxpayers to cheat, admitted in 1999 that the "tax gap," its euphemism for fraud and error, is now up to $195 billion a year.

But that estimate is based on tax data from the 1980s and does not remotely reflect current events. A more reasonable count of the revenue lost every year is upwards of $300 billion — the equivalent of the total income taxes paid annually by all individuals and families earning less than $75,000. And even that figure does not include lost taxes from illegal income such as drug trafficking, money laundering, gambling, and prostitution.

If Tax Dodging Inc. were a business, it would be the nation's largest corporation, eclipsing General Motors, which sits atop the Fortune 500 with revenue of $189 billion.

How do people escape paying the taxes they owe? They inflate their itemized deductions for everything from medical bills to charitable contributions. They manufacture deductions to cover expenses never incurred. They understate their income. Or they do both. They ship their money to foreign tax havens. They claim illegal refunds. They speculate in the stock market and don't report their gains. They charge off their personal living costs as business expenses.

And many don't even bother to file tax returns at all. For this group, April 15 is just like any other day of the year. There are no endless forms to fill out, no hurried visits to the accountant, no frantic search for receipts, no mad dash to the post office. Best of all, no taxes to be paid. Those who don't file are participants in the ultimate tax dodge. Their numbers are soaring. Superficial IRS studies turned up 3.4 million individual nonfilers in the 1985 tax year. Two years later, the number jumped 24 percent, to 4.2 million. By 1991, it was 6.5 million. Incredibly, 74,000 of them had incomes of more than $100,000.

How many nonfilers are there today? The IRS doesn't have a clue. In part, that's because Congress has slashed the agency's budget, halting the kind of audits that would make even crude projections possible. Informally, government tax authorities say there are 10 million nonfilers. In truth, there are many more, and here's why:

The IRS identifies a nonfiler as a person who fails to submit a tax return even though a third party has filed an earnings statement (W-2) or information return reporting interest or dividends (Form 1099) that shows the person received income during the year. This narrow definition ignores all those who leave no paper trail. These are the people for whom there are no W-2s or 1099s, no record of wages, annuities, gambling winnings, pensions, interest, dividends, or money flowing in from foreign trusts and bank accounts.

In addition to these people who deal only in cash, there is another larger group whose numbers have soared. They are wealthy Americans and foreign citizens who live and work in the United States and in other countries — multinational wheeler-dealers, independent businesspeople, entertainers, fashion moguls and models. They have multiple passports or global residences and therefore insist they are exempt from the U.S. income tax.

People like the Wildensteins of New York City. That would be Alec and his former wife Jocelyne, who became a staple of the New York tabloids during an unseemly divorce that raged from the fall of 1997 until the spring of 1999.

Alec, born in 1940, is an heir to his family's century-old, intensely private, multibillion-dollar international art business. Jocelyne, four years his junior, is best known for having undergone countless plastic surgery procedures that make her look more feline, permanently, than any member of the cast of *Cats*. Her bizarre appearance inspired the tabloids to dub her "The Bride of Wildenstein."

For the Wildensteins, the once impenetrable curtain that had protected the family from prying eyes for generations was unexpectedly pierced on the night of September 3, 1997, when Jocelyne returned to the couple's opulent Manhattan home after a visit to the family's 66,000-acre ranch in Kenya. Walking into the six-story townhouse on East 64th Street, next door to the Wildenstein gallery, a few minutes after midnight, she found her husband in bed with a nineteen-year-old, long-legged blonde.

Alec hastily wrapped himself in a towel, grabbed a 9mm handgun, and pointed it at his wife and her two bodyguards. "I wasn't expecting anyone," he screamed with a touch of understatement. "You're trespassing. You don't belong here."[1] The bodyguards summoned the police, who arrested Alec and charged him with three counts of second-degree menacing.

So it was that the French-born, aristocratic Alec Nathan Wildenstein, having traded his towel for an Armani suit and a monogrammed shirt, spent the night in the Tombs prison with some of New York's low life. If nothing else, the incarceration gave him time to plot his revenge. When he got out the next day, he moved quickly. He canceled his wife's credit cards. He cut off her telephone lines, locked all the rooms in the townhouse except for her bedroom and sitting room, shut off her access to bank accounts, directed the chauffeur to stop driving her around, fired her accountant, and, in one final act of retribution, ordered the household chefs to stop cooking for her, which proved a major inconvenience because she had never learned how to operate the stove.

Jocelyne responded by turning up the temperature a few hundred degrees on what had been one of the quietest divorce proceedings ever among the rich and discreet. As a result, life among the Wildensteins — a family that for more than a century had guarded its privacy with a pathological obsession — went on public display.

Jocelyne demanded a $200,000 monthly living allowance, payment of her personal staff's salary and expenses, and a $50 million security deposit pending distribution of the marital property. Alec pleaded poverty. He insisted that he had no money of his own and that the millions they spent came from his father.

The Wildenstein family circus that followed established conclusively, one more time, that the rich are very different from the rest of us, beyond the fact that they often pay comparatively little or no taxes. But first, some background on this intriguing family.

Alec is the son of Daniel Wildenstein, the patriarch of the enormously rich French clan. Daniel, born in 1918, controls the Wildenstein billions through a web of secret trusts and intertwined corporations. The Manhattan townhouses, for example, are owned in the name of the Nineteen East Sixty-Fourth Street Corporation, which in turn is controlled by "intermediate entities held in trust."[2] He continues to operate the private, secretive art business started by his grandfather in the nineteenth century, with galleries in New York, Beverly Hills, Tokyo, and Buenos Aires, catering to private collectors, museums, and galleries. And while he spends a lot of his time in Paris, a good chunk of his money resides in secret Swiss bank accounts.

Tucked away in family storerooms, notably in New York, is reportedly the world's largest private collection of the works of the masters — valued at $6 billion to $10 billion. The inventory includes thousands of paintings by Renoir, Van Gogh, Cézanne, Gauguin, Rembrandt, Rubens, El Greco, Caravaggio, da Vinci, Picasso, Manet, Bonnard, Fragonard, Monet, and others. Many have never been displayed publicly.

In 1990, Daniel's sons Alec and Guy took over management of the New York gallery. Their families maintained separate living quarters in the East 64th Street townhouse. They shared the swimming pool in the basement, the informal and formal dining rooms, the foyer, elevator, and the entrance to the townhouse.[3] Alec and Jocelyne lived on the third floor, their two children had bedrooms on the fifth floor, and Jocelyne used the sixth floor as an office. In addition to the Manhattan townhouse, they maintained a castle, the Chateau Marienthal, outside Paris, an apartment in Switzerland, and the Kenya ranch.

Wherever they happened to be, the Wildensteins pursued a lifestyle that was lavish even by the standards of the rich and famous. The details, as they poured from Jocelyne's lips in the divorce proceeding, told the story of a family of seemingly unlimited wealth and no hesitation about spending it. According to her, she and Alec "routinely wrote checks and made withdrawals" from their Chase Manhattan Bank checking account "for $200,000 to $250,000 a month." Jocelyne said that over the last twenty years they did "millions of dollars worth of renovations of the Paris castle and Kenya ranch," and she directed the management, hiring and staffs of those properties. The routine operating costs of the ranch alone ran $150,000 a month.

In New York, Jocelyne's staff payroll at the 64th Street town-house included $48,000 a year for a chambermaid; $48,000 for a maid who tended the dogs; $60,000 each for a butler and chauffeur; $84,000 for a chef; $102,000 for an assistant with an MBA; and $102,000 for a secretary.

In Kenya, their vast Ol Jogi ranch, with its two hundred build-ings spread over an area five times the size of Manhattan, required nearly four hundred employees to look after the grounds and the animals.

In France, the resident staff at the chateau, "the largest private home of its type within a fifteen-minute drive of Paris," included five gardeners, three concierges and three maids.[4]

Talk did not come cheap for the Wildensteins. The annual tele-phone bill in Manhattan alone sometimes ran as high as $60,000. And then there were all the other necessities, like $547,000 for food and wine; $36,000 for laundry and dry cleaning; $60,000 for flowers; $42,000 for massages, pedicures, manicures, and electrolysis; $82,000 to insure her jewelry and furs, and $60,000 to cover the vet-erinarian bills, medication, pet food, beds, leashes, and coats for their dogs. As for miscellaneous professional services, $24,000 went for a dermatologist, $12,000 for the dentist, and $36,000 for phar-maceuticals. Her American Express and Visa card bills for one year totaled $494,000.

Some of these bills were paid out of the couple's Chase Manhat-tan account. Some were paid out of "other bank accounts in New York, Paris and Switzerland." And some bills, Alec confirmed, were paid from "the Wildenstein & Co." account, "the Wildenstein & Co. Special Account, and family businesses."[5] Sort of like having your employer pick up the cost of your clothing, pets, and vacations.

And then there were Jocelyne's personal expenditures. Over the years, she accumulated jewelry valued at $10 million, includ-ing a thirty-carat diamond ring and custom pieces from Cartier. She attended fashion shows in Paris. Her annual spending on clothing and accessories ran to more than $800,000. She once spent

$350,000 for a Chanel outfit that she helped to design. All told, according to papers filed in the divorce case, the couple's personal and household expenditures added up to well over $25 million in 1995 and 1996 alone.

With all those tens of millions of dollars flowing out over the years to maintain a lifestyle beyond comprehension to most people — $60,000 in dog bills exceeds the annual income of three-fourths of all working Americans who pay taxes — you might think that Alec and Jocelyne also forked over millions of dollars to the Internal Revenue Service. But you would be wrong.

They didn't pay a penny in U.S. income tax.

In fact, they never filed a federal tax return.[6]

These admissions by a family accountant are spelled out in records of the acrimonious divorce and also entered into court opinions. They lived the tax-free life even though, by Jocelyne's account, they resided in the Manhattan townhouse for nineteen years, from shortly after their Las Vegas wedding in 1978 until the rancorous divorce proceedings began in 1997. Their children were born in New York and went to school in New York. Alec conducted the family art business through Wildenstein & Company Inc., a New York corporation, from the gallery next door. He had a U.S. pilot's license. He sued and was sued in the courts of New York and other states. He signed documents moving millions of dollars between Wildenstein companies, some located in the tax havens of the world. He transacted business in New York and other states. He was vice president of Nineteen East Sixty-Fourth Street Corporation, which owns the townhouse, gallery, and other properties. His New York pistol license identified him as an officer of Wildenstein & Company. And following his arrest for pointing the weapon at Jocelyne and her bodyguards, he insisted that he should be released on his own recognizance because of his substantial ties to the community.

Nonetheless, he filed no federal tax returns. And no one in Washington or New York noticed. Or cared. Under ordinary circumstances, even the complex tax returns of the very wealthy that are filed go unchecked. That's due to a deliberate decision by Congress to starve the IRS, both in operating funds and in manpower and expertise to conduct such audits. So forget about ferreting out serious nonfilers among the rich and prominent. That task doesn't even register on the tax fraud radar screen. Not surprisingly, representatives of Alec Wildenstein declined to discuss his tax affairs. Jocelyne's lawyer said she doesn't know anything about taxes, since Alec controlled the money. And the IRS can't comment on the tax matters of private citizens. Or in this case, the non-tax matters.

In the divorce case, Alec argued that he was not a resident of the United States, that he had a Swiss passport and visited this country on a tourist visa, and that he did not have a green card permitting him to work. Furthermore, he contended that he had "less than $75,000 in bank accounts" and that "my only earnings are approximately $175,000 per year."[7] On a net-worth statement, Alec listed his occupation as "unpaid personal assistant to father Daniel Wildenstein."[8] That stirred the ire of State Supreme Court Judge Marilyn G. Diamond, who presided over the hostilities. "He fails to explain why he is 'unpaid,'" said Diamond, adding that "this contention insults the intelligence of the court and is an affront to common sense."[9]

Judge Diamond was also angered that Alec never bothered to attend the divorce hearings. Shortly after Jocelyne began unveiling intimate details of the couple's private life, he fled the country. He ignored repeated court dates, failing to appear to answer either the gun charges or his wife's allegations. At one hearing, an irritated Diamond excoriated Wildenstein in absentia for his refusal to obey court orders and to attend depositions. His attorney, Raoul L. Felder, the New York celebrity divorce lawyer, offered an explanation for his client's behavior:

"It may not be his disinclination to appear before the court. You are aware there are substantial tax problems we believe created by the plaintiff."[10]

Judge Diamond agreed. "There are going to be more substantial tax problems," she said. "There are more substantial potential tax problems by people continuing to take certain positions. Make no mistake about it."[11]

If this conjures up visions of battalions of vigilant IRS agents engaged in a relentless search to identify tax scofflaws and, when they do so, dun them for the taxes they owe, assess interest and penalties, seize their bank accounts and cars, freeze their assets, and auction off their possessions, well, that's what they are, visions — at least when it comes to the very rich. For the double standard is to tax-law enforcement what rock is to roll.

Suppose you earn $40,000 a year and don't file a return. When the IRS catches up with you, it prepares a substitute return, estimates your income, calculates the tax you owe, tacks on interest and penalties, and sends you the bill. If you don't like their numbers, you must prove that they're incorrect. What's more, the agency may seize your bank accounts, your car, and whatever else you have of value.

Not so with the truly prosperous. First, the agency mails out a computer-generated letter asking the nonfiler to submit a return. When the reluctant recipient fails to respond, a second letter goes out. And then another. And another. If the silence persists, IRS resorts to another tactic: the telephone. It tries to find the number of the missing nonfiler and place a series of calls. When all that proves futile — it generally does nothing.

Nothing?

That was a finding of a 1991 study by the General Accounting Office (GAO), the investigative arm of Congress, that examined the IRS's handling of affluent nonfilers: "IRS does not fully investigate high-income nonfilers, which creates an ironic imbalance. Unlike lower income nonfilers in the Substitute for Returns program, high-income nonfilers who do not respond to IRS' notices are not investigated or assessed taxes. Even if high-income nonfilers eventually file tax returns, their returns receive less scrutiny than those who file returns on time."[12]

What's the IRS's explanation for the double standard? Incredibly, it told the GAO that it does not prepare a substitute return for rich nonfilers, as it does for middle-income people, because it fears that it might "understate taxes owed." In other words, no loaf is better than half a loaf. So do nothing. Second, the GAO said, "to pursue more high-income cases, IRS would need additional staff."[13] Which, of course, is precisely what Congress refuses to provide.

But things have changed since that critical 1991 audit tried to prod the IRS to act, right? Indeed they have. With each passing year, the number of affluent nonfilers has gone up while Congress has continued to slash the service's auditing capabilities. There is no better evidence of the agency's breakdown than the fact the Wildensteins went two decades without filing a tax return and the IRS knew nothing about it.

The Wildensteins also illustrate one of the weaknesses of the federal government's tax statistics. According to IRS data, more than 1,000 individuals and families with income over $200,000 paid no federal income tax in 1996. But the IRS counts only those people who actually file returns. The Wildensteins didn't. Nor did others in their class. As you might guess, the official estimates of the nontaxpaying rich are on the low side.

Dodging taxes, of course, is hardly a new phenomenon. For as long as there has been an income tax, there have been people who have sought by every imaginable means, and some means not so imaginable, to avoid paying it.

In fact, as far back as 1916 — just three years after the income tax was enacted — newspapers across the country published a syndicated series titled "The United States Income Tax Steal!" The first article began: "Three hundred and twenty million dollars of your money was stolen last year through income tax frauds and evasions, involving thousands of wealthy and prominent citizens and thousands of the most profitable American corporations."[14]

In the late 1930s, when the income tax still applied only to the more prosperous, and before it reached into the pockets of every working American through withholding, many of the wealthiest citizens devised various schemes to escape it. The top rate back then, by the way, was 79 percent on taxable income over $5 million. That's a rate that would double the tax bills of tens of thousands of today's billionaires and millionaires, like Bill Gates, Warren Buffett, and Wal-Mart's Walton family.

On June 8, 1937, Henry Ellenbogen, a Democratic congressman from Pittsburgh, took to the floor of the House to denounce the avoiders and evaders. "A few extremely wealthy individuals have resorted to every trick and every device which their lawyers could conceive to avoid the payment of taxes justly due by them," he said.

What kind of "tricks" was Ellenbogen talking about sixty years ago? He explained:

> [One] American millionaire organized no less than ninety-six personal holding companies all over the country so as to make it difficult, if not impossible, for the Treasury Department to follow his complicated financial transactions.
>
> Some of our multimillionaires have incorporated their yachts and their landed estates so that they can deduct the expenses for their upkeep from their incomes and escape a tax thereon. . . . Let me remind you that the ordinary citizen is not involved in these tax schemes.[15]

And thus it has been ever since. For more than eighty years, newspapers, magazines, and books have chronicled the stories of citizens who fail to pay their taxes. But these scofflaws represented an insignificant portion of the population — until the 1970s, when tax cheating began to move gradually into the mainstream.

In November 1979, Senator Lloyd M. Bentsen Jr., the Texas Democrat who would go on to become President Clinton's first Treasury Secretary, expressed concern that "an alarming trend" was emerging: Otherwise honest citizens were cheating on their taxes.[16]

In April 1983, then IRS Commissioner Roscoe L. Egger Jr., talking about tax evasion, said that "all the signs are that it has been growing and is continuing to grow."[17]

In April 1984, the *Wall Street Journal* reported that "the IRS is losing the battle against tax cheats. Its high-tech wizardry and strengthened legal arsenal can't keep pace with an ever-growing army of tax evaders hiding in a jungle of complex laws."[18]

What's the difference between 1916, 1938, 1984, and this first decade of the twenty-first century?

Just this: That "army of tax evaders," its ranks swollen by legions of fresh recruits, is on the verge of declaring victory. While once upon a time tax dodgers could be counted in the hundreds of thousands or a few million, they now number in the tens of millions and account for between one-third and one-half of the taxpaying population.

One reason for the dramatic increase: Lower- and middle-income taxpayers are frustrated with a system that is overly complex and that favors the wealthy. Congress has arranged the tax code in a way that allows those at the top to escape payment of taxes in lawful ways that are not available to average working people. Hence the attitude "If someone who makes twenty times or a hundred times or as much as a thousand times more than I do can legally reduce their taxes courtesy of Congress, why shouldn't I do the same illegally?"

This inequity between income classes has grown more pronounced over the last two decades, especially when federal, state, and local taxes combined are factored in. That's because Congress and the White House have shifted the cost of programs once funded by the federal government to the states and cities. Those governments traditionally have relied on taxes, such as sales taxes, whereby the burden falls as income rises. In addition, the explosive growth in self-employment has further aggravated tax disparities. The self-employed must pay both the employer and employee shares of Social Security and Medicare taxes — or 15.3 percent right off the top.

To better understand the inequities, consider the tax bills of two households: a single, self-employed health care worker living in Philadelphia, and Bill and Hillary Clinton of Washington, D.C.

On their 1998 tax return, the Clintons reported adjusted gross income of $509,345. They paid a total of $112,496 in local, state, and federal taxes. Their overall tax rate: 22 percent.

A Philadelphia woman working as a self-employed home health care attendant that year who earned $25,000 paid a total of $8,129 in local, state, and federal taxes. Her overall tax rate: 33 percent.

Thus, while the Clintons' total income was twenty times greater than that of the Philadelphia worker, her tax rate was 50 percent higher than that of the president and first lady.

To be sure, the Clintons' tax rate was held down because of hefty charitable contributions. But even Vice President Al Gore and his wife, Tipper, with an income of $224,376 and average charitable contributions, paid overall taxes at a rate of 24 percent — still 9 percentage points under the Philadelphia health care worker's.

Given a president whose tax rate is less than that of a working woman whose income is one-twentieth of his, and with people like the Wildensteins, who spend more money on food and wine alone in one year than most taxpaying families earn in ten years and who don't even file a return, it is inevitable that millions of people at the low end of the economic spectrum would be inspired to file returns and secure refunds fraudulently.

PHANTOM CHILDREN

The earned income tax credit (EITC) is one of the few antipoverty programs to survive from the 1970s that has won praise from Republicans and Democrats alike.

President Ronald W. Reagan, a Republican, called it "the best antipoverty, the best pro-family, the best job-creation measure to come out of Congress."[19]

President Clinton, a Democrat, asserted that "this is not a handout. . . . It gives some breathing room to people who day in and day out have done everything they could to take care of their families, to make their own way, to be self-supporting taxpayers."[20]

Although Congress has amended and expanded the program in the years following its enactment in 1975, its purpose has remained the same: to use the tax system to encourage the poor to seek employment rather than welfare, and to offset the impact of Social Security taxes on low-income workers with families.

Most qualified working individuals and families receive a check for the amount of the credit. Others reduce or eliminate the income tax they owe, depending on the number of eligible children and the amount of their income from jobs.

For example, for tax year 1998, workers who had two children and who earned between $9,390 and $12,260 received a maximum credit of $3,756. The credit phased out by the time someone's income reached $30,095.

Curiously, as the nation moved from recession at the beginning of the 1990s to a period that economists and politicians have labeled the best of all times, with a stock market that went in only one direction — up — tax returns with the earned income credit rose sharply instead of plunging, as might have been expected in a robust economy. From 1990 to 1997, returns filed by people claiming the credit — meaning they worked but said they didn't earn enough to maintain even a poverty-level existence — soared 56 percent, from 12.5 million to 19.5 million. Returns claiming an EITC refund check went up even faster, climbing 78 percent, from 8.7 million to 15.5 million. A majority of the returns were by heads of household; most were age twenty-five to forty-four.

Astonishingly, returns filed by all other individuals and families reporting wage income barely moved during the period, edging up a scant 1 percent — from 84 million to 85 million. Thus, in the eight years from 1990 to 1997, the number of tax returns by all other working taxpayers went up just 1 million.

This during a time when 14 million men and women joined a burgeoning workforce that grew by 13 percent, from 109 million to 123 million.

This during a time when personal consumption expenditures jumped 45 percent, from $3.8 trillion to $5.5 trillion.

This during a time described repeatedly by President Clinton as the "longest peacetime economic expansion in our history."[21]

How is it possible for the ranks of the working *poor* to shoot up during such a time? For the amount of EITC refunds paid out by the IRS to surge 400 percent, from $5 billion to $25 billion?

Two words account for much of the increase: *runaway fraud.* As many as 5 million earned income credit returns are fabricated or contain errors that favor the filer. That's the equivalent of every taxpayer in Arkansas, Delaware, Kansas, Nevada, Nebraska, and Wyoming filing a bogus or inflated return. The cost of the fraud: an estimated $8 billion. That's comparable to all the taxes paid by every taxpayer who earns less than $50,000 a year in Minnesota and Michigan. Think of it as a direct transfer, from workers in those two states to earned-income tax cheats.

The fraud takes many forms. Men "borrow" a child or two from the women they live with or date. Grandmothers claim the tax credit for their grandchildren, when mothers of the children are not eligible for it. Some invent children but use actual Social Security numbers. Some fabricate children and Social Security numbers. Some parents with children don't work, but submit mythical W-2 forms showing income from phantom jobs. In border cities like El Paso and Brownsville, where Mexicans cross legally each day to work in the United States and return home at night or on weekends, they file U.S. tax returns, claim their children as dependents, and collect the credit even though the children live in Mexico.

Tax statistics confirm that border states and other states with large numbers of illegal immigrants account for a disproportionate share of EITC returns. For the nation as a whole in 1997, 19 percent of all tax returns with wage income claimed the credit. In New Mexico, it was 28 percent. In Texas, 26 percent. Florida, 24 percent. Arizona and California, 21 percent. By way of comparison, in New Hampshire, a state with few illegal immigrants, just 12 percent of the returns sought the credit.

The variety and extent of the fraud are limited only by the imagination and ingenuity of those seeking the "refunds," or the tax preparers who encourage them to do so. In many cities, independent tax firms working out of storefronts have recruited people to file EITC returns and pocketed a percentage of the refund. The fraud has also been abetted by electronic filing, which eliminates paperwork and speeds up the refund.

But don't blame the IRS for all the earned-income fraud. Blame Congress, which gave what essentially is a welfare program to the tax collector to administer. Sort of like asking your lawyer to perform your root canal.

In this case, the fraud is the kind that, absent an investigation of each individual return, is nearly impossible to prove. As the General Accounting Office put it, EITC "eligibility, particularly related to qualifying children, is difficult for IRS to verify through traditional enforcement procedures, such as matching return data to third-party information reports. Correctly applying the residency test . . . for example, often involves understanding complex living arrangements and child custody issues."[22]

Translation: Unless the IRS sends an army of agents into the field to confirm the existence of children named on returns, and determine whether the filers actually supported the children and are otherwise eligible, there's no way to document individual fraud. Obviously, this kind of wholesale, intrusive investigation has never been an option. Even if the IRS had the personnel to do so, Congress, fearing public backlash, would never allow it. And that was before lawmakers in 1998 ordered the IRS to become a taxpayer-friendly, service-oriented agency, and to tone down its image as a tough enforcer.

Even before Congress curbed the IRS's enforcement powers, the GAO had concluded that "the incentive to file problematic returns is likely to increase as IRS' capability to verify information on the return decreases."[23]

SECRETS OF THE SYSTEM

The IRS's limited ability "to verify information" extends well beyond the tax returns of the working poor. Another growing bloc of tax dodgers consists of people who have structured their personal and business lives in a way that allows them to ignore the tax collector.

They do this through endless schemes. They move money between U.S. and foreign bank accounts to disguise its source and destination. They use other names on bank and brokerage accounts. They shift assets and money in a dizzying maze involving U.S. and foreign corporate entities. They arrange for third parties to pay their bills from tax havens. They buy stock at bargain-basement prices offered to insiders and sell it for large gains without reporting the income. They intermingle personal and business expenses. And when questioned about their finances, they offer explanations that are as disorienting as their deals. To unravel such a bewildering array of transactions and estimate the amount of tax owed would require a task force of IRS agents — one for each person or family.

Unlike the Wildensteins, whose very existence was unknown to the IRS, these people are well known to the agency. They are everywhere. Many are your next-door neighbors. People like Stanley and Jean Schulman.

The Schulmans, who until 1999 lived in a three-quarter-million-dollar house in a gated community in Bell Canyon, California, thirty miles northwest of downtown Los Angeles, have led a comfortable life. He's an investment consultant. She's a former computer analyst who retired from Blue Cross about 1986. They travel in Europe. They drive late-model vehicles. They have provided cars for their six children. They entertain. In 1994, Schulman said his yearly income had averaged about $300,000 from 1984 until that time. That would have placed him among the top 1 percent of the nation's taxpayers — if, that is, Schulman had paid taxes. But he hadn't, not in any of those years. As he explained in May 1994 during a deposition in a lawsuit filed against him by a businessman seeking to collect a money judgment: "I have not paid income taxes since 1968 and I cannot discuss my income taxes because I don't pay them. . . . I don't have any income that is taxable, so I don't pay income taxes."[24]

But then he paid income tax in another country, right? Wrong. "I have paid no taxes to any sovereign entity in the world since 1968. I have minimized my tax liability," Schulman said.[25]

Minimized indeed. But how? In part, by shuffling "large sums of money between various offshore accounts."[26] In part, by having offshore companies pay personal expenses.

Schulman worked as a consultant for a company called Albemarle Investments Limited, which maintained an office in London but was organized on Guernsey Island. Guernsey is one of several tiny islands in the English Channel that have been notorious tax havens for decades. Schulman once explained Albemarle's business this way: "It is a full-service financial company. . . . It provides each and every type of service that any full-service financial corporation would for individuals and corporations throughout the world."[27]

As for his role, Schulman said, "I arrange for them to invest money in various companies around the United States, England, Canada, Europe, and I help manage investments. I arrange individual clients to open accounts with them for tax limitation purposes."[28] In other words, he sets up deals so clients can drastically reduce or eliminate *their* taxes.

Schulman said he received about $250,000 a year from Albemarle, and that he pulled in another $50,000 for providing similar services to a second offshore company called Coubert Dennis

Limited in Ireland. From both, he received shares of stock as payment for his work, which he sold to generate cash.

To appreciate how the Schulmans lived the tax-free life, let's take a look at their household expenses. Typically, individuals and families work to save money for a down payment to buy a house. That money, naturally, represents earnings on which taxes have been paid. After moving into the new home, they pay the monthly mortgage charge, as well as utility bills, with wage income earned, once again, after taxes. Or more accurately, after the taxes have been withheld from paychecks. That's how the system works for most people.

Not so for the Schulmans and millions of others like them. In Stanley Schulman's case, Albemarle Investments, his self-described "employer," decided to take a flyer in California real estate late in 1993 because "everybody felt that the market was coming back and there would be a big upsurge in property value."[29]

In one of those happy coincidences, the Schulmans just happened to be in the market for a new home at the time. Stanley scouted out the area and settled on a $600,000 five-bedroom, four-and-a-half-bath home on a 2.65-acre lot in Bell Canyon, complete with spa and horse corral. On orders of Albemarle Investments of Guernsey, a California corporation was formed with the identical name, Albemarle Investments Limited, to hold title to the real estate. Schulman was president of California Albemarle.

At closing, Guernsey Albemarle wired $320,000 into a Bank of America account of California Albemarle for the down payment, and financed the $300,000 balance with a private loan. Did Schulman know how the offshore Albemarle came up with the $320,000? "No, I don't," he said.[30]

To sum up: Schulman selected a house for California Albemarle to purchase as an investment for Guernsey Albemarle, and signed all the papers as president of the California company. In addition to being an "investment," the house also would be the

Schulman family homestead, as well as the address for several businesses.

What does the rest of the California Albemarle investment portfolio look like? Not much. In fact, the Schulman house was Albemarle's only investment. But it wasn't the company's only expense. When the monthly gas, water, and electric bills and homeowner's fee arrived, all were paid out of an Albemarle checking account at the Bank of America, thereby relieving the Schulmans of the need to spend after-tax dollars on mortgage and housing expenses, as other people must.

Guernsey Albemarle was quite generous in other ways. The Channel Island company leased two cars in 1994 for Schulman and his wife — a 1994 Lincoln and a 1994 Ford Explorer, sparing the family yet another expenditure. Schulman received the cars, he said, "in exchange for the services" he provided to Albemarle.[31] And that wasn't all. Guernsey Albemarle also leased six additional Ford Explorers. Listen to this exchange during a deposition in March 1995 between Schulman and a lawyer representing one of his creditors, as the lawyer seeks to learn the whereabouts of the mini-fleet of vehicles:

Attorney: Does Albemarle Investments have any other automobiles?

Schulman: Yes.

Attorney: Can you tell me what those are?

Schulman: Ford Explorers.

Attorney: They have Ford Explorers? How many?

Schulman: Approximately six.

Attorney: Approximately six. Do you know where they are located?

Schulman: . . . Well, in L.A.

Attorney: All in Los Angeles? Do you have any idea who is in possession of them?

Schulman: Yes.

Attorney: Can you tell me who that is?
Schulman: My children.
Attorney: Your children. How many children do you have again, I'm sorry?
Schulman: Six.[32]

Schulman later explained that five of his children drove Ford Explorers leased by Albemarle, and the sixth car was on loan to a friend. His sixth child drove a Cadillac originally leased by Coubert Dennis. Why would a Guernsey Island company lease sport utility vehicles for Schulman's children, who did no work for that company?

Because the president of Albemarle, one William Daniel Dane, authorized it to do so. Schulman recounted events leading up to the leases: "The company owed me a fee at the time and [Dane asked] 'How do you want it?' I said, 'Well, why don't we just authorize the company to lease cars for my kids.' And he said, 'Go do it.'"[33]

Inside the Schulman house, Guernsey Albemarle provided the Macintosh computer and Coubert Dennis furnished the fax machine. The two companies also paid the monthly charges on Schulman's MasterCard and Visa accounts. On occasion, Schulman wrote the corporate checks on the California Albemarle bank account — at the direction of Guernsey Albemarle, of course, and as an agent of the company. As one might gather by now, Schulman owned nothing in his own name. He maintained no records of financial transactions. He wrote no personal checks. He destroyed all documents.

How did Schulman arrange his affairs so that he paid no income tax? A walk through one of his financial transactions is enlightening.

In late summer 1993, one of the brokerage accounts he maintained sold stock in Medgroup Inc. for $19,332. The company described itself as an operator of physical therapy clinics in California and Arizona. Schulman had received the stock from Albemarle in return for services he performed for Medgroup on Albemarle's behalf. Yet he never saw the cash. The $19,332 was routed back to the United Kingdom and into an Albemarle bank account that paid his credit card charges, car, and other personal bills.

Schulman also resorted to other tax-free practices. But let him explain:

"You have two things that you have to look at. If I take you to dinner and spend $300, I'll pay cash for it because nobody will ever know I spent the cash. If I buy a pair of shoes, I'll bill it to the company, because people can see the shoes."[34]

Schulman allowed that he did pay some personal expenses out of his pocket. "I pay for the dry cleaning, clothing . . . the vet bill on my dogs and cats. Just having one of our cats operated on . . . was $700 estimated. . . . I pay for my granddaughter's tutoring monthly. . . . It's just normal living expenses."[35] And he paid the tuition, books, and health insurance for one daughter attending UCLA.

Sometimes even basic needs — such as food — were mysteriously provided for, as this exchange between Schulman and a lawyer during a deposition in June 1995 demonstrates:

Attorney: Between March and today, how have you made a living?

Schulman: I haven't.

Attorney: You haven't made any payments toward living?

Schulman: None.

Attorney: You purchased any food in the past three months?

Schulman: My wife has.

Attorney: How does she make those payments?

Schulman: She has some cash in the bank and I believe she borrowed some money.

Attorney: When she was last here I recall that she testified while you were sitting here that she received all her money from you.

Schulman: Yes.[36]

To summarize, Jean Schulman has no income of her own. She gets her money from her husband. But he doesn't have any income either. Yet she pays for the family food that he can't buy because he doesn't have any money. But wait. There's more. Jean Schulman has her very own Bank of America Visa card, and uses it to pay the monthly bills in the same inscrutable way as the grocery bills. Listen to an exchange between a lawyer and Mrs. Schulman during a deposition:

> **Attorney:** Are there outstanding debts on the card?
>
> **Mrs. Schulman:** Yeah.
>
> **Attorney:** Can you give me a ballpark figure in your estimation?
>
> **Mrs. Schulman:** Roughly $5,500 because that is the max on it. . . . Uh, $4,000 maybe. I don't know. . . .
>
> **Attorney:** And you make the monthly payments on that account?
>
> **Mrs. Schulman:** No.
>
> **Attorney:** No, you don't? But it is your card?
>
> **Mrs. Schulman:** Right.
>
> **Attorney:** Who makes the payments?
>
> **Mrs. Schulman:** Stan.[37]

The Visa card was but one of the credit cards Mrs. Schulman used. There were at least four others for department and specialty stores. Those bills were handled in the same way as her Visa account. She never saw them. She didn't know the balances. Her husband paid them. She maintained that she had no assets, owned no stocks or bonds, and had no investments.

Amazingly, while Mrs. Schulman was unable to say how much she owed on her credit cards, indeed, that she never even saw the bills because they were paid by her husband, and that she didn't have any income or assets of her own, and that she didn't file state or federal tax returns because she didn't have any income, she did manage to come up with money to engineer the acquisition of a company. Once more, the story is best told through the deposition of her husband. He is explaining that when California Albemarle filed for Bankruptcy Court protection, he once again became president, at least temporarily. Remember, California Albemarle's only holding is the Schulman family home.

Attorney: You're still president of the Albemarle California Company?

Schulman: I am president until the day the bankruptcy is adjudicated at which time the new president is being appointed.

Attorney: How do you know that?

Schulman: The board told me.

Attorney: The board told you that? What does, who comprises the board?

Schulman: My wife.

Attorney: Your wife. How long has your wife acted as the board of Albemarle California?

Schulman: Approximately since May of this year, when she acquired the company. I believe that she has sold the company, I'm not certain.

Attorney: Oh, she sold the company already?

Schulman: I'm not certain. . . .

Attorney: Currently, as president you're not certain if the company has been sold?

Schulman: Yep. Not my business.

Attorney: How did . . . your wife acquire the company?

Schulman: She bought it.

Attorney: She paid money for the company?

Schulman: She advanced funds to the company. . . .

Attorney: And she did that with, she advanced the company whose funds or just, is it a loan or . . . ?

Schulman: As a loan. . . .

Attorney: As a loan. Was she to receive interest?

Schulman: I don't know. I wasn't a party to any of the transactions.[38]

To summarize once more, Mrs. Schulman, who by her reckoning had no income or investments and got her money from her husband, who himself had no income, advanced $67,000 to the company that owned the family home.

The Schulmans are just one example of why the federal tax system is crumbling. They enjoy a comfortable lifestyle in an upscale neighborhood, yet pay no income tax. To determine how much they owe would require a costly audit by teams of IRS agents. Multiply this one case by the millions and you get some idea why the words *tax law* and *enforcement* have become non sequiturs.

Not that the IRS hasn't tried to audit the family's finances. But by Stanley Schulman's own account, the efforts have been to no avail. "They try. They throw up their hands and they say, 'What do we do? We have no documents.'"[39] In his skirmishes with the IRS that he related in 1994, Schulman said: "Right now they're willing to settle for three years of tax returns, even if I give them a zero balance, and I'm not quite sure that I want to do that. That's my current status with the IRS."[40]

In April 1996, two years after Schulman boasted under oath that he paid no income tax, the IRS finally got around to filing liens against him, saying he owed $369,447 for 1990 through 1993. As of the summer of 1999, the liens were still outstanding.

Also that summer, the Schulmans and Albemarle sold the Bell Canyon house and moved to a new home in Devore, fifty-six miles east and north of Los Angeles. As a local business publication recounted the arrival of the newcomers:

> A horse ranch in Devore is now the headquarters of Albemarle Investments Ltd., a venture capital firm that looks for promising start-ups and helps them with financing, management and eventually takes them public. The firm's headquarters are essentially embodied in Stanley Schulman, its

founder and public representative. Schulman bought a five-acre ranch in Devore and moved from Ventura County in September. The business came with him.[41]

INVISIBLE WORKERS AND UNTAXED PROFITS

None of this is to suggest that you need establish a mysterious off-shore link and work for companies based in tax havens to avoid paying U.S. income tax. Truth to tell, many people in the computer field, especially programmers and systems analysts at the largest companies in America — from Chrysler Corporation to the Baby Bells, from Bank of America to Unisys — pay not a penny in income or Social Security taxes.

How can this be? Consulting and contracting firms recruit so-called temporary workers in other countries, especially India, and bring them to the United States under a special visa called H-1B. They farm out these foreign programmers to large U.S. companies that do not want to add permanent employees to their payrolls or to replace higher-paid American workers whose jobs have been eliminated. Still other clients are state governments that contract out computer work.

During the 1990s, nearly 1 million foreign computer technicians came to the United States to work for a maximum of six years under this program, and then, in theory, return home. Most decided to stay. If some members of Congress — and computer and software companies like Microsoft, Intel, and Hewlett-Packard — get their way, the ranks of the foreign workers will swell to 2 million this decade.

The reason: Computer companies are lobbying lawmakers to raise the cap limiting the number of such visas to 200,000 a year. Under existing law, the cap was slated to fall from a high of 115,000 in year 2000 to 65,000 in 2002. Fortune 500 companies complain they cannot find enough qualified American workers to fill openings. Critics charge the companies want to drive down wages by hiring cheap foreign labor. A computer industry magazine finds this perfectly acceptable: "Companies have a fiduciary responsibility to keep labor costs low. If U.S. technology companies cannot find highly trained, highly motivated American employees at a competitive cost, then a shortage does exist. And if companies say they want to hire more skilled foreign workers because those workers are cheaper, we should believe them — and increase the number of visas issued."[42]

In addition to their willingness to work for lower salaries — as much as $25,000 lower — many foreign recruits, at least when they first come to this country, enjoy another advantage over American workers competing for the same jobs: They don't pay U.S. taxes.

Visit most any large American company and you will find two people working on the same computer project. One is a permanent company employee who pays taxes through withholding. The other a temporary employee who enjoys the kind of payday that more than 100 million American workers can only dream about — a full paycheck with zero deductions.

Because they are employed by the consulting firm that recruited them, many of these foreign workers are paid either in cash or by check — and no money is withheld for U.S. income tax, Social Security, Medicare, state, or local taxes. What's more, they often live in rent-free apartments with free meals, all courtesy of the consulting firm that hired them. Still others receive a paycheck that is banked in India, and, while they're living and working in this country, they're paid an "allowance" that is also free of all U.S. taxes.

This widespread practice came to light during a little-noticed civil lawsuit in which one consulting firm accused another of raiding its employees from India. The legal action was filed by Tata Consultancy Services, a division of Tata Sons Ltd., of Bombay, against Syntel Inc. of Detroit in U.S. District Court in Detroit in 1990. The dispute dragged on for years, during which time numerous Tata and Syntel employees, most of whom had come to the

United States from India on temporary visas, testified about the tax-free life of foreign programmers.

Among those questioned was Sujatha Subramanian, a female programmer from India, who, like others, was brought to the United States by Tata but later left to join Syntel. Technically, she was employed by a company in India called Leading Edge, which subcontracted her to Syntel, which assigned her to computer projects at Ford and Chrysler. She received a paycheck from Leading Edge that was deposited in rupees in a bank in India and she received a living allowance from Syntel in U.S. dollars. The following exchange is with a Tata lawyer.

> **Attorney:** What other kind of benefits are you receiving?
> **Subramanian:** None from Syntel.
> **Attorney:** None? Do you get your cost of living allowance from them?
> **Subramanian:** Yes. And I'm covered by health, covered for health and medical. . . .
> **Attorney:** Do you pay taxes here in the United States?
> **Subramanian:** No.
> **Attorney:** Only in India?
> **Subramanian:** Yes. . . .[43]

In one of the cruel ironies that run through the American tax and labor systems, foreign workers who pay little or no U.S. taxes receive health care coverage through the contractors that place them, while millions of American workers in jobs with even lower wages pay taxes but have no health care benefits. Their employers do not provide coverage, and individual policies are too expensive. Yet the taxes they pay go in part to pay for the health care coverage of the poorest of Americans who qualify for Medicaid.

Another programmer, Rengaswamy Mohan, who was contracted out to work for Deloitte Touche in Florida, spoke candidly about his tax and employment status and the interwoven relationships between Syntel and other consulting firms in India. While working in the United States, Mohan received a paycheck from an Indian firm, Mascon, which was deposited in a bank in India, while Syntel gave him a living allowance. When asked during a deposition whether taxes were withheld from the monthly check of $2,270, Mohan replied:

"No. Actually, I was told that these were all the expenses and I was sitting as a consultant from India."[44]

And a nice place to sit it is, the tax-free life in America. But Mohan also enjoyed another fringe benefit. He received a finder's fee for referring another programmer to Syntel.

Attorney: How much did you get?

Mohan: I don't remember, but, you know, I get like, so long as she is in this [Deloitte Touche] project, 50 cents an hour.

Attorney: Fifty cents an hour for each hour she works on this project?

Mohan: Yes.

Attorney: . . . For how long? Is that forever? As long as she keeps working —

Mohan: So long as she is in this project.

Attorney: That's a good deal.[45]

A really good deal, considering the programmer was his wife.

None of this is to suggest that every Syntel programmer pays no taxes. Some eventually go on the company payroll and are treated like other permanent workers — taxes are withheld from their paychecks. But court records show that for many, such is not the case. In this, Syntel is not alone.

In 1998, an Indian programmer in Chicago, worried that he might lose his bid for American citizenship, wrote a letter to the U.S. Department of Labor expressing concern over his off-the-books income.

Employed by a computer consulting firm in Chicago and farmed out to Ameritech, the programmer explained that when he came to this country he had been compelled to become part of a complex scheme by the consulting firm to evade taxes. He was not clear on all the elements that made up the fraud, but a key component was that his pay came partly in cash:

> They told me that in this way neither they have to pay taxes nor I have to pay taxes on that amount. When I objected it, they told me that most of the other employees are paid in similar way. I asked my couple of colleagues . . . everyone communicated that they are paid in same way. Part of the payment [almost 30 percent of the salary] they receive is not taxable and paid to them every month. Now I realize that this practice . . . is illegal. I don't want to be part of this system, but presently I do not have any alternatives.[46]

Where, you might ask, is the IRS in all of this? The answer is: Nowhere. "Immigration is a big problem for IRS," confided a former high-level Treasury Department official. "It doesn't know how to track foreign workers."[47]

If Congress has guaranteed that the IRS is incapable of finding people who physically exist, whether they be foreign workers or the Wildensteins of the world, then what are the chances the agency will detect paper profits? Virtually none.

Of all the areas where fraud is easy to commit and most difficult to identify, capital gains income ranks near the top. Here's why.

The IRS receives a notice that you picked up $460,000 from the sale of stock. Let's say 5,000 shares at $92. You originally paid $30 a share, or $150,000. Subtract that sum and your capital gain — the amount on which you must pay taxes — totals $310,000. But the IRS doesn't know what you paid for the stock. They take your word for it. So you put down $75 instead of $30. Magically, $225,000 in taxable income disappears. That's a tax savings of $45,000.

Long before fraud became commonplace, the IRS never came close to collecting all the taxes owed the government from capital gains income. This was partly because of the complexity of the tax code, partly because of tax evasion by those who suspected, quite rightly, that the agency didn't have the resources to aggressively track underreporting.

Now it's much worse. In this first decade of the twenty-first century, the IRS is overwhelmed by securities transactions. Hobbled by inadequate resources, the agency poses little or no threat to people who understate their profits. As a result, capital gains fraud is skyrocketing.

From 1990 to 1997, the average capital gain reported on tax returns went up a modest 32 percent, from $13,400 to $17,700. That growth did not come close to matching the rise in the overheated stock market or the volume of daily stock trades. During those same years, the Dow Jones Industrial Average leaped 200 percent. Trading volume was up even more, spiraling 297 percent.

Other data are even more compelling. In 1990, wage and salary income reported on all tax returns totaled $2.6 trillion. By contrast, the value of all stock trades that year on the New York Stock Exchange, the American Stock Exchange, and the NASDAQ over-the-counter market added up to $1.8 trillion. Thus wage and salary income was 1.4 times greater than the value of stock trades, a pattern that had long been the norm.

By 1997, that ratio had been reversed, as the value of stock trades reached a staggering $10.4 trillion — or 2.9 times greater than wage and salary income of $3.6 trillion.

What all this means is that the opportunities for fictional accounting have never been greater. Just how great, you ask? Consider that in 1990, net capital gain income reported on tax returns was 6.8 percent of the value of stocks traded. By 1997, that figure had fallen off by half, to 3.3 percent — a seemingly impossible decline during an era of sizzling stock market activity.

What would capital gains income have totaled if the 1990 ratio had been in place in 1997? Over $700 billion, or double the reported sum of $348 billion.

To be sure, tax law changes and other economic factors may account for some of this difference. Also, the stock market is just one slice of the capital gains pie, albeit a large one. Sales of commodities, futures, real estate, and other capital assets must also be factored in. Nevertheless, a chunk of the difference is attributable to tax fraud.

Who's benefiting from this?

While Democrats and Republicans alike talk of the nation's booming economy, and how everyone is in the stock market, the IRS's tax return data tell another story. A comparatively small number of people report taxable income from the sale of capital assets, and only a tiny fraction of those rake in most of the profits.

In 1996, for example, 915,000 individuals and families with incomes of more than $200,000 reported receiving $171 billion from the sale of capital assets. They accounted for only 8 percent of the returns — but collected 67 percent of the money.

THE PERFECT TAX RETURN: ALWAYS A REFUND

While tax dodging among investors is rampant, fraud within another part of the population is even more widespread. That would be the fastest-growing segment of the U.S. economy: the self-employed.

Historically, this group has been a major source of taxpayer fraud and error. Studies have shown "they are less compliant" than other taxpayer groups, and that they "appear to be intentionally non-compliant more often" than taxpayers who receive a weekly paycheck.[48]

What accounts for this reputation? Many of these businesses are operated on a cash basis — nail salons, beauty salons, restaurants, mom-and-pop grocery stores, landscapers, child care providers, antiques dealers, independent auto repair shops, plumbing and heating contractors, truckers, painters, and electricians. In addition to depending on cash, these businesses are subject to fewer requirements for information returns, such as the 1099 notices that banks must submit to the IRS reporting interest payments. Also, there's usually no withholding in these or scores of other occupations and professions, such as lawyers, accountants, computer programmers, physicians, and nurses. Again, no paper trail.

That's why one study carried out in the late 1980s — and which has never been updated — found that even back then the self-employed did not report 25 percent of their income. Evasion and avoidance across the board have escalated since then. In 1994, another study found that fewer than half the self-employed paid the Social Security and Medicare taxes owed.

Let's put this in more personal terms. Suppose the self-employed now report 60 percent of their income, a charitable assumption. Multiply your annual income, say $45,000, which you receive in a weekly paycheck with taxes already deducted, by 60 percent. That comes out to $27,000, which you enter on your Form 1040. With the stroke of a pen, $18,000 of your income disappeared from the taxman's view. The savings: $1,377 in Social Security and Medicare taxes and $2,400 in income tax, thereby providing an extra $3,777 in spending money.

While fraud has always existed in this area, the volume and scope have been shooting up. One reason is the emergence of *involuntary* self-employed people, like the computer workers at large companies who are replaced by the nontaxpaying foreign computer workers. These displaced workers, who once paid taxes, are forced to go out on their own. They rent themselves out, doing the same work but for less money and no health care or other fringe benefits. These embittered former corporate employees often feel no special obligation to prepare an accurate tax return.

This is especially true when they see the effect their independent status has on their tax bill. It goes up. Remember the health care worker who pays total taxes at a higher rate than the president of the United States? Her largest tax bill is for Social Security and Medicare. She must pay both the employer's and employee's share, which adds up to 15.3 percent of her income. Add to that the federal income tax and state and local taxes.

Not surprisingly, the self-employed are keeping a larger share of their income for themselves than in the past. A Los Angeles economic development official says, "It used to be 'a dollar for the IRS, three dollars [in unreported income] for me.' Now it's 'a dollar for the IRS and eight for me.'"

The data bear this out. From 1980 to 1997, the average amount of receipts reported by the self-employed inched up a meager 10 percent, from $46,000 to $50,700 — lagging far, far behind the inflation rate of 95 percent and other economic yardsticks. During the same period, average wage and salary income on all tax returns rose 116 percent. Gross domestic product per capita jumped 148 percent.

These and other statistics suggest that the self-employed are understating their income by upwards of $250 billion — a sum that grows yearly. That's a tax loss of $50 billion, the equivalent of the income tax paid by everyone who earned less than $50,000 a year in Connecticut, New Jersey, New York, Ohio, Pennsylvania, Maryland, Massachusetts, Indiana, Virginia, West Virginia, and Delaware. That $50 billion, by the way, is calculated on unreported income only. It does not take into account inflated, phony, or inappropriate deductions that allow business owners to escape billions more in taxes.

Some of the self-employed do their own creative accounting. Others take their make-believe numbers to a tax preparer. Increasingly, accountants say, the business owner tells them how much he or she wants to pay in taxes and instructs the tax preparer to arrive at that figure. Sort of like the ordinary working person deciding how much he or she would like to pay in taxes, and then adjusting income and deductions accordingly.

A veteran IRS examiner confirms the practice is widespread and adds that the goal of many self-employed persons is to pay no taxes at all. As an example, the examiner pointed to the operator of a fast-food franchise who lived with his family in an affluent neighborhood, sent his child to a private school, and paid not a penny in income tax. When the IRS examiner questioned the tax preparer about the return, the preparer replied: "If I don't do what he wants, he won't pay me. He'll go to someone else."[49]

That's the way the system works. If one tax preparer declines to produce a return showing the desired result, some other one will. Opportunities for this kind of fraud have multiplied. Tax returns filed by those who report income from a trade or business have shot up four times as fast as those filed by individuals and families who report wage and salary income, spiraling from 9 million in 1980 to 17 million in 1997.

Not all errors on self-employed returns come from cheating. Some individuals are genuinely confused by the complexity of the Internal Revenue Code and make honest mistakes. For others, their perceptions of what should be considered legitimate deductions or income lead them to make mistakes — almost always in their favor. One way or another, it costs the Treasury and other taxpayers.*

So who, exactly, are we talking about here?

These are people like the Los Angeles–area lawyer whose extracurricular horse-breeding business racked up $132,253 in expenses over seven years while bringing in only $752 in income. The lawyer used the $131,501 in losses from the horse venture to offset taxable income from her law practice and reduce her tax bill. Over seven years, she reported that net profits from her law busi-

---

* One might ask what difference fraud makes in an era when record tax collections are pouring into the U.S. Treasury and members of Congress and the president are debating how to spend the surplus. Putting aside the gross inequities created by people who cheat and the fact that taxes could be reduced if fraud were eliminated, the truth is there is no budget surplus. The $124 billion "surplus" for 1999 hyped by President Clinton was, in fact, an $88 billion deficit in the government's general fund.

Current and future "surpluses" are attributable to excess Social Security and disability insurance tax collections, along with excess collections in other trust funds. The Social Security tax dollars collected in excess of Social Security benefits paid out are merely spent for other government purposes — like congressional salaries, foreign aid, and radioactive waste management. Then the trust fund is stuffed with IOUs. Ultimately, you will redeem them with higher taxes. Or else Social Security benefits will be trimmed and the retirement age raised. Or all three.

In the 1990s, Presidents Bush and Clinton diverted nearly one-third of a trillion dollars in Social Security and disability insurance taxes to run the U.S. government. These taxes are paid overwhelmingly by working people in the middle and at the bottom of the economic pile. From 2000 through 2005, the U.S. government budget calls for another half-trillion in Social Security tax dollars to be siphoned off for other purposes.

ness averaged just under $20,000 a year. In one year, 1995, she reported a loss of nearly $39,000. Expenses of her horse business averaged slightly under $19,000 a year. In addition, the lawyer filed her tax returns from one month to seven years late. And she understated the income from her law practice by $32,000. The IRS concluded — and the U.S. Tax Court agreed — that she owed $34,000 in back taxes and $8,500 in penalties.

A New York opera singer wrote off over five years $70,000 for travel and entertainment, $18,000 for meals, $23,000 in commissions, $7,400 for insurance, and $5,500 in bad debts. In all, he claimed $126,525 in business expenses that the IRS disallowed. That was in addition to $90,825 in other deductions that were disallowed, including $49,839 in employee business expenses. He filed his tax returns from one to five years late. He ignored appointments with tax examiners. He failed to appear at tax court hearings. And he produced no records to substantiate his expenses. The tax court sided with the IRS and disallowed the business and other deductions, ordered the singer to pay $46,000 in additional taxes, and levied a $15,000 penalty.

An aging Hollywood screenwriter and his actress-wife wrote off expenditures made to revive their dormant careers. They reported business income of $1,574 and expenses of $34,942. A net loss of $33,368 offset other income and reduced their taxes. Among their deductions: $3,120 for trips to Branson, Missouri, and Las Vegas and Laughlin, Nevada, where they watched country and gospel performers to inspire him to write song lyrics. He didn't sell any. They deducted $1,140 for tickets to movies, concerts, and plays because he planned to write the book and lyrics for a Broadway musical comedy. He didn't. They wrote off $4,615 to cover the cost of research trips to Alaska and Mexico. The purpose of the Alaska trip was to obtain onsite photos — taken by the wife — and collect other material for a screenplay. The trip to Mexico was to meet a comedienne for whom he hoped to write material. Neither worked out. They wrote off $2,480 for business use of their travel trailer — including campground fees, repairs, insurance, and registration — and $8,540 for use of their 1970 Ford truck on business trips. They wrote off $5,132 in home office expenses, including pool service, cable television, home improvements, and yard service. They deducted $1,114 for their home telephone, including all long distance calls. They wrote off $569 for two television sets, a VCR, and videotapes. And they carried over a net loss from the previous year of $15,892. The tax court disallowed all these deductions. Over five years, the couple claimed net losses of $142,000 from their "business."

By now, you get the idea of the pleasant tax advantages enjoyed by the self-employed, at least those who never see an IRS examiner, which is the vast majority. Unlike average paycheck-drawing Americans, they often write off personal expenses incurred by everyone and label them business expenses, and they engage in hobbies masquerading as businesses that seldom earn a profit. These expenses and losses, in turn, are subtracted from other income, thereby reducing or eliminating the taxes they owe.

One of the more brazen cases that shows how pervasive fraud has become among the self-employed is the story of Gail Carlette Dixon of East Palo Alto, California. Dixon was a tax preparer who also provided property management and notary services. From 1990 to 1992, her income from this work totaled $368,000, or about $123,000 a year. That should have placed her among the top 5 percent of tax-return filers. But it didn't. Dixon did not file returns for those three years. She was one of more than a million self-employed nonfilers — one of the few to get caught.

As it turned out, Dixon's personal fraud was incidental to her contribution to the great American tax dodge. People who turned to her Cozy Home-Dixon Tax Service for professional tax help in those years were never disappointed. In fact, they must have felt like they had won the lottery.

In one of those tax miracles that occur far more frequently than the IRS, the Treasury Department, and Congress will ever let on, Dixon achieved the equivalent of pitching not one perfect base-ball game, but a perfect game every day of the season for her clients. Every single person who walked into her office in 1990 car-rying tax papers walked out with a return showing a refund owed by the IRS: 2,336 returns in all. It was Dixon's best performance. In the next two years, 99 percent and 98 percent of her clients col-lected refunds.

The returns were models of ingenuity, with phony claims for the earned income tax credit, as well as child and dependent care credits, and phantom deductions for mortgage interest, real estate taxes, charitable contributions, medical and dental bills. The amount of the false claims ranged from $375 to $17,599, and totaled more than $200,000 overall.

This impeccable refund record finally attracted the attention of the IRS. An agency spokesman observed with some under-statement at the time that "a 100 percent rate would be unusu-ally high."[50] The IRS raided Dixon's office and seized sixty boxes of records. She subsequently was indicted and convicted on four-teen counts of aiding and abetting the filing of false returns. After eighteen months in a minimum-security facility, Dixon was released with the understanding that she would file her per-sonal returns for 1990, 1991, and 1992. She owed $92,000 in back taxes, plus $28,000 in penalties, bringing her total tax bill to $120,000.

Tax preparer Dixon said she failed to file her own tax returns because she was "too distraught over her husband's death" in October 1990, and that she was taking a lot of medication while under a physician's care for stress.[51] But apparently not so much stress as to interfere with production on her refund assembly line. In 1991 alone, she managed to prepare 2,765 tax returns.

Let us review. Tax preparers who craft phony returns for others and don't bother to file themselves. Self-employed persons who write off their personal expenses or deduct their hobby losses from their income. Concealed capital gains from the sale of stocks.

Immigrant workers who live tax free. Independent businesspeople whose living expenses are paid for by offshore corporations. Poor people — and some not so poor — who collect earned income tax credit refund checks to which they are not entitled. Rich people who file returns and don't pay taxes. Rich people who don't even file.

As for the IRS cracking down on these schemes, there's not much chance, given the agency's current level of funding. That's really good news for those who are engaged in the latest mass tax-dodging craze: stashing money and assets in secret accounts in the tax havens of the world — beyond the reach of the IRS.

CHAPTER 2

TREASURE ISLANDS

MYSTERIOUS ENTITIES

F orty years ago, a visitor to Road Town, the only town in the British Virgin Islands, found himself in one of the sleepiest backwaters of the British Empire. "As unassuming as its name," Road Town, on the island of Tortola, was little more than a jumble of rundown stores, bars, hotels, and restaurants, hugging a single paved road between the harbor and the hills behind, wrote a correspondent for the *Saturday Evening Post.* The only structure of any consequence was Government House, home of Her Majesty's government, a white, square-shaped little edifice on a rise above the harbor. But even Government House couldn't disguise the reality. Anyone walking around could plainly see that the British Empire had "sputtered out" by the time it reached Road Town, leaving behind a colonial relic hopelessly out of touch with the modern world. Someday, perhaps, the writer speculated, "time is going to catch up" with the place. But in the meantime the British Virgins would remain "overlooked islands," charming oddities preserved by their isolation.[1]

A visitor arriving in Road Town today is struck by much the same languor of 1960. There are, of course, more shops, hotels, restaurants, and cars. Paved roads now lead from the waterfront into the foothills that come right down to the town. A cruise ship pier brings tourists to browse in the modest shops and boutiques, or to stroll along the harbor where sailboats and island packets busily come and go. But for all these superficial changes, Road Town still exudes an air of quiet detachment and tropical torpor, the feeling of a place that is still very much off the beaten path, especially when compared to its nearby American cousin, bustling Charlotte Amalie on St. Thomas.

It is not until one ventures a few blocks from the center of town, to a modern, two-story building of West Indian design in Pasea Estate, a neighborhood just up from the harbor, that one discovers time has finally caught up with the British Virgins. This is the office of the British Virgin Islands' Financial Services Department, the government agency that oversees the corporate registry. Inside, tight-lipped clerks efficiently go about the task of processing applications to establish so-called international business corporations, or IBCs.

Although they sound very official, IBCs exist only on paper. For starters, they don't usually engage in any business activity. There's no chief executive officer or board of directors. They don't publish financial statements. An IBC's books, if it has any, can be kept anywhere in the world, but no one can inspect them. IBCs are not required to file annual reports or disclose the identity of owners. So just what are they? Basically, they're paper shells, clandestine arrangements that allow an individual, a family, or even a business to hide assets offshore.

As recently as the late 1980s, the British Virgin Islands (BVI) had roughly 10,000 IBCs on the books. Now they register many times that every year, and by the year 2000 more than 350,000 such creations were crowded onto their registry, more than on any other Caribbean isle. Indeed, there are more incorporations in the BVI than in any state, including Delaware, the corporate domicile of choice for American businesses. But of course, those Delaware companies are real companies, unlike IBCs.

As pioneered by the BVI in landmark legislation in 1984 and subsequently copied throughout the Caribbean, the international business corporation has mushroomed into one of the most popular tax-avoidance devices. It's a kind of personal holding company for an individual's assets. An IBC formed in the semi-autonomous British Virgins may engage in any financial activity outside the islands — own real estate, trade stock, hold bank accounts and patents, receive commissions, dividends, rents, and royalties — all tax free. It operates in total secrecy, beyond the reach of the IRS and any other tax authorities. All interest, dividends, or capital gains remain confidential; nothing is reported to the IRS.

Every so often, word seeps out about one of these secret entities. Martin Frankel, the smooth-talking insurance scammer who purportedly took off with $300 million and fled the United States in 1999 before being apprehended in Germany, funneled some of his ill-gotten gains through a BVI corporation. Asif Ali Zardari, husband of Pakistan's former prime minister Benazir Bhutto, used a BVI corporation to hide millions of dollars in payoffs from foreign businesses operating in Pakistan. But the island registrar never disclosed the existence of these corporations; word leaked elsewhere.

"Once your assets are there," says an envious tax lawyer on nearby St. Thomas in the U.S. Virgin Islands, "they can't be located."[2]

What's happening in the BVI is being replicated all over the world. Secret corporations, trusts, and bank accounts are forming as rapidly as registrars can process paper or download e-mail. While once this activity was confined to relatively few places — the Isle of Man, the Cayman Islands, and Liechtenstein, for example — today just about every tropical island as well as a number of landlocked principalities are eagerly trying to grab a piece of this phenomenal growth industry.

Sleepy islands where commerce once consisted of locals leading dive trips to offshore reefs now boast sophisticated financial-service

industries with savvy financial planners, full-time legal depart-
ments, and branches of international accounting firms — all connected via sophisticated telecommunication networks to the States
and Europe.

To cater to those who want to move money out of the taxman's grasp, the tropics have made the process as effortless as rent-
ing a car. "Some people have the impression that sheltering assets
offshore is difficult or cumbersome to achieve," says a Belize-based
service, which reassures that in fact, it's "easy, convenient, confidential and secure."[3] In a Costa Rica Internet directory, amid
entries on how to book a hotel or sign up for a rain forest tour, is a
handy guide to setting up your own personal corporation or trust.
"Experienced professionals" are standing by in Costa Rica, the
directory asserts, to help you tailor a variety of programs to your
needs, including a "tax deduction."[4]

To the throngs of sun worshipers and scuba divers who flock to
the Caribbean every winter has been added another class of
tourists: wealthy Americans attending seminars on "asset protection" or "wealth preservation," workshops that show them how to
move money offshore.

One such event was the British Virgin Islands Offshore Strategies Conference held at the posh Biras Creek Resort on Virgin
Gorda in January 1998. The stunningly beautiful, intimate thirty-
two-suite resort, reachable only by boat, was closed to the public
after participants — weary of the "heavy breath of government,"
as the conference organizer put it — forked over $6,950 a couple
to hear "international experts" explain the "latest techniques for
using offshore structures . . . for privacy, protection and growth."[5]

So sophisticated have these programs become that some are
devoted to such arcane subjects as the rapidly evolving technology
that facilitates the offshore flight of capital. The Leeward Island of
Anguilla, 100 miles east of the U.S. Virgin Islands, is the site of an
annual conference on financial cryptography, where papers are
presented that are "devoted to finding the best way to use the

Internet to ship money from place to place."[6] At the 1999 gathering, speakers discussed "Playing Hide and Seek with Stored Keys," "Improved Magic Ink Signatures Using Hints," and "Anonymous Investing: Hiding the Identities of Stockholders."[7]

Offshore promoters have their own annual trade show, "Shorex, the International Money Show." Held every fall, usually in London, it attracts 2,500 exhibitors, practitioners, clients, and visitors from more than fifty nations. Participants attend seminars on "New Offshore Financial Vehicles," "The Tax Implications of Internet Trading," and "Money Laundering Through the Internet."[8] Says Philippe Gelin, the show's founder and managing director: "We have now established a real forum from where professionals in the offshore industry can openly market their services."[9]

For American citizens, there is nothing inherently illegal about parking assets offshore. What is illegal is not reporting to the IRS all income earned by those accounts. And that's why the offshore flight of assets has such ominous implications for taxpayer compliance. Once money leaves the country, the IRS loses track of it. Unlike U.S. banks or corporations, which are required by law to report to the IRS on all interest, dividends, or securities sales, an offshore corporation or trust doesn't. In fact, laws in offshore jurisdictions usually prohibit such disclosure. Thus, while U.S. tax law requires American taxpayers to report all income, wherever earned, the IRS has no way to track income earned abroad. The decision on whether to report it is left solely to the taxpayer.

In the Caribbean alone, hundreds of thousands of international business corporations have been chartered in the past decade. An equal, if not greater, number of secret trusts and bank accounts have also been created. How much U.S. wealth has gone offshore? Nobody knows. The Organisation for Economic Cooperation and Development (OECD) in Paris tried to come up with an estimate in 1998, but eventually gave up. Nevertheless, the OECD turned up substantial anecdotal evidence that the use of tax havens is widespread and that "participation in such schemes is expanding at an exponential rate."[10]

Unofficial estimates put the value of assets held offshore at $5 trillion. A chunk of that belongs to corporations, which use it for legitimate business purposes as well as a way to reduce or eliminate their corporate income tax bills. Another slice belongs to citizens of other countries. And a piece is owned by individual Americans for just one purpose — to evade taxes. Assuming that their holdings amount to only one-tenth of the total, a conservative assumption, their offshore arrangements allow these people to escape payment of income taxes that add up to the equivalent of every tax dollar paid by everyone in New York State and New Jersey who earns less than $200,000 a year.

For the United States and other developed countries, the OECD warned, the growing popularity of these offshore centers poses a grave threat to their tax systems:

> Because tax havens offer a way to minimize taxes and to obtain financial confidentiality, tax havens are appealing to corporate and individual investors. Tax havens serve three main purposes: they provide a location for holding passive investments ("money boxes"); they provide a location where "paper" profits can be booked; and they enable the affairs of taxpayers, particularly their bank accounts, to be effectively shielded from scrutiny by tax authorities of other countries.
>
> All of these functions may potentially cause harm to the tax systems of other countries as they facilitate both corporate and individual income tax avoidance and evasion.[11]

THE ENTREPRENEUR

Ronald D. Preston knows all about engaging in activities that will cause harm to the U.S. tax system. That's his business. An American living in self-imposed exile, Preston is the impresario behind an outfit in Costa Rica called the Magna Charta Society, whose mission undermines tax collection in the United States.

Like offshore promoters everywhere, Preston is getting a big assist from an idea that is spreading like an epidemic through the tropics and that is going to be increasingly bad news for the U.S.

Treasury. The idea goes something like this: For years, wealthy Americans have been making out like bandits by sending their money out of the country; now it's time for average Americans to do the same.

"Do what the rich do," Preston advises Americans who are considering sending assets offshore. "Take the lion's share of your wealth outside your home country's legal reach. Watch your investments or retirement fund compound tax free in a Tax Heaven environment, safe from attacks by potential creditors, even tax collectors."[12]

Preston operates from San José, the capital of Costa Rica, which has become a magnet for offshore money just like its Central American neighbors Belize and Panama, and the Caribbean islands to the east. Named for the historic document English nobles foisted upon an unwilling King John in 1215, Preston's Magna Charta Society is dedicated to reining in the power of government — in this case, the power to collect taxes.

Inviting people to cheat on their taxes once was done with a certain amount of discretion or secrecy, but Preston proves those days are gone forever. "Placing assets outside one's home country jurisdiction, beyond the reach of the courts is the essence of this program," says a society circular. "You never lose control. Eliminates probate, estate taxes, and income taxes."[13]

To bring about this tax-free state of bliss, Preston peddles a smorgasbord of financial products: international business corporations in the British Virgin Islands, an offshore trust (a "financial fortress" shielding your identity), and an offshore bank account, which Preston will set up for you right there in Costa Rica.[14] To achieve maximum protection and tax minimization, Preston recommends all three. He describes his role in bringing all these things to pass as a little like being a symphonic conductor. "All I do is orchestrate [this process.]"[15]

Preston says he got his start in the early 1980s in Seattle, putting together offshore asset-protection trusts for doctors and other professionals. A native of the Pacific Northwest from a "lower-middle-class family," Preston lied about his age and enlisted in the Army when he was fourteen, according to a biographical profile.[16] He was soon sent to Korea, where, by his account, he was among the few to survive Pork Chop Hill, one of the bloodiest and most famous battles of the Korean War, later dramatized in a movie starring Gregory Peck.

After the war, Preston claims to have been variously a deputy sheriff, an entrepreneur, and then an offshore-trust developer for clients of a large Seattle law firm. He soon ran afoul of the IRS because "we were stupidly operating in the United States." After waging a losing battle with the agency, he decided the time was right to actually move offshore.

"If we were going to offer asset protection, we better do it the right way and that means you get the hell out of the United States and you do it where you're domiciled," he said. "People who offer offshore services inside the States are crazy. We learned the hard way."[17]

He went first to Belize, where he established the Magna Charta Society in 1992. He also chartered two trusts, Avalon Trust and Central American Trust. Everything went well in Belize and business boomed, he said, until 1995, when he became disenchanted with the Belizean government and moved his operations to Costa Rica.

The heart of Preston's pitch is a strategy that he maintains will outwit the most determined revenue agent and allow Americans, and anyone else for that matter, to keep their money out of the hands of tax collectors, creditors — indeed, anyone at all.

Send Preston as little as $1,000 and he'll set you up offshore. He starts by buying a share of stock in something called PANAFIN, a Costa Rican financial services agency. PANAFIN in turn opens a numbered account for you in the Banco Del Pacifico, a Costa Rican chartered bank with offices in downtown San José, an account that promises "absolute privacy," says Preston. "Our clients' accounts are like Swiss secrecy accounts, numbered, therefore no client's name resides within our office nor in our companies."[18]

You're then issued a PANAFIN debit card, which Preston calls a MonyCard. With this you make deposits and withdrawals. Because the system is based on a debit card, the owner's name need not appear on the card. "Your name is not exposed," Preston assures. "MonyCard is a numbered debit card in the Electron (Visa) System. Your name is not shown on the face of the MonyCard, unless you specifically request it."

Deposits are made by the cardholder with Citibank, New York, with a stipulation that they be transferred to the numbered account at the Banco Del Pacifico, one of the myriad correspondent banks used by Citibank around the world.

But isn't it illegal to send money out of the United States and not report it to the IRS? Ah, that's the beauty of it, at least in Preston's mind. He claims: "Funding . . . is accomplished by depositing funds at Citibank N.A. New York, where funds remain . . . in the in-transit account of Banco Del Pacifico."

Since the "deposited funds never leave . . . New York," Preston maintains, "there is never a need to send money offshore creating a paper trail. . . . With MonyCard you will never have to repatriate funds. Therefore, foreign account reporting is not required by government and no taxes are owed nor due." In addition to cash, Preston also encourages U.S. taxpayers to deposit other holdings into their accounts, such as stocks and any other interest or dividend-bearing assets. "All interest that accrues is foreign-earned interest," he claims, "and not subject to U.S. taxes. . . . It doesn't get any better than this."[19]

Just how successful Preston has been is anybody's guess. He says his business is booming. Are more and more Americans going offshore? "Absolutely," he answers. "One short sentence summarizes what's going on. The tighter the government squeezes you, the harder you are going to look for an out, and you're being squeezed like you can't believe."

Preston pauses in his diatribe against taxes. "I love my country," he says with passion. "I just don't have any love for the government."[20]

STRICTLY CONFIDENTIAL

The Magna Charta Society and hundreds of purveyors like it operate under the protection of foreign-government-sanctioned secrecy. "Your name is never attached to the account in any bank," the Magna Charta Society assures prospective clients. "The laws of Costa Rica forbid revealing the names."[21]

Costa Rica isn't alone. An iron-clad code of confidentiality governs most offshore centers. In Anguilla, the secrecy law is called the Confidential Relationships Ordinance. In St. Kitts–Nevis, it's the Confidential Relationship Act. In St. Vincent, it's the Confidential Relationships Preservation Act. In the Cayman Islands, any government official or bank employee who divulges the identity of a Cayman account beneficiary can be sent to jail for violating the Confidential Relationships Act.

This means that if you assign cash or some other asset to one of these jurisdictions, there is virtually no way the IRS can pry that information out of the local authorities. Most people who go offshore transfer cash, certificates of deposit, stocks, and bonds to a corporation, trust, or bank account. But another popular asset turning up in portfolios is real estate — U.S. real estate.

In some of Manhattan's fashionable neighborhoods are condominiums registered to companies in the West Indies. The real estate rolls in other affluent areas across the country also are peppered with names and offshore addresses that conceal the identity of the true owners. Some of the properties are owned by foreign citizens who live part time in the United States. Others are owned by Americans who prefer Caribbean tax havens over those in Europe or Asia. In one of the few instances when the nationalities of depositors in secret accounts have surfaced — the 1999 Guardian Bank and Trust Company scandal in the Cayman

Islands — the chief figure in the investigation, Guardian bank founder John Mathewson, told authorities that more than 90 percent of the depositors in Cayman banks are American citizens.[22]

Just how far Caribbean countries will go to guarantee secrecy was demonstrated by Belize in 1995, when it blocked efforts by U.S. authorities to inspect the records of a fraudulent offshore bank. The Belize-based Swiss Trade & Commerce Trust Ltd. was created by two American promoters and had served as a conduit for U.S. taxpayers to funnel money away from the IRS. When the U.S. Securities and Exchange Commission, looking into separate charges, sought to review the bank's records, the supreme court of Belize refused to allow it. Evidence abounded that Swiss Trust was a scam — a federal judge in Washington, D.C., later ruled the bank was a fraud and one of its founders is now a fugitive from U.S. authorities — but the Belize court held that the country's confidentiality laws outweighed all other factors and thus barred U.S. authorities from reviewing bank documents.

Secrecy in tax havens has become so secure that once a U.S. citizen creates an offshore account, there is little likelihood that jurisdiction will divulge the name, especially when taxes are involved. While the Caymans, the BVI, and other isles will sometimes cooperate with U.S. authorities when drug money is suspected as the source of a deposit, they won't help when the investigation concerns taxes. That's because the offshore world doesn't consider tax evasion a crime.

Escaping taxes levied by the United States or other developed countries is viewed by tax havens as an inalienable right, much like free speech or freedom of assembly. So if you park assets offshore and you do it with great care, chances are you're home free. "Unless revenue authorities discover papers which point to hidden offshore assets, they have nothing to go on," says one British Virgin Islands financial planner. "The chances of being caught are largely dependent on an individual's own actions. Has he left a paper trail?"[23]

That's exactly what happened to flamboyant financier, antiques collector, and scourge of the Hamptons, Barry Trupin. He first loomed into view in the early 1980s when he and his wife bought an oceanfront estate in Southampton and began renovating the Georgian mansion into a French Gothic castle complete with turrets and towers. He called it Dragon's Head, an apt name for what his neighbors regarded as a monstrosity taking shape in their midst. In addition to violating the town's building code, Dragon's Head's new pink and purple additions and underground shark tank clashed with his neighbors' sense of decorum. Trupin also imported a sixteenth-century Normandy pub, cramming it into space once occupied by the mansion's library, and installed an indoor pool and freshwater grotto equipped with oxygen jets for scuba divers.

Trupin's financial planning business fell on hard times by the late 1980s, and he was later forced to sell Dragon's Head for $3.3 million. Some of the proceeds were wired to a Canadian bank, which in turn sent a portion to an account that he controlled in the British Virgin Islands.[24] Trupin failed to report the proceeds on his personal income tax return, but he left a trail and the IRS stumbled upon it by accident. He subsequently was indicted, and in August 1999 a federal jury in New York found him guilty of failing to pay $6.6 million in taxes that he owed.

As you might expect, the phenomenal fascination with everything offshore is opening up untold opportunities for operators anxious to make a buck. They're a colorful lot who see the brightest of futures. As a group, they espouse an abiding hatred of the U.S. government, with their fiercest indignation and scorn reserved for the biggest bogeyman of all, the IRS. Most are pretty fair salesmen, with a gift for turning a phrase. They invariably come up with catchy names for the organizations or causes they lead, which in turn become effective marketing tools to lure yet more taxpayers into their secret world.

They are folks like John Pugsley, who with his wife Kiana are known in offshore parlance as "PTs." That stands for Permanent

Travelers or Permanent Tourists, a phrase that denotes a person who "arranges his or her paperwork in such a way that all governments consider him a tourist."[25] The Pugsleys say they are still U.S. citizens, but they now live in the British Virgin Islands, usually aboard their fifty-foot-long sloop, *Eris Island*.[26] For the Pugsleys, being a "PT is the only path to true freedom and happiness."[27]

Pugsley is chairman of something called the Sovereign Society in Waterford, Ireland, where the famed crystal bowls, candlesticks, goblets, and chandeliers are made. The Sovereign Society arranges offshore bank accounts, trusts, and paper companies. Pugsley, who calls himself an economist, issues periodic reports on "why you must begin moving assets outside your own country now, before it's too late" and "how to hold assets abroad and legally not have to report them to your government."[28] All this is necessary, he maintains, because of the government's "heinous attacks on our personal wealth and privacy." [29]

Before turning offshore, Pugsley launched his reputation with a couple of best-selling financial advice books. In 1974, *Common Sense Economics* made a hit by forecasting a rise in inflation. He followed in 1980 with *The Alpha Strategy,* which exhorted readers to stockpile common items — toothpaste, shampoo, razor blades, fan belts, and underwear — as a hedge against inflation. His general advice was to buy everything you needed rather than paying higher prices for the same stuff later.

"If it were possible to create a perfect savings account," Pugsley advised, "it would consist of a lifetime supply of every item you'll ever use. With such a stockpile, you would have reached financial independence and eliminated forever the risks of external economic forces such as inflation or recession."[30] Hopefully, investors passed on Pugsley's advice. The price of toothpaste and razor blades has barely moved since 1980. That same money invested in the stock market would have appreciated more than 1,000 percent.

In the late 1980s, while living in Newport Beach, California, Pugsley created a kind of upscale meals-on-wheels business that delivered delicacies from quality restaurants to homes, businesses, and boats. His Restaurant Express got off to a good start in Orange County. But plans to expand into Beverly Hills and other wealthy enclaves proved too costly and the business foundered after two years.

Pugsley then found his true calling — offshore promotion. His first vehicle, *John Pugsley's Journal,* a $100-a-year newsletter featuring "Private Conversations with the Money Masters," quickly established him as an ardent "Freedom Philosopher," in the words of one admirer.[31] Pugsley describes all governments as being run by "ruffians and schemers" out to "plunder" the wealth of their citizens, whose only recourse is to transfer their holdings to an offshore tax haven. Such places, according to Pugsley, are a "legal refuge to the assets of the richer citizens of the bigger nations [who] flock to these offshore sanctuaries by the hundreds of thousands, carrying with them the titles to their assets. And the big nations are effectively powerless to stop them."[32]

Pugsley's Sovereign Society hawks the usual goodies, but gives special emphasis to another emerging tax avoidance tool — second passports. "Your government does not want you to know this," he says,

> but you can get an instant, legitimate, lifetime passport from a Caribbean tax haven for as low as $55,000 for a family of five.
>
> A large discount has been guaranteed for you on two of the world's best economic citizenship programs. These unique programs are only known to a handful of well-informed people — some of whom are among the wealthiest people in the world.[33]

Sovereign doesn't identify the islands, saying the U.S. government has "forbidden" the two from advertising. But don't worry. Sovereign assures you that it knows who they are and "has made it possible for you to access these programs easily and directly."[34]

Why would you want such a thing? To dodge taxes, of course.

"This passport can act as a powerful tax-planning tool," says Pugsley, and can help reduce your tax burden and "give you the option to live, do business, or retire on tax-free, sun-soaked, affordable Caribbean islands."[35]

These claims notwithstanding, a second passport, as far as U.S. laws are concerned, does not lawfully reduce one's tax liability on current income. But that hasn't stopped the flow of applications to the Caribbean from taxpayers who hope otherwise. Grenada, Belize, St. Kitts–Nevis, and Dominica have been especially active marketers. The latter regards its "economic citizenship programme" as a major component of "national development."[36]

In St. Kitts, so many applications surged into the office of the Ministry of Trade, Industry and CARICOM Affairs in 1998 that the small nation quintupled the price of passports from $50,000 to $250,000 to dampen demand. Even so, it remains one of the most popular passport providers and is featured prominently on the Web pages of brokers dealing in second passports. While the St. Kitts government does not release data on the national origin of the purchasers, many are U.S. citizens. Asked where his clients come from, the otherwise reticent M. Irvin BonCamper, a St. Kitts–based consultant who establishes trusts, personal holding companies, and offshore bank accounts, doesn't miss a beat. "They are mostly United States citizens." And why is he getting their business? "Because they want to save money on their taxes."[37]

The tropics are honeycombed with small businesses like BonCamper's that work with U.S. depositors through their ties to local law firms and banks. Alongside these entrepreneurs you find offices with familiar names that illustrate just how pervasive offshore accounts have become — names such as Citicorp, Chase, Peat Marwick, and PricewaterhouseCoopers. All the big management, banking, accounting, and financial service firms have set up shop in tax-free havens to create secret accounts. Counting on their established reputations, they cater to wealthy clients around the world who are eager to shift assets offshore, but who are reluctant to entrust their holdings to strangers.

Raul Salinas, the brother of the former president of Mexico, turned to Citibank, one of the world's richest and most prestigious, to help him move more than $90 million out of Mexico in a way that "effectively disguised the funds' source and destination, thus breaking the funds' paper trail," according to the General Accounting Office (GAO).[38] Citibank officials bent over backward to accommodate Salinas, whose wealth has been suspected of coming from illegal drug profits, by helping him establish a dummy corporation in the Cayman Islands through which funds were routed to Citibank accounts in London and Switzerland.

Touch down just about anywhere offshore and you're likely to find an international financial services provider ready to create a variety of instruments that can be used to hide assets. KPMG Belize in Belize City, which sets up bank accounts and shell corporations, stresses the company's affiliation to the vast KPMG network as a reason to trust its operation: "KPMG Corporate Services (Belize) Limited is an affiliate of Belize's premier accounting and consulting services firm, KPMG. We are part of the extensive global KPMG network comprised of 6,561 partners and more than 85,291 total staff across 155 countries."[39]

But these connections, while useful to hustle business, can be made to seem tenuous if law enforcement officers come inquiring about customers. Manhattan District Attorney Robert M. Morgenthau found that out in a frustrating case prosecuted by his office in 1995.

One of the few high-profile law enforcement officials who have publicly voiced concern about the rise in offshore activities and their potential for tax evasion, Morgenthau uncovered a complex scheme of kickbacks and tax fraud orchestrated by an international bond trader in New York involving the sale of millions of dollars in bonds of developing nations.

The trader, Waldemar N. Jezler, bought and sold bonds, paid off certain banking officers for the business, and shipped the proceeds to a secret account in the Caribbean, defrauding both the banks and taxpayers. When Morgenthau investigated, the trail led to the international accounting firm of Price Waterhouse on Antigua. It turned out that the island office of Price Waterhouse had established and run something called Merlin Overseas Ltd., a company that Jezler used to conceal millions of dollars in taxable income.

But when Morgenthau turned to Price Waterhouse's home office in New York City for help in ferreting out details about Merlin, he got no cooperation. Although the Antigua operation clearly was related to the giant accounting firm, Manhattan officials contended they had no say over their foreign offspring. "Even McDonald's has more control over its franchises," Morgenthau fumed. "They advertise the services of its Antigua office, they use the same logo, same stationery, then they say, 'We have no control.'"[40]

Nevertheless, Morgenthau pushed ahead and eventually secured an indictment of Jezler and his company. Under the terms of a plea bargain agreement, Jezler pleaded guilty to the charge that he "knowingly filed a false tax return" with New York State, and Merlin pleaded guilty to commercial bribery.[41] Although Price Waterhouse (now PricewaterhouseCoopers) was not charged with any offense, Morgenthau believes the firm had played a pivotal role in helping the trader hide his millions. "This accounting company was complicit," Morgenthau said.[42]

THE HIDDEN WORLD AROUND YOU

Lest you think all this offshore investment activity takes place offshore, think again. Some of the aggressive promoters are onshore, in places that might surprise you — in suburban shopping malls, in modest bungalows on typical streets, in small towns you've never heard of, in numbered post office boxes, and in some of America's exclusive residential communities.

Unlike Ronald Preston, who left the United States because he believed it was safer to operate from offshore, others who practice the craft do so quite nicely without ever leaving the States. And they have encountered few, if any, difficulties with the IRS. Most operations appear to be small, often just one or two people. Together, they represent a disconnected patchwork of promoters functioning independently. About the only thing they have in common is the sales pitch they direct at people who want to send money offshore. But the ranks of these promoters are growing in a spontaneous movement that has been ignited by mounting discontent with the U.S. tax code and sustained by the ease with which an offshore account can be established.

These days you can find an offshore operator just about anywhere you look.

Prairie Village, Kansas, is about as Middle America as you can get. A suburb of Kansas City, Missouri, it has 25,000 people, a median family income of roughly $50,000, few minorities or poor people — and at least one offshore promoter, Research Press Inc. A clearinghouse of newsletters, books, and timely advice, Research Press publishes *Offshore Tax Strategies* and maintains an "Offshore Tax Library" with information about tax havens, trusts, expatriation, permanent tourist status, and secret bank accounts. It also periodically conducts what it calls an "offshore boot camp" to answer such questions as "How do I transfer money offshore?" and "How can I be sure it's safe offshore?" Research Press assures that its advice is sound and that the IRS is welcome to send representatives to the boot camps "because there won't be anything discussed . . . that isn't totally legal."[43]

Carson City, Nevada, is the state capital and a place where prospectors and gunfighters once roamed the streets. Mark Twain lived there for a time and failed at every get-rich-quick scheme he tried before turning to writing. Carson City is also home to the National Asset Protection Institute, an offshore provider whose Web page pictures a winged dollar sign flying toward a tropical island, leaving little doubt as to the institute's mission — to show you "how to legally disinherit Uncle Sam."[44] By signing up with the Institute, "you can learn the same insider secrets once known only by elite investment bankers and lawyers for the super-rich."[45]

Sunnyside Road in Clackamas, Oregon, a suburb of Portland, is home to the International Privacy Corporation, which promotes secret accounts in Belize and in the Turks and Caicos. The two nations offer "more privacy, are less complicated, and less expensive than anywhere else in the world," says IPC.[46] The group supplies how-to kits to open offshore accounts. Don't know what to call your "company"? No problem. IPC has already reserved a bloc of names. How about Buccaneer Assets Ltd., or Tiger Tales Ltd., or Serendipity Assets Inc.? IPC will process all the paperwork and no one will know who actually owns the company. "We don't even have to know your name," IPC says.[47]

Cantera Avenue is a quiet, little-traveled ribbon of asphalt winding through the exclusive Hope Ranch neighborhood in Santa Barbara, California. Ninety miles northwest of Los Angeles, Santa Barbara abounds in beautiful homes. But even by local standards, Hope Ranch is a place apart. With towering palm trees, a private golf course, and houses with breathtaking views of the Pacific Ocean, Hope Ranch is the epitome of genteel living. It is also, in a house in the 1500 block of Cantera, the locus for an aggressive offshore information service. Offshore Outlook Inc. spews out articles, newsletters, and advice on "Moving Profits and Income into Offshore Financial Centres," "How to Choose an Offshore Tax Haven," and "Getting the Most From Your Offshore Structures."[48]

Sierra Bonita Avenue runs north from Hollywood Boulevard, climbing into the Hollywood Hills. It is a typical pre–World War II West Hollywood neighborhood, with small one- and two-story bungalows, many in the architectural style of the Midwestern cities their builders left behind. One house in the 1500 block serves as a distribution center for mailing the brochures of an especially energetic promoter called Offshore Information Services (OIS).

"Welcome to the hidden world of offshore business!" says one OIS promotion. "Offshore is where the money is at!" OIS recommends that clients create bank accounts, corporations, and trusts in separate jurisdictions so that there is no "link or paper trails between them."[49]

Show Low, Arizona, in the White Mountains, 175 miles northeast of Phoenix, takes its name from a legendary card game that two early settlers played to see who got the town. Today, it's a popular resort where vacationers flee the summer heat to fish, hike, golf, and swim. Others flee something entirely different. On the town's main drag, Deuce of Clubs Street, there's an address for Administrative Consultants Ltd., the U.S. branch of a Nevis-based offshore trust creator. "Offshore trusts are available to anyone," says Administrative Consultants. And it boasts that its profits "are not connected with the U.S. or a U.S. citizen. Therefore, profits are not taxed. . . . Who doesn't want you to go offshore? For obvious reasons, the IRS!"[50]

Aloma Avenue in Winter Park, Florida, is home to the usual suburban shops and strip malls, plus PILL — Prosper International League Ltd., which peddles Belize and Antigua trusts. From a small, sporadically manned office, PILL provides easy-to-follow instructions to help the little guy create an offshore trust. For years, PILL claims, only the wealthy had the wherewithal to establish offshore trusts, but "now it's your turn," thanks to the explosion in offshore connections and low-cost providers like itself.[51]

By the time you've read this, some of the operations discussed will have moved, changed their names, or gone out of business. That's part of their nature. The offshore sands are constantly shifting, with promoters always on the move, sometimes in the mistaken fear that the IRS is about to shut them down. These promoters are a mixed bag. Some are outright hustlers who take people's money and run, while others clearly provide services and want to be around in this booming business for years to come. In any event, new promoters spring up faster than old ones disappear. This assures an ever-growing nightmare for the IRS. While the agency doesn't like to talk about the torrent of money flowing into foreign accounts, it has acknowledged the severity of the problem and the implications for the U.S. tax system.

In an off-the-cuff speech before tax professionals in Miami Beach in January 1999, John T. Lyons, IRS assistant commissioner, railed at the "explosion" in the use of trusts, both domestic and foreign, for tax avoidance and evasion.[52] "Unlike in the past," he said, "havens are being used not only by criminals and the very rich but by doctors, lawyers, and other successful professionals for tax avoidance and to shelter assets for other purposes."[53]

One of the few times the IRS has actually placed a dollar figure on the cost of offshore evasion and avoidance was in 1995, when the agency successfully appealed to Congress for a law to tighten up reporting requirements for U.S. citizens using foreign trusts. "The IRS estimates that in 1993 only $1.5 billion of foreign trust assets were reported," Sam Gibbons, then a Democratic congressman from Florida, told his House colleagues. "Treasury estimates that tens of billions of dollars of assets could easily be contained in foreign trusts created by U.S. persons. It appears to me that the rate of noncompliance exceeds 85 percent.... Treasury estimates that my legislation would result in $3.4 billion in additional revenues over 10 years."[54]

The IRS doesn't want it known how easily money can be shipped offshore and how difficult it is to trace transactions.

How is the transfer actually made? Every scheme has its own trademark. In one, a taxpayer turns over cash or other assets to a broker in the States. The broker in turn divides the assets into smaller increments and deposits them in a series of accounts in multiple banks, then wires the funds from those accounts to secret accounts offshore. Ultimately, the money is wired back to the States to yet another set of accounts, and later redeposited in the client's account. The idea is to create a byzantine trail that the IRS couldn't follow even if it had the agents, which it doesn't. This is more or less the scenario three California men cooked up, one that might still be operating had they not gotten too greedy.

Ronald L. Chappell, an accountant, and Todd C. Gaskill, a lawyer, began peddling offshore accounts and trusts in the early 1990s from Roseville, California, near Sacramento. Using names such as Forest Estates Planning Associates and Heritage Estates Lifetime Planning Services, Chappell and Gaskill solicited doctors and other professionals with stunning success. A Redding, California, cardiologist and his wife turned over hundreds of thousands of dollars to the promoters. Investigators later determined that Chappell, Gaskill, and a third accomplice, Martin L. Goodrich, funneled at least $687,000 of the couple's income through a maze of offshore accounts to evade taxes.

Once the trio signed up a client for one of their offshore packages, they implemented a dizzyingly complex series of steps to cover their tracks. First, using cashier's checks and bank accounts with phony names, they deposited a client's money in numerous bank accounts under their control in California and Nevada. The money was then wired to banks in the Caribbean and Central America, and then back to the States for deposit in yet another string of bogus accounts, from which it would be secretly returned to the clients. Once the money had completed the full onshore-offshore cycle, it was said, in the trio's lingo, to have made a complete "pass."[55]

What eventually tripped them up had nothing to do with their offshore activities. It was the outrageously excessive amounts and types of deductions that Chappell, Gaskill, and Goodrich entered on their clients' tax returns. It wasn't enough to shift money offshore untaxed; they also concocted huge write-offs using the offshore trusts to generate fraudulent tax deductions. According to the U.S. Attorney's office in Sacramento, clients transferred their "businesses, homes and other assets into the trusts." On their returns, they wrote off various personal expenses, including "lawn care, house cleaning, and 'scholarships' for their children, as deductible expenses of the trusts. The clients also depreciated the value of their residences and passed losses from the trusts onto their personal tax return."[56]

Chappell, Gaskill, and Goodrich were indicted and convicted of tax fraud and sentenced to federal prison in March 1999 for terms ranging from three to seven years.

A fourth defendant, Lloyd Winburn, skipped the country during the trial and is now a fugitive from justice, reportedly living in Mexico. A former California state legislative aide, Winburn was the point man of the scam, routing the money in and out of dozens of offshore accounts to camouflage the trail.

The IRS likes to point to the Sacramento convictions as sending a "clear signal" to other tax cheats that they're playing with fire.[57] "For those who market tax evasion schemes involving the use of trusts and sham transactions," said Paul L. Seave, the U.S. Attorney in Sacramento, "the sentences in this case should put them on notice that their conduct is criminal, and that if convicted, they will serve time in prison."[58]

Truth to tell, Chappell and his crew are the exception to the rule. Very few get caught. No one, especially the IRS, has the slightest idea how many offshore trusts exist. Unlike IBCs, which are at least registered on the islands where they're created, trusts don't even have to be recorded. Merely executing the documents with an offshore agent who keeps them in his or her possession is all that's needed to activate a trust.

Of all the lures that are scoring big with tax-avoiding, litigation-conscious Americans, the home run may be secret foreign trusts. Offshore purveyors sell them as the one vehicle immune to seizure, confiscation, or pillaging by U.S. authorities. Once you turn your assets over to a trust, they say, no one — not your spouse, not an aggressive lawyer, not a judge, and especially not the IRS — can get their hands on them. The promoters say that even if you — the trust's creator — would like to release the assets, you can't. Your hands are tied because all authority over the trust resides with the trustee.

While every offshore promoter has a full array of products for sale, from secret bank accounts to your own personal corporation, a few specialize in trusts. Like EHMT.

That would be Entrepreneur Holdings Management Trust of Orlando. EHMT will help you establish a trust in Belize with one of its "Do-It-Yourself Offshore Trust" packages, which come "with a customized template that is ready to go. You just plug in the right names, get their signatures and it's finished! It is now a LEGAL OFFSHORE ENTITY, ready to conduct business!" Best of all, you need not designate a foreign bank or attorney or someone else you don't know to act as trustee. Just assign yourself. As EHMT explains, "The rules are different Offshore. 'You can have your cake and eat it too!'"[59]

The cost of a Belize trust is a "one-time fee of $950" that also entitles you to "unlimited on-going support from EHMT via phone, fax, email, etc." The "Complete Offshore Trust Package," as EHMT describes it, "comes with a very thorough and explicitly thought-out thirty-page Trust document with 'easy-to-follow' instructions . . . We'll take you through every page, one step at a time."[60]

EHMT's "international division" is located at 2457-A South Hiawassee Road, Suite 327, in Orlando. What do these international offices of a global financial services company look like? Well, they're a little cramped, measuring about four by six inches. Inches?

The address turns out to be a mailbox at U.S. Pak-N-Ship in Orlando's Metro Park Village, bracketed between Subway sandwiches and Metro Cigars, and a few doors down from Sam Snead's Tavern, where Slammin' Sammy's golf clubs are on display, which is more than can be said for EHMT's managers. A clerk at Pak-N-Ship allowed that someone from EHMT merely picks up the mail delivered to its private postal box.

OPEN SECRETS

The offshore world has always attracted hustlers and con artists who operate in the shadows. But another breed of promoters poses a far greater threat to the IRS. These are the people who have boldly established headquarters in the open, thereby proclaiming that they're here to stay. They exude an aura of stability, permanence, and respectability. If you look, you'll find them in plain sight.

One little-known organization, the Oxford Club, occupies an elegant brownstone in Baltimore's historic Mount Vernon neighborhood, an architecturally rich area of museums, churches, restaurants, parks, and nineteenth-century townhouses.

The club has its headquarters in a four-story, twenty-three-room mansion at 105 West Monument Street. Built by a wealthy merchant on the eve of the Civil War, the townhouse abounds in exquisite architectural details: rich walnut paneling, ornate plaster molding, marble fireplaces, high ceilings. For most of the twentieth century the Episcopal archdiocese owned the mansion, and a small chapel on the first floor has been preserved as a meeting room.

From this imposing base, the Oxford Club reaches out to its 40,000 members, most of them in the United States. Club employees help form local chapters, book foreign trips, arrange seminars on "wealth preservation" and "expatriation," and publish a slick twice-a-month newsletter, the *Oxford Club Communiqué*, that offers tips on investments, privacy preservation, and taxes — especially nuts-and-bolts advice to members on "how to keep . . . money invisible from the IRS."[61] The *Communiqué* brims with stories and photographs of euphoric Oxfordians on outings — a Family Wealth Cruise to Alaska, an Investors' Expedition to Turkey, a Global Investment Gala and Symposium in San Francisco.

The club describes itself as "one of the most successful and profitable financial fellowships in the world."[62] Just how successful is anybody's guess. The club doesn't release financial information, and members pledge not to divulge any of its advice on taxes or other matters. A guiding principle for Oxfordians is that membership makes them privy to exclusive information. "The best information will never be aired publicly," the club confides in its annual

report. "We won't read about the safest, most lucrative investments in our local newspapers. This is knowledge shared by only a
few."[63]

The club has a Members' Exchange to flash alerts about "extraordinary investment opportunities" and a Members' Real Estate
Exchange to post properties for sale, rent, or swap. The club also
publishes an annual confidential membership directory, the Blue
Book.

All this creates the impression that the Oxford Club is, well, a
club. But it isn't. The trips, seminars, and investor safaris, real as
they are, are just window dressing for what Oxford really is — a
fancy name for a slick investment newsletter that advocates,
among other things, tax avoidance and sets forth ways to achieve
it. The message is clear: "We believe taxes are the biggest single
threat to your wealth."[64]

The club delivers a steady diet of articles about the latest tax-
avoidance gimmicks and ways to outwit the IRS. These aren't con-
ventional tax tips. They're about "How to safely keep cash in an
offshore bank"; "How to transfer cash. But not in your name";
"How to open tax-free foreign bank accounts."[65]

The brains behind the Oxford Club is a newsletter guru, William
Robert Bonner, a tall, lanky Marylander whose flair for bombast has
built an $80-million-a-year direct mail empire. The founder and
principal owner of Agora Publishing Inc., Bonner churns out scores
of newsletters, books, and audio and videotapes on subjects from
alternative medicine to global travel, all with a definite point of
view. As *Worth* magazine characterized his approach: "Hype, when
Bonner is doing the hyping, has the power to bend reality —
his way."[66]

Bonner launched Agora in 1979 after a stint with the National
Taxpayers Union in Washington, which was founded by an old
high school buddy from Annapolis, Maryland, James Dale Davidson. Having started with one newsletter, Bonner now publishes
forty, edifying 900,000 subscribers about taxes, financial manage-

ment, travel, and health, including *What Doctors Don't Tell You, International Living*, and *Health & Longevity*. Agora is located in Baltimore, but Bonner lives in France, in a centuries-old nineteen-bedroom chateau three hours south of Paris, set amid two hundred acres of gardens, woods, and orchards.

Of all Bonner's enterprises, the Oxford Club occupies a unique niche. Its membership list is one he won't sell. It's part of the club's special allure of exclusivity, of belonging to an elite circle of a favored few in the know who are disenchanted with federal taxes and willing to actively do something about it.

Becoming an Oxfordian is a little like joining a cult. The philosophy that "we're all in this together" infuses club literature. But just who "we" are remains a secret. In keeping with the club's code of confidentiality, members who are quoted in club publications are usually identified only by their initials or first names. Oxford claims its members are "venture capitalists, award-winning entrepreneurs, attorneys, presidential candidates, artists, former members of Congress, best-selling authors, physicians, corporate executives and some other 'ordinary' people with great ambitions."[67] Beyond that, it doesn't say who they are. "To do what we need to do," the club solemnly explains, "it is essential that we keep a low profile."[68]

Like most details about Oxford, its origins are a bit murky. Club literature says it grew out of upheavals in the Far East in 1968, when American businessmen in Hong Kong and Macao banded together to ride out the economic turbulence spilling from mainland China's Cultural Revolution. Faced with potential ruin, according to Oxford lore, a small group of Western businessmen formed an "exclusive society" to design strategies to "protect and grow wealth despite any chaotic environment."[69]

Exactly what strategy they hit upon to stave off ruin is never revealed, but it somehow involved the "discreet sharing of valuable information" which "enabled them to take advantage of the chaos, and, in fact, create personal fortunes. . . . The trials of

Macao taught them secrets few others would understand. That was the origin of the Oxford Club."[70]

Whatever the veracity of this stirring tale, the club's more recent history is a good deal less inspirational. Bonner took over the name in the early 1990s from a South Florida stock promoter and investment newsletter mogul named Joel Nadel, after Nadel ran afoul of authorities over deceptive business practices. The U.S. Securities and Exchange Commission in 1990 accused him of accepting hundreds of thousands of dollars in cash and stock in exchange for touting new issues.[71] The Better Business Bureau of West Palm Beach also concluded that one of Nadel's newsletters, titled *The Royal Society of Liechtenstein,* was highly misleading because it was not in the least royal and had no connection to Liechtenstein.[72] After the bureau ordered him to stop publishing the newsletter, Nadel simply changed its name to *The Oxford Club.*[73]

Sometime in 1991, Bonner apparently bought the name or obtained the right to use it, and changed the title of one of his existing newsletters to reflect that. Members have been flocking ever since, no doubt enticed by the club's patrician-sounding name.

The club's publications are obsessed with promoting tax avoidance — both income and estate — and advise members that there are three essential steps for creating financial security:

- An overseas bank account that provides safety, privacy, and investment flexibility.
- A source of retirement income that is secure from politicians, lawyers, and economic failure.
- A low-cost offshore trust that protects assets, reduces taxes, and provides an effective way to transfer assets to children and grandchildren.[74]

Oxford will help members set up their own offshore trust through a program called the "passport financial trust."[75] Oxford seminars feature speakers who explain offshore instruments, from bank accounts to annuities, and the steps necessary for Oxfordians to "create a fortress" around their wealth.[76] Still others promote "experts" who extol "the wealth of opportunities afforded by expatriation and becoming a tax exile," and who put participants in touch with those who will help them carry out their plans.[77]

The Oxford branch that deals with taxes is its "Wealth Defense Initiative," led by a committee of money managers, lawyers, and investment authorities. From time to time the chairman has been the aristocratically named James Boxley Cooke, who also happens to be chairman of the Oxford Club itself. A Baltimorean, Cooke was formerly a vice president for institutional sales for T. Rowe Price Associates Inc., the huge Baltimore-based mutual fund. Another committee member is James Dale Davidson, Bonner's high school chum from Annapolis who founded the National Taxpayers Union and is the author of a widely read newsletter on investing.

Perhaps the best known of the committee's members over the years has been Robert E. Bauman, the director of the club's Wealth Defense Initiative.[78] Bauman served three terms as U.S. congressman from Easton, Maryland, and once was a bright light of the Republican Party. A member of an old family from Maryland's Eastern Shore, he seemed destined for a long and rewarding political career.

While in college, Bauman helped found Young Americans for Freedom, a national organization of conservative Republicans. Elected to the House in a special election in 1973, he quickly established himself as one of the party's rising stars, the author of a steady stream of pithy one-liners. On Congress: "Any time the House is in session, America is in danger." On abortion: "The ultimate child abuse." On liberal Republicans: "Democrats in drag."

Bauman endeared himself to conservative Republicans by opposing liberal lawmakers, abortion, and especially homosexuality. Reelected in 1974, 1976, and 1978, he seemed to have nowhere to go but up — until 1980. That spring, law-enforcement agents in

the District of Columbia, while trying to crack a child pornogra-
phy ring, picked up reports that Bauman was cruising gay neighborhoods in Washington and propositioning teen-age boys for sex.

A few months later, just weeks before the November general
election, Bauman was formally charged with soliciting sex from a
sixteen-year-old youth who worked as a nude go-go dancer at a
Washington gay bar. A few days later an emotional Bauman admitted to the "twin compulsions" of "alcoholism" and "homosexual
tendencies."[79] Bauman later worked out a deal with prosecutors to
accept six months of counseling, after which the charges would be
dropped. Not surprisingly, he was defeated in his conservative
rural Maryland district.

After leaving Congress, Bauman became active in the Oxford
Club, helping the organization devise a "first-of-its-kind wealth
protection kit" that spells out the various offshore instruments
members must establish to "start protecting their personal
wealth."

Oxford Clubbers who pursue one of these strategies should, in
Bauman's words, do so with the utmost caution, making sure they
don't leave a paper or electronic trail. As Bauman wrote in 1996:
"Your digital cell phone . . . [should be] used only for unimportant
conversations. Similarly, your voice mail box is with a private company, not the record-keeping local phone company, and your
unlisted home phone number is sparingly given. You assume every
phone call is monitored, so you choose your words accordingly."[80]

The prudent Oxfordian, says Bauman, has his computer
equipped with encryption software to provide a "secure firewall"
to block outside entry. And one more thing. Make sure the return
address you use on e-mail messages "shows up as a third-party
remailer in an offshore country."[81]

Paranoid? Alarmist? However one might characterize this
advice, it's pretty strong stuff from someone who, not so long ago,
was an influential policymaker in Congress. More important, it's a
sign of the income tax's troubles, and evidence of how those bent

on dismantling the tax thrive by openly advocating radical measures that would have been inconceivable a generation ago to all but a handful of splinter groups.

The aggressive efforts of the Oxford Club, the Magna Charta Society, Citibank, and scores of other outfits to promote foreign accounts are only going to further erode income tax compliance. Whether they operate from distant islands, suburban shopping malls, anonymous post office boxes, or enclaves of respectability in upscale neighborhoods onshore, these promoters represent an ever-increasing challenge to the IRS. And it's about to get much worse. For a powerful new tool for tax avoidance has appeared, and it is turning out to be the most corrosive of all.

CHAPTER 3

THE INTERNET: AVOIDANCE MADE EASY

ESCAPING THE TAXMAN

*T*he offshore tax haven was once an exotic world open only to jet-setters. But no more. Technology has transformed the process that used to require a plane trip or the services of a high-priced lawyer in the tropics. Now a few keystrokes will take you there.

Just about anyone who owns a computer has new opportunities to cheat on taxes, because anyone can visit corporate registrars' offices on sandy isles at any time of the day or night without ever leaving home. The Internet has democratized offshore tax evasion and avoidance.

Log on to the World Wide Web and see for yourself how easy it is to open a bank account, establish a personal holding company, or create a trust on some distant island or in a faraway country. The promotions are pitched in a variety of ways, but they all add up to the same thing: an invitation to send your money offshore, where, in the words of one Internet promoter, "your assets will be safe from the Tax Authorities in your local country."[1] Chances are, given the IRS's weakened state and primitive system for monitoring Internet finance, they're right. The IRS probably won't find out about them, and you could get away with it. Every day, more and more Americans do.

The options are endless, and the speed with which you can establish your own offshore structure is limited only by the speed of your modem. The Web page of Offshore Secrets Network is indicative of what you can find without looking very hard. The Internet site bills itself as an independent group of entrepreneurs — the only named individual is one Eytan Gold of Israel and Canada — that "is based in many different locations on the Globe," from Vanuatu to Israel.

Offshore Secrets offers "fully anonymous bank accounts, diplomatic passports, second passports, citizenship programs, offshore banks, trusts and corporations, and much more."[2] Declaring that "the best protection against informers and tax hounds is a virtually anonymous bank account," it says that it will establish a clandestine account for you through its Latvian Offshore Bank. The account can be accessed with a debit card from an affiliate of MasterCard that is "valid at millions of ATM terminals worldwide." As for the possibility that the IRS or some other tax agency might secure information about your account, the Web page assures that banking laws "make it impossible for even their own Police to obtain account information. As for revealing account information (even if known) to 'foreign' tax authorities . . . you must be joking!"[3]

To further assure the confidentiality of your transactions, Offshore Secrets offers a mail drop service so that mail can be sent to you at one location and then forwarded to where you really live. Sometimes the mail drop is "in the same city, other times in another continent many hours away." You may have your mail directed to drops in Costa Rica, the Bahamas, and Israel, among other countries, where it will be "placed unopened into another envelope" and forwarded to you. Among the site's other offerings:

alternate identification products such as a "genuine government issued" driver's license that is "accepted by banks for opening bank accounts"; a college degree, and titles of nobility — "become a Duke, Knight, Sir, Lord or other form of Nobility. . . ."[4]

For the convenience of consumers, the Offshore Secrets Network sells "Package Deals." That's right — trusts, corporations, bank accounts, and other services all bundled in assorted packages with varying prices. For example, "The ULTIMATE GLOBAL BUSINESS PACKAGE," a $6,500 value, goes for $4,499. It includes a Belizean trust, major credit card (no identification required), a Panamanian international business corporation complete with directors and bearer shares, a Visa debit card, and a Costa Rican mail drop.

The Finor Organisation in the British Virgin Islands makes it as easy as buying airline tickets to create a personal trust to hide assets from Uncle Sam, a spouse, a creditor, or anyone else. Advertising itself as a "one-stop" shop, Finor has posted an application on its Web site for viewers to create a trust online, without traveling to the Caribbean. The cost: $700.

Even the American legal profession has turned to the Internet to promote offshore accounts. The law firm of Michael B. Nelson in Walnut Creek, California, near San Francisco, provides an hour's worth of legal advice over the telephone for $750 on "establishing, setting up and applying for your own Offshore Bank Account," according to the firm's Web page. The firm will help you fill out a "bank application form and advise you on various jurisdictions in which your Offshore Bank Account may be located."[5] You can charge the fee on a credit card.

In opening such an account, Nelson stresses, it's important "not to use a foreign bank with U.S. affiliations. If you use such a bank, it will be subject to subpoena action from U.S. courts and forced, through the means of huge penalties [assessed] daily on the bank, to release your confidential banking information, including your initial application forms and all transactions, deposits and disbursements, for the life of your foreign bank account."[6]

As do many offshore specialists, the Nelson firm emphasizes that it's committed to providing "tax and offshore advice that is of the highest caliber and to develop a relationship to [help] you accomplish your tax objectives, legally."[7] Nelson's operation also reflects how mainstream the promotion of offshore instruments has become. Among his credentials: He was chairman for the American Bar Association's 1999 Offshore and Asset Protection Conference.

Offshore providers on the Internet have embraced the latest marketing tools of online retailers who sell everyday consumer items like flowers, computers, or toys. But some of the sales pitches have all the polish of a used car dealer's. The Shelf Shop, a purveyor of paper corporations, is typical. Supposedly based in Monaco, the Shelf Shop will sell you for an "unbelievable price" a company that has already been named and registered. The cost ranges from $250 for a Belize corporation to $845 for one in Cyprus. "The Shelf Shop is the most spectacular company to hit the Internet in a long time," it boasts. "We combine the benefits of communications technology and long established offshore experience and expertise. The Shelf Shop is your one-stop low cost shop for offshore shelf companies and related services. Shop no further."[8]

The Web page of Antigua International Business Companies claims to create secret offshore corporations "for people from all walks of life" so they can protect their "real identity" and "operate TAX FREE." Form an international business corporation on Antigua "to mask your real identity in business dealings" or open an offshore bank account "which can be used to transfer and store assets securely and invisibly."

To secure either or both services all you need to do is click on the hypertext. What appears next is a form similar to a credit card application that asks for your name, address, phone number, e-mail address, the name of the corporation, and its directors and shareholders. Once that information is entered, click on the box

"Submit" and, after you've paid $2,750 in startup fees, you're in business.[9]

Online consumers now have so many offshore options that Global Money Consultants, which says it's in Greece, has added a "shopping cart" to its Web page. As you browse its offshore supermarket, you can click on certain goodies and add them to your cart, just as if you were buying a book or compact disc from Amazon.com. You can choose a BVI international business corporation — $1,350; an offshore ATM bank account — $800; a private bank in St. Vincent — $27,500; a Panamanian trust ("one of the most valuable tax avoidance vehicles available") — $900; a confidential, numbered credit card — $700; a second passport from an undisclosed country — $5,000. When you've made your selections, click on "Go to checkout now" to view your order, the cost, and make arrangements to pay.[10] It's that effortless.

The Internet has made the IRS's traditional approach to audits obsolete. To enforce the tax code, the agency relies on a paper trail of documents. Businesses report wages paid. Banks and financial institutions report interest payments. Brokerage firms report income from the sale of stocks and bonds. Companies report payments to independent contractors. There are reports itemizing payments from retirement accounts, state and local tax refunds, royalties, currency transactions involving cash sums of more than $10,000, and canceled debts. Then there are all the receipts and checks — for goods and services purchased, charitable contributions, and payments to state and local tax authorities.

All these pieces of paper can be authenticated and traced. If your bank pays you interest of $1,000, the bank will mail you a written record (Form 1099) of the income and send a copy to the IRS. This reporting requirement is the major cog in the IRS's enforcement machinery. The agency can compare the dollar amounts you enter on your tax return with the dollar amounts reported on the 1099s. If they don't match, you may be audited. Similarly, if large sums of cash or checks representing unreported income flow into your account, the IRS can subpoena those records to determine whether you declared the money as taxable income.

But Internet transmissions create no paper trail. In place of documents are hundreds of billions of electronic blips that course through cyberspace daily. To sift through those blips to determine who is moving money around the globe would be a daunting task requiring an army of investigators. To identify them if they are using high-tech encryption would be impossible. What's more, unlike paper records, electronic transactions can be amended or erased without leaving a trace.

Historically, the IRS's audits have focused on bricks and mortar, real places such as a house or office building, a physical location where an agent can walk in, serve a subpoena, and look at the books. The Internet, of course, is anything but that: It's amorphous, with no central authority or operating center. It is here, there, and everywhere. Matters that ordinarily are easy to verify, such as where a taxpayer lives or conducts business, can be ambiguous, sometimes impossible to pinpoint. An individual's Internet address may indicate who registered the site, but it won't tell you where the computer maintaining the site is physically located. As a Treasury Department report explains:

> Even if an e-mail address is clearly associated with a certain person and computer, that person and [his or her] computer could be located anywhere in the world. This makes it difficult to determine a person's location and identity. . . .
>
> If Anne, who lives in Australia, is running a commercial site on the Internet for U.S. customers, using a computer located in Canada, Anne can control the Canadian computer from Australia through a series of computer programs which can be configured to leave no audit trail. Moreover, if the need arises, operations can be shifted to somewhere else on the Internet.[11]

OPC International, which calls itself an "international online organization," illustrates just how hard it is to know the actual location of one of these Internet sites. OPC says its "world headquarters" is in Venezuela, but then hastens to add that it doesn't really have an office anywhere. Instead, it relies on agents in "multiple jurisdictions" around the world. "An offshore provider doing business from a permanent onshore address will always be vulnerable to government pressure," says OPC. "We have decided to do business 100% online and not to run any offices that are open to the public."[12]

OPC sells Panamanian corporations, "tax busting" bank accounts, offshore credit cards, mailboxes, and trusts. Its Web page states: "When you order a Panamanian corporation from us, we will forward your name choices, but not your name or address, to the Panamanian incorporation agent. Once the corporation is ready, it gets sent to us. Then we forward it to you and delete all records related to you. This completely eliminates any kind of paper trail between Panama and you."[13]

OPC describes its Web site as offshore, "far away from robber jurisdictions like USA and EU."[14] Just where that might be is anybody's guess. OPC uses an Internet domain name, nu, issued by a tiny island in the South Seas called Niue (pronounced *nee-OO-way*). With fewer than 2,000 residents, Niue is the smallest self-governing nation in the world. The technical personnel who are registered to oversee the site are supposedly in Caracas, Venezuela, some 8,000 miles away. But there's no information about the location of the actual equipment that maintains the Web page or who pays the bills.

The Internet thus disarms the IRS's most time-tested and dependable enforcement weapon — the system of tracking money through its audit trail — and allows the old paper trails representing billions of dollars of assets to vanish into thin air. "As all users of computers know," a Treasury report notes, "[electronic documents] create the possibility for tax evasion and fraud because computerized records can be altered without a trace."[15]

Hiding assets from the IRS electronically will only get easier. A metamorphosis in currency itself is speeding the flow of money into secret accounts. Just as paper trails are disappearing into cyberspace, paper money is giving way to electronic money.

To facilitate the transfer of currency, the wired age has produced an ingenious vehicle — electronic cash. Banks have used it for years. Now you can, too. With e-cash, you can store money in a microchip implanted on a so-called smart card, about the size of a credit card. You can purchase goods and services with it, or send money over the Internet. Think of it as an electronic wallet or purse in which you can carry an unlimited sum of cash, with one major difference: The source of the money is untraceable.

The smart cards offer new opportunities to break the law with impunity. Individuals are now able to move money around the world anonymously, according to one technology expert, "literally at the speed of light, from one bank to another or to a creditor, without the bank knowing to whom the money was paid, or the creditor knowing from which bank or even country the money came."[16]

Law enforcement officers are justifiably worried. A federal official who monitors currency transactions, Stanley E. Morris, director of the federal government's Financial Crimes Enforcement Network, told a House Appropriations subcommittee in 1996 that the Internet's new cyberpayment systems are going to create vast opportunities for consumers and criminals, in part because of "virtually untraceable financial dealings. . . . This technology is a money launderer's dream."[17]

Of course, this means vast opportunities for tax evasion as well. It's a lot easier, and a lot less risky, to carry around unreported cash on a smart card than in hard currency. By using the Internet to transmit cash, anyone can create a secret overseas bank account or trust. "Unlike paper currency, electronic money can be securely and instantaneously transmitted anywhere in the world," Treasury warned in its report on electronic commerce. "It is now possible to open a bank account over the Internet in a bank secrecy jurisdiction, without actually traveling to the bank's location. Electronic money could be instantaneously and anonymously transferred to such an account, thereby eliminating the risks and reporting requirements involved in transferring cash."[18] In other

words, says a leading technology executive, the "cybermoney revolution makes some forms of tax evasion very easy."[19]

For the public record, officials of the IRS and revenue authorities in other developed countries are trying to put the best possible
face on this threat. When questioned about how they plan to combat the erosion of their tax base, they express optimism that new
technology will enable them to catch the evaders. But when
pressed as to how that will be accomplished, they confess they
don't know. Perhaps the most revealing and candid comment
came from an official of Inland Revenue, the IRS's counterpart in
the United Kingdom. Asked by *Tax Notes* magazine how the agency
hoped to tackle noncompliance problems posed by the Internet,
the British taxman replied: "We haven't got a clue about how to
solve them."[20]

SECRET CODES

Just as the Internet has linked average Americans to obscure tax
havens, a related development may prove even more pivotal in
channeling the flow of tax dollars out of the country. This is the
emergence of low-cost, easily installed encryption software that
can transform a personal computer into an instrument of secret
coding more powerful than any device used in World War II or at
the height of the Cold War.

While there is no shortage of U.S. taxpayers who would gladly
ship money offshore to escape federal taxes, fear of detection by
revenue agents keeps many Americans honest. Failure to declare
income from offshore accounts is a crime, and an offshore transaction carries a risk of detection, if only by accident. But if a computer message is encrypted — transmitted in a code that can be
deciphered only by a party on the other end who possesses the
same code — it will remain secret from even the most diligent law
enforcement authorities.

For two thousand years, encryption was of interest only to
governments and the military. It was a way to transmit secret

information without fear of it falling into the wrong hands. An intercepted message was worthless without the code to decipher it, and some of the most memorable chapters from the First and Second World Wars center on efforts by combatants to crack each other's codes.

Encryption uses mathematical formulas to scramble data so that only parties who have the formulas can read the coded exchanges. Any digital message can be encrypted, including e-mail, telephone calls, photographs, and computer files. Encryption provides, as one writer puts it, "the locks and keys of the information age."[21]

This once arcane technology is now mainstream. Businesses use it to transmit sensitive data, and inexpensive encryption software is widely available for installation on desktop computers. Critical to its success was the development of a new technology called public key cryptography. To use this, a participant must have two complementary keys, a public key and a private key. Anyone can use a public key to encrypt a message. But only the intended recipient with the private key can decode it. No one else has access to the private key — not even the person who encrypted the message. It's not uncommon to find the public key of many offshore operators posted on their Web pages.

In the last few years, the number of encryption programs available for installation on home computers has mushroomed, giving average citizens entrée to a clandestine world once inhabited only by secret agents. Programs such as Super Snooper, Lock Up, Hide Anything, ABI Coder, Data Lock, Invisible Files 2000, F-Secure, Top Secret Messenger, Encrypt-It, WinXFiles, Encrypted Magic Folders, Navaho Lock, Winzap, Privacy Guard, and OfficeLock all promise to keep e-mail and other communications strictly private.

Encryption enables anyone to preserve the confidentiality of online personal letters, family communications, private affairs, and business dealings — all the legitimate personal and business matters you just don't want anyone else in the world to know about other than those with whom you choose to share your secrets. But the same technology that allows law-abiding citizens to maintain their privacy can also be used by tax evaders to establish secret accounts the IRS can't trace.

Of all the encryption programs that have become popular in recent years, the runaway favorite is PGP. That stands for Pretty Good Privacy. It has become a kind of everyman's encryption program — a readily accessible piece of software that allows consumers to safely transmit credit card numbers to buy goods over the Internet, and that also enables tax evaders to correspond in secret with offshore agents. Many offshore firms urge clients to install PGP if they want to do business with them. "The only way to protect your privacy and anonymity is to use PGP encryption," warns Offshore Life Corporation, a typical Internet operator.[22]

Computer magazines that evaluate encryption programs, just as consumer agencies test household appliances, invariably give it the highest marks. *PC/Computing* wrote in November 1999:

> There are inevitably times when you must share your secrets with others. That's when you need PGP Personal. PGP stands for Pretty Good Privacy, a name that's entirely too modest for a powerful cryptographic suite that's used in professional applications. Use it to secure files, disks, and network connections, or to encrypt messages so they are available only to people who know the magic password. PGP also provides authentication so your partner in secrecy knows a message really came from you.[23]

PGP is so good that it is now the preferred way many government agencies transmit confidential information. Hard to get? Expensive? Not at all. It's available from many Web sites. Anyone with a modem can download it for free.

The program was created by a onetime antinuclear activist, Philip R. Zimmermann, whose motivation had nothing to do with taxes. A 1978 graduate in computer science from Florida Atlantic University, Zimmermann in the early 1980s was convinced that the world was headed for a nuclear holocaust. He joined the

Nuclear Weapons Freeze Campaign, and during one protest at the Nevada nuclear test site he was arrested along with astronomer Carl Sagan and others.

Zimmermann's experiences in the antinuclear movement convinced him that grassroots political groups in the United States needed encryption because of their "adversarial relationship" with the federal government.[24] His goal was to give all citizens the means to protect their privacy. As he would later write:

"In the information age, cryptography is about political power, and in particular, about the power relationship between a government and its people. It is about the right to privacy, freedom of speech, freedom of political association, freedom of the press, freedom from unreasonable search and seizure, freedom to be left alone."[25]

Zimmermann began creating his encryption program in the late 1980s, while living in Boulder, Colorado. By 1991, the software was ready for release. He called it Pretty Good Privacy, a name inspired by Ralph's Pretty Good Grocery, a fictional sponsor of Garrison Keillor's popular *Prairie Home Companion* radio program.[26] Rather than license his program commercially, Zimmermann, correctly fearing that the U.S. government would ban the sale of such a powerful tool as a threat to national security, asked a friend to post it on an Internet bulletin board. Zimmermann's life hasn't been the same since.

Almost instantly, PGP was downloaded by privacy fanatics, Webheads, free-speech advocates, and entrepreneurs. Zimmermann became something of a folk hero to political liberation groups around the globe, for whom PGP provided a magic cloak to keep their secret communications hidden from oppressive governments that were trying to squelch them. Others — notably U.S. law enforcement and security agencies — viewed the issue in a different light: By releasing his program to the world, Zimmermann had given aid and comfort to terrorists, who could use it to avoid detection. The U.S. Customs Service began investigating

Zimmermann to determine whether he had violated software export laws. Eventually, after three years, federal authorities called off the probe and declined to indict him. By then, millions of hands held the key to PGP.

The experience made Zimmermann a cyber hero, but defending himself against the U.S. government had also left him virtually broke. Although millions of copies of PGP were in use, the program still needed refinement. Zimmermann founded PGP Inc. in 1996 to market enhanced versions of the software, but then sold the business to an established Silicon Valley company, Network Associates, Inc., of Santa Clara, marketers of the popular McAfee Virus Alert and other network security programs. "It was a fire sale," Zimmermann said later. "We were out of money and we had to sell the company."[27]

Zimmermann stayed on as a consultant to assist in developing the next generation of PGP software and to serve as a kind of roving ambassador for the company as it offered an upgraded PGP to buyers. Since then, newer versions have been released, and today PGP is the most popular encryption software in the world.

Between the commercial program sold by Network Associates and the free version still available from Web sites, including one maintained by the Massachusetts Institute of Technology, PGP will soon be in use on more than 10 million computers, many of them owned by ordinary Americans for whom the concept of encryption was once an exotic subject only read about in James Bond novels.

The messages these people send, whether to friends, coworkers, lovers, businesses, or offshore financial agents, are so secure that anyone who intercepts them will end up with incomprehensible gibberish. To unravel a single communication from the billions that soar through cyberspace every day would require the round-the-clock services of a supercomputer for years. And there would be no guarantee of success.

Imagine the closing scene in the Indiana Jones movie *Raiders of the Lost Ark*, where the camera pans over a seemingly limitless warehouse of crates, one of which holds the Ark of the Covenant. Multiply the number of crates in that image by the largest number you can write, and that will give you an idea of the chances that the IRS will be able to retrieve and read your Internet mail.

GNOMES IN CYBERSPACE

The increasingly widespread availability of PGP and other sophisticated encrypters produces both winners and losers. If the biggest loser is the U.S. Treasury, the runaway winners are the thousands of offshore operators who freely display their wares on the Internet and the legions of taxpayers who take the plunge by going online to order from them.

The sheer number of Internet operators is staggering. The Web crackles with their easy-to-follow instructions for opening an offshore account. They're all over the globe, from the Caribbean to the Pacific, and the equipment operating them is located everywhere from densely populated central cities in America to isolated archipelagos in the Indian Ocean. Each Web site has a specialty, but they all rely on the power of the Internet to lure customers in search of a secret haven to stash assets.

In the Bahamas, New Providence Estate Planners Ltd. has a convenient online form to establish an offshore company or trust. While some offshore providers promote asset protection as the reason to ship money abroad, New Providence's Thomas Azzara is more candid on why most taxpayers open foreign accounts: to avoid federal taxes.

"The IRS cannot seize, lien on or investigate bank records here," says Azzara. "I've never witnessed an IRS proceeding of any type in this country." He says "thousands of Americans" use the Bahamas "to shelter income from the IRS. . . . It is our conclusion that 99% of the upper middle class type family IBCs registered offshore are not paying federal income taxes; and are not filing federal income tax returns." And there's little or no danger of running afoul of the IRS by going that route: "The IRS doesn't know, or can't prove, that the money even exists offshore."[28]

With Global Privacy Management Trust (GPMT) in the Cayman Islands, you don't have to give your name to open an account. Using its online form, you can establish an anonymous account in an Austrian bank, and when it comes to anonymity, *sparbuchs,* as the Austrian accounts are called, are the best anywhere, GPMT claims.

"This account is one of the best kept secrets in the banking world," says GPMT's Web page.

> No ID, no mailing address, no bank references, not even a single professional reference is required to open this account. . . . It does not need to carry any name. It can be issued to ANY name. . . . No paper trail is created, which means nothing can be intercepted by money-grubbing tax fiends, ex-wives, police, creditors, and other sorts who would love to ruin your day. . . . It is absolutely, unquestionably impossible to establish just who opened the account (and who owns it).[29]

With few exceptions, the most active Web sites post online forms that allow taxpayers to place offshore orders as if they were buying patio furniture for the backyard. In Panama, PrivacyWorld Online, which says its mission is to "protect your ass and your assets," has one form to fit all orders.[30] It comes with what Privacy-World calls an "iron clad money back guarantee." It also warns that customers should install PGP encryption if they want to assure privacy in their dealings with PrivacyWorld.

While it's often difficult to determine who is behind Web sites, PrivacyWorld is an exception. Although the server that maintains the site is in Switzerland, the actual company is in Panama, and is connected to Marc M. Harris, an American expatriate who has built an impressive offshore organization, relying heavily on the Internet to bring him customers and cash. PrivacyWorld.com is but one of Harris' entities, which also include www.marc-harris.com and www.escapeartist.com.

One of the most visually appealing Web pages is maintained by Offshore Globe Corporate Services Ltd. in the British Virgin Islands. Enhanced by dramatic graphics in blue, yellow, beige, green, and red, it leads customers through a series of short steps to form a secret corporation. By tapping the power of the Internet, the company says, it saves "the cost and time of travelling to an offshore tax haven to incorporate in person."[31] Offshore Globe has even linked up with Amazon.com, the online retailer, to sell books extolling the wonders of offshore accounts.

The most out-of-the-way places have become wired into the burgeoning offshore Internet industry. If you think the outer Bahamas are isolated, then consider the Seychelles, a sprinkling of coral and granite outcrops 1,000 miles off the coast of East Africa. Composed of more than 100 small islands spread over 175 square miles of ocean, the Seychelles are little more than tiny dots on a map of the Indian Ocean. Known for their pristine beaches, exceptional snorkeling, spectacular peaks, and exotic birdlife, the sparsely populated Seychelles are making a name for themselves in the offshore field as well — as a sympathetic haven to conceal cash and other assets.

International Attorneys Ltd. in Victoria, the capital of the Seychelles and its only port, has a full-fledged Internet center that can open bank accounts or charter corporations in other jurisdictions. Its Web site declares:

> Freedom from taxation and exchange controls are important reasons for the formation of an offshore bank and usually these will be of significant advantage and mutual benefit to both the offshore bank and its client. . . . A tax free or low tax environment will not only allow the offshore bank to generate a better bottom-line but will also provide it with a stable operating base by avoiding the vagaries or contingencies of onshore fiscal policies.[32]

Typically, the Seychelles are only the point of entry for offshore banking. The actual banks are elsewhere — in places such as Vanuatu and Nauru in the Pacific and the Turks and Caicos in the Caribbean. Whatever location one selects, International Attorneys Ltd. says it has "several ready made offshore banks available."[33]

If the proliferation of Web sites urging you to funnel your money into cyberspace is proving a nightmare for the IRS, developments in a financially respectable part of the real world promise to be even more disturbing. As one upstart promoter after another beckons from remote islands, the bankers who invented offshore banking have decided to get in on the act.

In the fall of 1999, one of Switzerland's most aggressive private banks, MFC Merchant Bank of Geneva, made a startling announcement. Within weeks, the bank said, it would begin accepting applications over the Internet to open accounts with deposits as low as $5,000. Peter Jessop, the bank's first vice president, explained that MFC had tailored the program for individuals with "substantial assets but with insufficient funds for a traditional privately managed offshore account."[34] Translation: Courtesy of cyberspace, you no longer need to be rich to have a Swiss bank account.

Like other Swiss banks, MFC had been developing an Internet-based system to give clients the option of reviewing their accounts and making financial decisions online. But the October 1999 announcement went considerably beyond that by opening the once exclusive world of Swiss banking to a mass market.

Using the bank's Web site, SwissNetBanking.com, customers can log on and go offshore under the umbrella of one of the most secretive and respected banking organizations in the world. "MFC Merchant Bank SA," claims the bank's Web page, "is offering to clients world wide the tradition of Swiss Confidentiality and Security in all services offered to its clients by using the convenience of the Internet without the high level of investment typical to this type of account. . . . The primary focus is to make available totally confidential Private Banking services and trading opportunities via the Internet to investors that wish to participate in confidential banking, as well as investment in liquid equities."[35]

The bank devotes special attention to promoting its encryption program: "SwissNetBanking.com has invested a great deal of time and money to protect all of your private information and transactions. We believe [we] employ the latest encryption technology, firewalls, and digital certificates to protect your information from accidental eavesdropping or criminal hackers."

Even if a customer's message were intercepted, MFC says, it would be virtually impossible to decode. "Designers of encryption software believe that an advanced computer could take billions of years to grind through enough calculations to break [the] encryption. If a hacker did manage to break the code, he would still only have access to that one session! As the bad guys gain ground with faster computers, you can be sure we will stay one step ahead with newer, faster technology." [36]

The bad guys in this parlance include, of course, the IRS. When the Swiss bank's plans were announced, Peter Jessop told a reporter for *USA Today* that the bank would never give the IRS "details on our clients unless our clients ask us to."[37] Not much chance of that, of course.

MFC's move proved a resounding success. The bank's Web site was awash in applications after it went online in late 1999, as a bulletin posted on the site attested:

"The response has been overwhelming, and judging from the consistency of the weekend requests, our site was in demand day and night. It was simply impossible to keep up with the demand, so we would like to apologize to those who were obliged to visit our site more than once in order to register. We have re-tuned the servers to provide uninterrupted service as of today."[38]

MFC Merchant Bank's success in small offshore accounts won't be ignored by larger Swiss banks that have long catered to a secretive moneyed class. The Swiss, after all, have a natural bent for attracting other people's assets. Depending on who is counting, they oversee from 30 percent to 40 percent of the world's private wealth, a good part of which is held by Americans. By opening their doors to the affluent upper middle class around the globe, Swiss banks will be welcoming many U.S. residents among their new customers.

If a significant number of Americans are now funneling money into secret accounts in strange-sounding banks on out-of-the-way islands, imagine how many more would open a Swiss account if it could be easily done. Beyond a glamorous reputation and a tradition of strict confidentiality, the Swiss offer something few of their offshore rivals can guarantee: stability. For more than a hundred years, the Swiss have been compiling an enviable record of banking solidity and first-rate service to their depositors — large corporations and wealthy individuals. Now, they believe, it's time to do the same for those who would like to be rich.

CAVEAT EMPTOR

In the mysterious and unregulated world of secret global banking on the Internet, everything is not what it sometimes seems. While many entities that specialize in offshore financial dealings deliver what they promise, just as the big brick-and-mortar banks do, you run one risk in cyberspace that is far greater than the chance of being detected by the IRS: Your money could disappear. A visit to one Internet bank, and a look at the family behind it, may be instructive.

It is the summer of 1998. On the World Wide Web, scores of pages are popping up like kudzu, advertising the wares of the Caribbean Bank of Commerce Ltd. on the island of Antigua. Anyone trolling the Web for investment opportunities abroad would encounter the Caribbean Bank promotional pages again and again. Emblazoned with an impressive crest, its Web page proclaims: "The Caribbean Bank of Commerce Ltd. has established itself as an off-shore World Class Financial Institution which provides old-fashioned one-to-one personal banking services to a wide range of customers through the use of state-of-the-art technology. This new breed of Cyberbanks of the 21st Century will allow all access to the benefits of offshore financial services."[39]

Like many of its competitors, the bank offers a broad range of services — personal offshore corporations, secret trusts, second passports, "secure" credit cards. It's all aimed at helping you move assets outside the United States — out of the reach of litigants, creditors, angry spouses, and, of course, the IRS. There are many reasons to go offshore, says one of the bank's linked Web sites, but one of the most compelling is "tax avoidance, legal and simple."[40]

Calls to the Antigua telephone number listed on the main Web page elicit a recorded message saying the bank is busy helping other customers, and would you leave your name and number. On one occasion, a man answers: "May I help you."

Caller: I'm trying to reach the Caribbean Bank of Commerce.
Man: This is it.
Caller: Can you tell me a little about the bank?
Man: We usually don't comment on our bank's situation. Our Web page speaks for itself. We basically provide all commercial banking services similar to other offshore banks, except we allow international clients to access these services via the Internet.

When asked where most of the bank's business comes from, the man can't discuss that. "By Antiguan law we're not allowed to comment on that. Antiguan law is very firm about what you're allowed to say, and we can't comment on that."

Although the man acknowledges only that the bank is on Antigua, he talks freely about one subject: the Internet. "I think it's a very successful medium. . . . It provides a lot of information, lets you contact individuals you would ordinarily not be able to reach. It lets small banks have an even playing field with the large competitors."[41]

So what does the Caribbean Bank of Commerce look like? In March 1999, a visitor travels to the island's capital, St. John's, for an unannounced meeting with executives of the bank on dusty Nevis Street, at the Dollar Building — named for Dollar-Rent-A-Car, the anchor tenant. On the second floor, Suite 9, the bank's official address, the visitor encounters an efficient young woman who has never heard of it.

"This is not their address," she says with the air of authority of someone who knows the occupants of the small two-story building.[42]

The visitor produces the Antigua telephone directory. He points to the listing sandwiched between Caribbean Auto Appraisal Services Ltd. and Caribbean Banking Corporation Ltd.: Caribbean Bank of Commerce, 9 Dollar Building, Nevis Street (463-0959).

The young woman is genuinely surprised. "This is right here," she says, seemingly amazed that she is standing in the middle of a bank that doesn't exist. She can't explain the phone book entry. All she knows is that "there is no bank here." Best to get the correct address from the government, she advises.[43]

But the Antiguan government isn't much help either. Strict confidentiality laws, you know. Government employees who disclose information about corporations chartered on Antigua could go to prison. The official who heads the government office declines to answer any questions.

The bank's Web page offers a clue. A detailed financial statement enumerates the bank's assets and assures that it "has significantly exceeded" the U.S. government's capitalization requirement of $5 million. "The capitalization as of December 31, 1997, is $100.2 million. This capitalization is in a form of cash, cash equivalents, securities, real and personal property."[44] The bank's rock-solid financial condition is authenticated by an opinion from a certified public accountant, James H. Chance, Suite 401 at 545 Eighth Avenue, New York City, care of the Liechtensteinische-Amerikanische Union Bank Corporation. That's the same bank — at the very same location — according to the Web page, which holds Caribbean Bank of Commerce stock in "safe keeping."[45]

The Eighth Avenue address turns out to be an aging building in the city's garment district, a few blocks from Madison Square Garden. Visitors take the ancient elevator to the fourth floor, where a dim and cluttered corridor leads to Suite 401. The sign says it is the home of EFLS Answering and Mail Service. The room is filled with computers and phone cable and occupied by a half-dozen or so persons busily answering telephones and sifting through mountains of mail.

One visitor asks a man seated at a desk just inside the door if this is the Liechtensteinische-Amerikanische Union Bank.

The man is curious about the visitor and his companion.

"Who are you?" he asks. "Are you a government agent?"

"No," one of the visitors says. "We're just trying to find the bank."

"We're just an answering service and a mail drop for many companies," the man says. "We have more than twenty-five thousand companies. We're almost to thirty thousand and ready to expand."

And the bank? one of the visitors reminds him.

"We don't know them," the man says. "They just come in and pick up their mail."[46]

As for James Chance, the man at the desk says, he never heard of him.

A further study of the Caribbean Bank of Commerce Web page leads to three other addresses. The Web page is registered to a company called International Financial Holdings Ltd., 79 Main Street, Hackensack, New Jersey. But that's a law office. The people there, like the young woman on Antigua, know nothing about any bank.

The second address is that of the firm that manages the bank's Web site, cdalton.com. It's located on West Drive in North Bay Village, Florida, a tiny community (population 5,000), about fifteen minutes north of downtown Miami. The address is a thirty-plus-unit apartment complex that resembles the two-story roadside motels found everywhere in America. The people living in an apartment on the second floor invite a visitor in. They introduce themselves. They are Otto Carl Neusch and his wife, Christina Dalton. They are from South Africa. They provide Internet services to businesses across the United States and around the world. All from their cramped apartment jammed with computer equipment and linked to cyberspace with a T-1 line, the high-speed data transmission connection used by America's largest corporations. One of their clients is the Caribbean Bank of Commerce.

The couple say they have never met anyone connected with the bank. All their conversations have been by telephone or via the Internet. They can't discuss their clients, but all correspondence is directed to the bank in care of 17 Chestnut Street, Ridgewood, New Jersey, a suburb of New York City.

This address is a three-story office building in the center of Ridgewood, a well-kept town of 24,000 in Bergen County, about twenty miles northwest of Manhattan. It doesn't look much like an offshore banking center. It houses a Fred Astaire Dance Studio, a computer service, the office of an accountant, a sports bar, and something called World Headquarters Corporation.

A visitor wandering through the building finds no evidence of the Caribbean Bank of Commerce. But then, in an unmarked room on the third floor, a casually dressed man emerges from a warren of computers to throw light on the subject.

Asked if he can direct a visitor to the Caribbean Bank of Commerce, he says: "This used to be their representative office. They're in the process of moving their offices offshore . . . back to Antigua. I used to represent them."

He says the Ridgewood office was closed because it "just wasn't profitable." It was a very "small bank," he says. "They had a very small presence here in the United States. It was basically an informational office."

Does he know the source of the bank's business?

"I wouldn't know," he says.

"You just rented them the space?"

"I rented them the space."

"So you don't really have any connection with the bank?"

"No."[47]

Reluctant to say more, the man discloses one bit of information: his name. He identifies himself as Gene Chusid.

As it turns out, Chusid has more of a connection with the Caribbean Bank of Commerce than he had let on — much more. While the bank's main Web page doesn't contain any individual names, a search of the World Wide Web yields a message that Chusid posted about the bank on another site:

> We at the Caribbean Bank of Commerce specialize in providing a full line of banking services both corporate and personal. Our correspondents include Bank of New York, Citibank NA and Chase Manhattan Bank among the many. We have full telex capabilities. We are owned by a USA publically [sic] owned holding company with over 300 shareholders. Our offices are located in the Caribbean and the USA. Our executives speak fluent English, Russian and other languages and will be happy to assist international companies and individuals in any banking requirements. Annomous [sic] accounts, bearer instruments, and numbered accounts are available (where permitted by law).[48]

The notice, which urges readers to visit the bank's main Web site, is attributed to Eugene Chusid, Caribbean Bank of Commerce Ltd., 17 Chestnut Street, Ridgewood, New Jersey.

Eugene Chusid is a member of an intriguing and enigmatic Russian immigrant family that has operated a network of domestic and international companies out of the family-owned Ridgewood building since the 1980s. The family starts up businesses faster than a six-year-old moves from one toy to another, and routinely shifts millions of dollars from one investment to another, inside and outside the United States.

But before recounting the bewildering business dealings of the Chusids, it's important to keep in mind the purpose for doing so. That is the role played by family member Eugene in the Caribbean Bank of Commerce, one of those Internet financial operations that are encouraging you to ship your money abroad.

Eugene, a younger brother, and their parents, Gregory K. and Svetlana Chusid, emigrated to the United States from Russia in the early 1970s. The family patriarch, Gregory, was born in 1938 in Odessa, Ukraine. An electrical engineer by training, he ran all sorts of strange businesses from 17 Chestnut Street, including Import Export International Engineering Company Inc. (IEIEC). Although few people in Ridgewood were aware of its activities, IEIEC was an international dealer in armaments. A financing statement buried in voluminous New Jersey court records describes it this way: "International operations include the wholesale of combat vehicles, guided missiles, firearms and ammunition, computers and medical equipment and supplies, and commercial flight carriers."[49]

IEIEC held a license issued by the Bureau of Alcohol, Tobacco and Firearms of the U.S. Treasury Department, authorizing it to manufacture and import firearms, including assault weapons. It also was "[licensed] by the Russian Federation to deal in arms."[50]

Gregory Chusid called himself an international trade consultant. He spent much of his time in Russia or in countries that once made up the Soviet bloc. His passport shows that in the late 1980s and early 1990s he traveled in and out of Paraguay, long a crossroads in the global arms market.

According to sworn depositions, he made money "from the sales of arms from Russia to third-world countries."[51] But the full extent of his consulting business is not clear. Indeed, a federal judge who once reviewed his financial dealings said he was mystified as to how Chusid made his money.

"You know, I don't know what underlying economic or business activities were going on here," said U.S. Bankruptcy Judge Joseph L. Cosetti. "I find it amazing, but I don't know what they were."[52]

Whatever they were, by the late 1980s Gregory Chusid was a multimillionaire. A personal financial statement submitted to a major bank in 1989 put his net worth at $15.9 million. His assets included an art collection valued at $3.2 million and real estate worth $13.9 million. A similar statement two years later placed his net worth at $18.1 million, with $2.1 million in a Swiss bank account. In 1994, a credit reporting company fixed the net worth of Chusid's IEIEC Inc. group of companies at $58 million. He maintained homes in Ridgewood, an apartment in Moscow, and a condo in Tel Aviv.

Svetlana Chusid, the matriarch, also owned real estate, including the 17 Chestnut Street building in Ridgewood, which she held through a company called the IEIEC World Headquarters Corporation. Through another company, Russian White House Restaurant Inc., she owned the liquor license for the All American Sports Bar, a combination bar and restaurant in the same building. By Eugene's reckoning, the business provided his mother with an income of about $240,000 a year. The bar was the subject of numerous police reports. In 1997, the Ridgewood Village Council, acting on "multiple complaints of improper, illegal, and outrageous behavior emanating from the bar-restaurant," denied renewal of the liquor license. The state later overturned the decision and the bar was permitted to remain open.[53]

In addition to her real estate holdings, Svetlana owned a company called IJV Inc., originally set up by her husband and based, naturally, in the 17 Chestnut Street building. The initials stood for International Joint Venture Inc. IJV owned 50 percent of a company called Inter Lotto International Inc., which ran an instant lottery in the Russian Federation. She also owned a mini-fleet of vehicles — three BMWs, two trucks, one Isuzu, and one Peugeot. They were all registered in her name, according to Eugene, because "she has the cleanest license of all of us. So she has the least insurance payment of all of us."[54] She drove one of the BMWs. Eugene drove another and his wife drove the Peugeot. His brother drove the Isuzu. Until the early 1990s, Svetlana also worked as a microfiche clerk for Bergen County, New Jersey, at a salary of about $20,000 a year, and "maintained [an] account with a Swiss bank." In January 1994, her account with Swiss Bank

Corporation in Zurich showed a balance of $673,813, according to documents that surfaced in one legal action involving the Chusids.[55]

Of all the Chusids, the one of most interest to this story is son Eugene, born in 1963. Graduated from Rensselaer Polytechnic Institute in Troy, New York, with a degree in biomedical engineering in 1985, he also attended Albany Medical College, a small medical school in Albany, New York, for two years. A credit report states that Eugene worked as a doctor in New York from 1981 to 1987. On personal stationery and in other papers dated through the 1990s, the letters *M.D.* often appear after his name. He has been identified in court records as a medical doctor. Not true. He was never licensed to practice medicine in New York State. Indeed, a college spokesman said Chusid never received a medical degree. But while he left college without the degree, he did walk away with something else: a bill for part of his college education that he's never paid. The tab is $30,000 with interest and penalties.

Eugene had a penchant for launching businesses which, by his own account, never quite made it. He was the sole shareholder of Urban Construction Redevelopment Corporation. It was in the construction business, but never built anything. His wife was sole shareholder of a company called W.U.S. Corporation, which owned a shell building in Jersey City. The couple planned to rehab the structure and rent it out. They never did. There was the 14 Park Street Development Corporation, which was set up to develop a vacant building in Jersey City. It didn't.

In this, Eugene had a role model: his father. In Moscow, Gregory invested in a company called Compass Inc., a joint venture he formed with about "six different admirals and generals from Russian Armed Forces." The company supposedly was going to use money derived from Russian Navy scrap sales to build housing for returning military personnel. It didn't.[56]

There was a company called GKCC Inc. The initials stood for Gregory K. Chusid Consulting. It was formed to work on behalf of

American companies interested in doing business in the old Soviet Union, but the various projects never seemed to pan out. And there was another company called International Joint Venture High School Technologies Inc., a joint venture in Moscow between Gregory and a Russian partner "to sell computers to various educational institutions in Russia." It didn't.[57]

Yet another company in which Gregory owned a half-interest, Belle Mead International Telephone Inc., held the cellular telephone license for Moscow. Belle Mead sold the license to Bell Atlantic for an undisclosed sum. But after Gregory and his partners pocketed an initial payment of $500,000, the deal unraveled and Belle Mead, according to Eugene, lost the Moscow license.

While Gregory was spending much of his time in Moscow, Eugene in 1988 began to actively oversee his father's investments. In 1990, his father gave him "the full power of attorney to manage all his business(es)."[58] He negotiated acquisitions, leases, and loans. One deal in 1990 would eventually prove a flashpoint in the family's financial life. On behalf of his father, Eugene "purchased a one-half interest in a company known as Orka Associates Inc., which owned a 25-unit apartment building in Newark."[59] As part of the deal, Gregory guaranteed payment of a $950,000 mortgage held by First Fidelity Bank in Newark.

In 1993, Orka failed to make mortgage payments and the bank sued. Gregory would later say he was in Russia and preoccupied with his consulting business and had left management of the property and his other investments in the hands of Eugene. Whatever the case, the Chusids disregarded the legal action and on May 18, 1994, a Superior Court judge in Newark entered a default judgment of $815,997. Ever since, First Fidelity, the bank that made the loan, has been trying to get its money back.

In court, the Chusids, father and son, proved to be masters at stalling, giving evasive answers, refusing to provide documents, and ignoring court orders. The court record is laced with testimony or statements by both in which they cannot recall what happened to the assets. Typical is this 1994 exchange between Gregory Chusid and a lawyer representing First Fidelity:

> **Lawyer:** This shows also that you had loans receivable, notes receivable in the amount of $2,300,000. . . . Do you know anything about that?
>
> **Gregory Chusid:** I don't remember.
>
> **Lawyer:** Do you know if you ever received that money, the $2 million?
>
> **Gregory Chusid:** I never received [the] money.
>
> **Lawyer:** This also shows you had stocks and bonds in the amount of $41,000. Do you still hold such stocks and bonds?
>
> **Gregory Chusid:** No.
>
> **Lawyer:** Did you sell them?
>
> **Gregory Chusid:** I don't know. I don't remember even what . . . happened to them. . . . I don't know where it went.
>
> **Lawyer:** This also shows that you own real estate in the amount of $13,901,900. Do you know what this figure comprised?
>
> **Gregory Chusid:** I don't remember.[60]

The Chusid family's individual and corporate tax affairs were as obscure and perplexing as their business dealings. It isn't even clear that all the required tax returns were filed over the years. Copies of tax returns submitted to banks to secure loans or produced in response to subpoenas, it turned out, were not genuine. Witness this exchange between a lawyer for First Fidelity Bank and Eugene Chusid concerning the 1992 corporate tax return of the IEIEC Group of Companies Inc.:

> **Lawyer:** I see this tax return was prepared and dated March of '93. Whose signature is that on the first page?

Eugene Chusid: Mine. . . .

Lawyer: That says president?

Eugene Chusid: Yes.

Lawyer: . . . It shows that the gross receipts and sales for this company for 1992 was approximately $6 million. Do you see that?

Eugene Chusid: Un-huh. Yes.

Lawyer: It also shows that . . . your father, Gregory Chusid, was the sole shareholder for that corporation. Do you see that?

Eugene Chusid: Yes.

Lawyer: The amount of compensation received by him from this corporation for 1992 was $475,000, is that correct?

Eugene Chusid: Correct. . . . This tax return, if you take a look, it incorporates the net worth of all the subsidiary corporations, which were not really subsidiaries, which filed independent tax returns. This [return] was really prepared as an internal composite return which was never filed with the IRS.

Lawyer: Why would you prepare and sign an internal composite return that's not filed?

Eugene Chusid: Because my accountant asked me to do that. . . .

Lawyer: Is there a reason why you signed it, if it was solely for in-house purposes?

Eugene Chusid: I always sign everything.[61]

A copy of the 1990 personal income tax return of Gregory and Svetlana is even more puzzling. It shows that Gregory's real estate business produced a net profit of $635,000. In addition, the couple reported wage and salary income of $18,507.63 and taxable interest income of $47,055.23. Total income from those three sources:

$700,562.86. But the Chusids, or their accountant at the time, arrived at a different figure, one very much in the couple's favor. The tax return shows adjusted gross income of $475,075.86 — or $225,487 less than they said they actually received. It's possible that like the corporate return this one was never filed with the IRS. It's also possible that the return was filed and the IRS never checked it. Whatever the case, the Chusids have a cavalier attitude toward taxes. Eugene conceded that as of December 21, 1994, his parents had not yet filed their 1993 tax return. Then again, someone submitted two very different 1992 tax returns of Gregory and Svetlana to two different banks. One return showed a negative income of $21,137. The other return showed income of $548,000.

After all the legal wrangling, father Gregory and son Eugene say they are broke. The tens of millions of dollars in cash and real estate and other assets have mostly vanished, they say, in failed business ventures in Moscow and in the United States. Gregory filed for bankruptcy. Eugene filed for bankruptcy, listing among his few assets a loan for his kidney. Even James Chance, the accountant who certified the sound financial condition of the Caribbean Bank of Commerce, filed for bankruptcy. The IRS said he owed $4 million in taxes. Among his remaining possessions of value: a Lionel train set.

Gregory has accused First Fidelity Bank of conducting a "witch hunt" and persecuting his family. The bank's attorneys say the Chusids are engaged in a "massive fraud" involving "secreting assets fraudulently transferred by Gregory Chusid" to other family members. "There is this constant haze over everything that the Chusids do," said Edward J. Butler of the Newark law firm McCarter & English, which represents the bank, "because that's the way they want it."[62] And as a federal bankruptcy judge put it: "He [Gregory] has never explained to any court what happened to those assets."[63]

There is at least a partial explanation. Earlier in the 1990s, Gregory transferred his holdings, including the $3.2 million art collection, to his wife. Eugene described the transaction during questioning by the First Fidelity Bank lawyers:

"My father made a settlement with my mom, more or less, that he would be transferring all his big assets to her because they were having personal problems."

Lawyer: Do you know what the basis of the settlement was?

Chusid: Basically my mom would not kick him out of the house and would not divorce him.

Lawyer: If he gave her all of his —

Chusid: All of his assets.

During the period when Gregory transferred assets to his wife, and Orka Associates stopped making payments on the mortgage, the Caribbean Bank of Commerce came into being on Antigua. Incorporated on March 10, 1993, the bank was known first as the Commerce Bank of Antigua. Two years later, its name was changed to the Caribbean Bank of Commerce Ltd. And two years after that, in July 1997, the bank became a subsidiary of International Financial Holdings Ltd., based in the Chusid family complex in Ridgewood. In a financial statement dated December 31, 1997, the bank and its parent claimed assets of $194.6 million, including deposits of $161.7 million. The accountant who audited the bank statements was the same James Chance who was once identified with the Liechtensteinische-Amerikanische Union Bank Corporation at a Manhattan mail drop and who also maintains an office in the Ridgewood building.

As for the Caribbean Bank of Commerce, it vanished into cyberspace, just like the Chusid millions. By late 1999, its Web site (www.caribbank.com) no longer existed. Also missing was $350,000 that had been wired to the bank between August and October 1998 by a New Jersey company, Construction Drilling Inc. (CDI). Thomas R. Crofts, a CDI representative, opened an account and transferred the money only after obtaining a financial statement showing the Caribbean Bank of Commerce and its parent, International Financial Holdings, had total deposits of $651.7 million.

In April 1999, Crofts traveled to Antigua but "was unable to locate any presence" of the bank. His company demanded repayment of the $350,000. A month later, Eugene Chusid "informed Crofts that he was resigning as senior vice president of Caribbean Bank" and that the money would be returned to him on June 11, 1999. The day before the transfer was to take place, another Caribbean Bank official advised Crofts that the bank "was on the brink of insolvency." Crofts never got his money.[64]

There is no way to know how many other people wired money to the Caribbean Bank of Commerce, only to see their deposits disappear. No doubt some who may have encountered the same fate have chosen to remain silent rather than talk about their offshore activity.

Crofts is not the first person to have been stiffed by Eugene Chusid. On the island of Antigua, Darryl Belizaire is owed several months of unpaid rent. Belizaire manages a luxury development called Bay Heights in the hills on the island's west coast. There, Eugene leased a two-bedroom condo with breathtaking views of the harbor at St. John's, and of the turquoise Caribbean to the north and west. The condo came fully furnished "down to the pillowcases, silverware — everything," Belizaire said. It rented for about $1,650 a month. For a while, Chusid's father, Gregory, no doubt weary from court battles back in the States, lived in this idyllic setting. But sometime in 1998, the Chusids abruptly pulled out without paying their rent.

"I think he has disappeared. He left me holding the bag," Belizaire said in March 1999. After Eugene Chusid, who had described himself as an "overseas banker," skipped town, Belizaire filed a complaint with Antiguan police that could serve to bar his reentry to the country if he came in under his own name. "If you find him please let me know," he implored an interviewer.[65]

While Chusid and his Caribbean Bank of Commerce are long gone from Antigua, the bank's disappearance from the Internet is not quite what it seems. For one of the marvels of the Internet is its ability to give birth to new institutions as quickly as old ones die. Or seem to die. So in place of the old Caribbean Bank of Commerce is a new entity called the Corporate, Bank and Credit Ltd. — CBC Ltd. (www.cbcltd.com).

The Web page bears all the trappings of a Eugene Chusid enterprise. It uses the same monogram and the same impressive crest as its predecessor. It offers many of the same offshore services to potential clients. It will form "offshore corporations and asset protection trusts"; buy existing offshore banks and insurance companies or set up new ones; establish Visa, MasterCard, and American Express accounts, and arrange for citizenship papers in other countries.[66] It assures that the company's "private consultants are all international financial systems specialists that have worked for either multi-national firms and/or international banks developing and structuring offshore investment, banking, tax reduction and asset protection strategies."[67] And finally, it promises that "our clients will work with seasoned financial professionals who are dedicated to fully understanding and discreetly executing the client's wishes. A climate of esteem and courtesy — which characterize valued, long-term relationships — is the hallmark of our company."[68]

Although CBC Ltd. is not based on sunny Antigua, it has maintained one of the Caribbean Bank of Commerce's ties to an entirely different part of the world — Alaska. The bank says it is "the exclusive representative of the Kuiu Thlingit Nation of the Kuiu Kwaan Island of Alaska." The CBC Ltd. Web site describes the Kuiu Thlingit Nation as "one of the 32 Ihuingit speaking nations of the region known as Southeast Alaska, British Columbia, and the Yukon Territory. . . . 'Thlingit' means the people who travel with the tide."[69]

Does CBC Ltd., like the Caribbean Bank of Commerce, have an office in the United States? You bet. Its New York office, the company says, is located in Suite 249 at 1202 Lexington Avenue. And what does Suite 249 look like? Even by Manhattan standards, it's small, about three inches by five inches. It's a mailbox in one of Manhattan's ubiquitous commercial postal drops called Mail Boxes Etc. By the time you read this, the company may have changed its name and moved on again. But it's safe to assume that as long as there is an Internet, there will be opportunities for those who know how to exploit it.

CHAPTER 4

CONGRESS'S HIDDEN AGENDA

DEMONIZING THE TAX COLLECTOR

*I*n Washington they make laws, entertain heads of state, and erect monuments to honor great figures in the nation's history. But what the city does best is stage spectacles. One of the more successful of these in recent times took place the week of April 28, 1998, in the spacious hearing room of the Senate Finance Committee on the second floor of the Hart Senate Office Building. Room 216 is where tax law is crafted, the place where senators haggle over "subpart f income," "pass through entities," "constructive dividends," and other dry and arcane subjects that determine who does and does not have to pay more in taxes. But during that week in April, it was transformed into something quite different — a carnival sideshow designed to amaze and appall viewers.

In four days of public hearings, choreographed by the most unlikely of impresarios, the rather lackluster Senator William V. Roth Jr. of Delaware, the committee room became a chamber of IRS horrors. A veteran senator not previously known for his showmanship, Roth departed from script to put together a production worthy of Cecil B. DeMille. He skillfully built up suspense, promising startling testimony from secret witnesses, telling reporters they would be surprised by what they were about to hear, refusing to divulge the slightest details of the upcoming drama — even keeping secret from other committee members the names of witnesses. When the spectacle began to unfold on the morning of April 28, Roth did not disappoint.

Spectators heard the story of a small-business owner from Virginia Beach, Virginia, whose restaurant and home had been raided by the IRS. "Armed agents, accompanied by drug-sniffing dogs, stormed my restaurant during breakfast, ordered patrons out of the restaurant and interrogated my employees," he testified.[1] He told the committee that agents impounded his records, cash registers, and computers, and later ripped the door off his house in search of incriminating evidence. "I used to believe that such things could only happen in a Communist bloc country, or a police state," he told the senators. "I don't believe that any more."[2]

A Tulsa accountant testified about the day armed IRS agents wearing brightly colored SWAT team jackets descended on the office of his tax-preparation company, seizing client records, computers, and personal papers. "It was the intent of IRS to break me emotionally and financially," he told the senators.[3]

An oilman from Fort Worth described how IRS agents "stormed" his office "like an army landing on any enemy beachfront." He told the committee that employees heard agents shout: "IRS! This business is under criminal investigation! Remove your hands from the keyboards and back away from the computers. And remember, we're armed."[4] Agents seized records and hounded him for years. The oilman claimed he had done nothing wrong, but said he later settled with the IRS for $23 million just to get them off his back.

This vivid picture of a rogue agency using Gestapo tactics to browbeat taxpayers created high drama in a hearing room crowded with reporters and television cameras. But some witnesses weren't exactly what they seemed. The Virginia Beach businessman had grossly exaggerated his story. The IRS was only one of several law enforcement agencies investigating his business affairs, and the probe had been launched by Virginia authorities, not the IRS. The explosive abuse charges that delighted anti-IRS senators fizzled out when the case came to court a year later. A judge in Norfolk, Virginia, dismissed the charges against the IRS agents who had been accused of acting abusively, and the businessman's lawyer later backed away from his accusations, telling the *Wall Street Journal*: "I don't think they did anything wrong."[5]

But at the time of the hearings, when senators were hammering out details of a new law that would sharply curtail the IRS's powers, the case studies were all accepted at face value — as true accounts of taxpayers victimized by an agency run amok. Few in the media bothered to look into the background. The Senate committee's mission was to put the IRS in the most unfavorable light possible, and on that score the hearings were a resounding success. As the horror stories aired on TV and radio and appeared in newspapers and magazines, senators expressed outrage over the IRS's tactics and called for reforms.

"We must demand that taxpayer complaints about unfair treatment are promptly heard and that abusive IRS employees are dealt with appropriately," thundered Daniel K. Akaka, a Democrat from Hawaii.[6]

"To the agents at the IRS, who have been out of control, and to the management who is protecting those agents, I want to say watch out," warned Mississippi's Trent Lott, the Republican majority leader. "We are on to you, and we will not let you do this sort of thing to the American people."[7]

"Its unlimited power has made the IRS a wasteful, arrogant, incompetent, intrusive, and abusive agency," said Rod Grams, a Republican from Minnesota.[8]

"Many tax collectors, in their zeal to catch those among us who don't pay their taxes, seem to have lost sight of the most important truth about our tax system — that citizens have rights that must be protected," said Max S. Baucus, a Democrat from Montana.[9]

Even IRS Commissioner Charles O. Rossotti, no doubt taken aback by the congressional broadside, had little choice but to chime in. "Should even one of these allegations prove true, that's one too many, and I won't tolerate it," he assured reporters after the hearing. "The IRS must conduct itself properly in all dealings with taxpayers, including criminal investigations."[10]

The media echoed the theme, calling on lawmakers to swiftly enact legislation to protect taxpayers. "Cleaning up the nation's tax collection agency and restoring public confidence in it is not a partisan issue," editorialized the Los Angeles Times. "The priority for both parties must be to enact effective reforms, including the machinery to bring under control and punish severely those in the IRS who are tempted to abuse their authority and terrorize taxpayers."[11]

The Memphis Commercial Appeal intoned: "An unaware observer who wandered into the committee hearings might reasonably have assumed from some of the anecdotes that the subject was the Mafia and the gangsters it employed to do its dirty work. . . . Congress should pass whatever bills are needed to ensure the proper controls are in place to help protect crucial freedoms."[12]

One week after the hearings, the Senate passed the Internal Revenue Service Restructuring and Reform Act of 1998. The vote was 97 to 0. Similar to a bill enacted earlier by the House, the measure pointed the nation's tax collector in an altogether new direction. For the first time, a nine-member board, including six members from outside the government, would oversee the agency and set policy. Tax penalties would be slashed or suspended in certain cases. The burden of proof in many disputes would shift from the taxpayer to the IRS. And the IRS's ability to seize property was curtailed.

Most important, the law imposed a rigid new standard of conduct on IRS agents in their dealings with taxpayers. Soon to be known pejoratively within the service as "the ten deadly sins," Section 1203 of the new law set forth ten actions that could be grounds for dismissal. Few could quibble with some of them: IRS agents could be fired for falsifying documents, assaulting taxpayers, or trying to extort money. But other "sins" were ambiguous and open to interpretation: Act No. 6 called for dismissal of any IRS agent who harassed a taxpayer or his representative. What is harassment? Some reluctant taxpayers could easily interpret it as an IRS agent's attempt to collect taxes rightfully owed.

An IRS employee found guilty of committing any one of these acts could be summarily fired. This provision would have enormous implications. But in Congress there were only smiles and back-pats as lawmakers congratulated one another for imposing stringent controls on an agency so many love to hate. "This plan will give David the taxpayer an arsenal of powerful slingshots to use against Goliath the IRS," said Bill Archer of Texas, chairman of the House Ways and Means Committee.[13]

No one was happier than the legislation's architect, Bill Roth, who called the bill the "most extensive reforms ever made" to rein in an agency he described as having "too much power, and not enough sunshine."[14] Roth was particularly proud of the bill's broad bipartisan support: "I believe the future will remember the work we have done here."[15]

As dramatic as it was, there was one thing wrong with this scenario: Lawmakers had their guns trained on the wrong suspect. For all the IRS's shortcomings, and it has plenty, the worst abuses of the income tax system are not traceable to the agency. The chief culprit is Congress.

Over the last two decades, Congress has systematically chipped away at the supports that underpin the tax system. Through erratic decision making, zigzag policies, and blistering attacks on the IRS, Congress has hobbled the service's efforts to enforce tax law. In doing so, it has created widespread contempt for the income tax and made it socially acceptable for Americans to cheat on their taxes. In fact, congressional actions have actually encouraged tax dodging.

Congress's assault on the IRS has been broad and relentless. Legislators have cut back on personnel, programs, and appropriations. The IRS had 116,400 employees in 1990. By 1998, the total had fallen to 97,400, a 16 percent decline — the first significant drop in manpower in its history. By contrast, the service had added employees in the 1960s, the 1970s, and the 1980s to keep pace with increased tax filings. Long-term programs announced amid great fanfare in Congress one year are abolished the next. IRS efforts to measure taxpayer fraud and error are blocked by congressional opponents before they get started. Congress funded a multimillion-dollar commission to barrage IRS with criticism, even though most of the troubles could be traced to Congress itself. Lawmakers clamor for a better IRS, then slash its budget. Congress has told the agency to lighten up, to treat taxpayers like "customers," not like, well, taxpayers.

Running through Congress to its highest levels is a contempt for the agency unlike anything in the past — a disdain for its basic function and for everything it does. An offhand comment of Trent Lott expressed this open disrespect. After hearing tales of alleged mistreatment of taxpayers by IRS agents, Lott offered this theory as to the supposed cause: "Quite often it appears to me that this abuse comes from the fact that they do not have enough to do."[16] Constantly being sabotaged by foes on Capitol Hill, the service has been in a tailspin for years, unable to satisfy lawmakers or meet its obligation to collect taxes owed.

To see how congressional policy plays havoc with tax administration, let's look at the way lawmakers handled an innovative IRS attempt in the mid-1990s to narrow the tax gap —the difference between the amount the agency says taxpayers owe and the amount they actually pay. In May 1994, after lobbying by the IRS, Congress approved a five-year, $2 billion "compliance initiative" to beef up enforcement. With the additional staff and other resources, the IRS estimated it could bring in $9.2 billion more in taxes over a five-year period. As a revenue raiser, the program would be an off-budget appropriation, meaning that the IRS wouldn't have to compete with other agencies in the annual tug-of-war for additional funds that stalls many long-range plans.

Speaking for the bill, Senator Dennis DeConcini, an Arizona Democrat, told colleagues: "I pay my taxes. You pay your taxes. Most of the people we represent pay their taxes. Why should we not go after those who do not? . . . [There] are over 14 million who do not pay their taxes and nobody asks them any questions or goes after them. I think we should go after them."[17]

Congress decided to do just that and appropriated $405 million for the first year. The IRS hired 3,000 agents and redeployed 2,000 others to implement the effort. From all signs, the program went exceedingly well, bringing in far more tax revenue than the IRS had projected. Collections totaled $803 million, and prospects for the following year, when all the freshly trained help would be in place, looked even brighter.

But when it came time for the second-year appropriation, Congress reversed course and killed the program. The compliance initiative was, in the words of Nebraska Democratic Senator J. Robert Kerrey, "zeroed-out." According to Kerrey, the action reflected a general attitude in the Senate that the agency must fundamentally change its ways. He added that most senators think: "I don't get my votes back home from IRS increases."[18] Thus, a year after the compliance offensive began, the IRS was compelled to abandon it and fire or reassign 6,000 agents.

Jubilation reigned on the floor of the Senate. "I am pleased to see that our efforts have achieved a success for the taxpayers," said

Iowa Republican Senator Charles E. Grassley. The Senate's action to force the IRS to fire 6,000 agents would, he said, mean fewer "agents looking through your files."[19]

A similar result befell a longer-running, more pivotal enforcement tool, the TCMP.

The acronym stands for Taxpayer Compliance Measurement Program, and it was the IRS's most comprehensive yardstick for measuring the extent of tax avoidance and to determine whether tax laws should be amended. Through the TCMP, the IRS would select a sample of individual and small-business returns every few years for intensive audits. Each was examined in depth to determine whether it accurately reflected the filer's tax liability. The result enabled the IRS to estimate compliance for the entire population. Virtually all of the IRS's estimates on the size of the tax gap come from TCMP studies.

No one has ever claimed the TCMP is without flaws. It was always a limited sample, usually around 50,000 returns, or less than 4/100ths of 1 percent of those filed. It never included the returns of large corporations, only businesses with sales of less than $10 million a year. For taxpayers who were selected for audit, it could be time-consuming and costly. Even IRS agents despised the TCMP because it piled more work on them. But in the opinion of tax professionals, it was the best single mechanism the IRS had to chart the health of the tax system. As a former IRS commissioner, Lawrence Gibbs, put it in 1995: "No one has come up with a better overall, comprehensive, credible approach to provide answers to the questions that everyone wants to know about our tax system."[20]

After the first TCMP audit in 1964, the IRS conducted it every several years — until the 1990s, when congressional opponents finally caught up with it. The showdown came in 1995, in a battle that illustrated why taxpayer fraud, once a rarity among Americans, is only going to increase.

Early in 1995, the IRS informed Congress that it would begin a new TCMP study that fall. It was to be the first since 1988 and would examine tax returns for 1994. It was to be the largest study ever, auditing 153,000 returns, and for the first time it would include all major groups: individuals, corporations, and partnerships. The returns would be reviewed over a thirty-month period, and the resulting data would be used by Congress, federal and state agencies, and researchers to formulate tax policy, estimate revenue, and calculate the extent of taxpayer fraud and error. Underscoring the need for TCMP data, IRS Commissioner Margaret Milner Richardson testified that Americans fail to pay more than $2 billion in federal income taxes every week. To improve compliance, she said, "we need to know where the problems are."[21]

Congressional opposition began to build immediately. One of the first salvos was fired by House Speaker Newt Gingrich, who described the TCMP as "a little bit like the return of the Inquisition."[22] Gingrich added that the IRS, "not having succeeded in irritating enough people in the normal course of business, has now come up with a compliance lottery, where they randomly pick people to go and persecute."[23] Gingrich's solution: Eliminate the TCMP.

That summer, a House Ways and Means subcommittee hearing explored doing just that, with lawmakers questioning the fairness of subjecting taxpayers to the "audits from hell." Representative Nancy L. Johnson, a Republican from Connecticut, spoke for many of the critics:

> TCMP audits are costly for taxpayers, whether it is the cost of the taxpayer's own time, or that of a hired tax professional. In addition, the audits are seen as unfair for those whose returns show no indication of a need for audit. We have to ask ourselves, "Is it fair for the government to place a burden and expense on innocent people in order to better identify those who may not be so innocent?". . . We have to do something to make sure that the subjects — or victims — of these audits are not unduly punished.[24]

Johnson's point was a fair one. And if that had been the legislators' true concern, the solution would have been simple: Provide funds to reimburse those taxpayers who had been subjected to the intensive audit — and who ultimately owed no additional taxes. The cost would have been minimal. But Congress had a hidden agenda. It was determined to kill the TCMP, but in a way that would not be quite so obvious.

Against a background of growing attacks, lawmakers slashed the IRS's enforcement budget for the next fiscal year, a move that made it impossible to conduct the TCMP. In September, with audits slated to begin the next month, the IRS postponed the start for two months. But a month later, facing an intractable Congress and a reduced budget, the agency called off the study, noting almost matter-of-factly: "It is clear that the 1996 budget will require the IRS to limit its compliance programs."[25]

It was a momentous decision, and one that has proven catastrophic to the service's ability to pinpoint certain areas of taxpayer fraud and error. So hostile is Congress to such audits, the IRS hasn't even proposed another one. After resigning as commissioner, Margaret Richardson was able to say in 1998 what she had been unable to say as head of the IRS: "Congress has made it virtually impossible to continue with that type of program."[26] Nor has the agency been able to fund an alternative, because Congress considers any examinations to be "intrusive." Consequently, the IRS has no idea how many Americans are cheating on their taxes.

This isn't to say that there is no money available to assess the tax system. At the same time Congress cut the IRS's budget for audits, lawmakers came up with funds for one of their own pet projects: a multimillion-dollar study commission to explore ways to reform and restructure the agency.

Originally triggered by the outcry following massive computer glitches, the National Commission on Restructuring the IRS was to be the most comprehensive review of its operations in years.

The commission was given a one-year mandate to take a wide-ranging look at the service to see how it could be overhauled or possibly even replaced. The thirteen-member bipartisan commission, cochaired by Democratic Senator Bob Kerrey of Nebraska and Republican Representative Robert J. Portman of Ohio, was to review the agency's organizational structure, computer system, returns processing, and collections. Congress also directed the commission to look into ways of changing the culture of the IRS to make it "customer-oriented" to help restore the "public's faith in the American tax system."[27]

Although that sounded noble, the commission became the means to turn the IRS into a congressional punching bag. Its deliberations stretched into more than a year of testimony from tax preparers, lawyers, legislators, accountants, academicians, and other citizens. Apart from the occasional halfhearted criticism of Congress's annual ritual of changing the tax code — the single largest factor complicating the IRS's job — the attacks were aimed squarely at the agency. Continuing the practice that many members of Congress would follow throughout the 1990s, the commission gathered extensive testimony portraying the agency as insensitive to taxpayers, destructive, and even evil.

To change all that, the commission put forth a range of recommendations, including placing the IRS under the control of an outside board of governors, a move hotly opposed by both the Treasury and the Clinton administration. The commission issued a 200-page report in June 1997 aimed at forcing the IRS to become less aggressive with taxpayers, even though by that time IRS audits, based on a percentage of the tax-paying public, were falling to an all-time low. The report is filled with directives on how the IRS must become "user friendly," improve "customer service," and promote "taxpayer satisfaction."[28] What's more, to push the IRS to become more responsive, the report called on Congress to "provide taxpayers with adequate and reasonable compensation for actual damages incurred for wrongful actions by the IRS."

Meaning, if agents didn't treat taxpayers with kid gloves, then citizens could sue.

Typical of the sweeping pronouncements: "As a guiding principle, the Commission believes that taxpayer satisfaction must become paramount at the new IRS and that the IRS should only initiate contact with a taxpayer if the agency is prepared to devote the resources necessary for a timely and proper resolution of the matter."[29]

The report reads like an Orwellian satire: "Customer satisfaction must be a goal in every interaction the IRS has with taxpayers, including enforcement actions." Just how IRS could promote "customer satisfaction" among taxpayers who have been audited and found to have cheated or underpaid their taxes is never spelled out.

Furthermore, the report said, the IRS's customer service operations lag behind those of banks, mutual funds, and others in the private sector: "The Commission believes most citizens compare the service they receive from the IRS with the service they receive from financial service institutions."[30] In other words, the IRS doesn't score as highly as the helpline, for example, at Fidelity Investments. Of course, the subject discussed with a Fidelity representative will invariably be warmer to the caller's heart than that of a chat with the IRS. How will the IRS ever rank the equal of a financial institution when its goal is to collect money, rather than to disburse it? The commission's unrealistic report is a master plan for future IRS failures, so impractical are its expectations for a tax collection agency.

Nevertheless, many in Congress were ecstatic. "This is truly a blueprint for ending the IRS as we know it," said Portman, the Ohio Republican who cochaired the commission. "If we make the IRS more customer-driven, we'll see more compliance."[31] House Speaker Newt Gingrich called the report "extraordinarily important" and said he "absolutely" supported placing the IRS under an independent board.[32]

The commission's report was yet another assault on the IRS, and would form the basis of the IRS Restructuring and Reform Act that was orchestrated into law by Senator Roth in 1998. The largest single consequence of these attacks on the service, along with the decrees by Congress to be more customer-oriented, has been to deemphasize audits — which are the only way to enforce the tax code. But is a kinder, gentler IRS the way to promote compliance? When taxpayers know there's little chance they'll be audited, will they be as conscientious about reporting their income and deductions?

No way. In fact, at a time when taxpayer fraud already is out of control, the reduced audits are a signal that it's open season for tax cheating. Think about it this way: When New York City experienced a surge in crime, soiling the city's reputation and hurting tourism, the city's response was simple and direct: Flood crime areas with additional police, including teams of plainclothes officers. The result, as everyone knows, is that the crime wave ended, the city's reputation bounced back, and tourism rebounded. Now, think about what would have happened if the city had *reduced* police presence instead. That's the decision Congress has made for the IRS.

And it has had devastating consequences. Congress's broadbrush attack on the service in the 1998 restructuring law has been especially catastrophic for enforcement. With its list of "ten deadly sins," the overt actions for which an IRS agent can be fired, the law sent a chill through the ranks. The number of liens, levies, and seizures by enforcement agents plummeted overnight.

Fear of being accused of the sixth deadly sin — harassing a taxpayer — has become a matter of grave internal concern. Of the 449 cases lodged against IRS agents in the law's first year, 269, or 60 percent, were in this category.[33] "The language in 1203 in our opinion invites allegations from those who are not fond of IRS," said Colleen M. Kelley, president of the National

Treasury Employees Union. "So listing the 10 Deadly Sins is an open invitation and it institutes a fear factor that just isn't necessary."[34]

Are IRS agents overreacting? Hardly. To further remind agents that they are now on a short leash, Congress authorized an entirely new police force within the Treasury Department to keep tabs on them. The restructuring bill created the office of Treasury Inspector General for Tax Administration (TIGTA). At the same time Congress slashed the IRS's manpower, it appropriated millions of dollars for TIGTA, which soon had "1,000 auditors, investigators, and support staff" on board.[35] TIGTA, according to the first inspector general, David C. Williams, "is committed to ensuring that complaints or allegations of criminal wrongdoing and serious misconduct are thoroughly and objectively investigated."[36] In other words, Treasury now has hundreds of new investigators — not to look into tax fraud, but to investigate IRS agents.

To carry out its mandate, TIGTA will investigate a percentage of IRS agents each year accused of harassing taxpayers. The *New York Times* reported in November 1999 that under TIGTA goals, those cases may soon "equal the number of cases against Americans for tax crimes."[37] While it remains to be seen just how thoroughly TIGTA will pursue its mission, IRS agents are understandably worried. An agent found guilty of harassment can lose his or her job and can make no appeal. Faced with such a draconian choice, most agents opt to play it safe.

Congressional attacks on the IRS are symptoms of a broader agenda by lawmakers in Washington and their allies around the nation. As much as many lawmakers hate the IRS, there is something they hate more — the income tax itself. There have always been those who clamored for repeal, but today's critics are more numerous and more strident. Beginning in the late 1990s, efforts to scrap the income tax gained more ground than in any previous sessions of Congress, and the rhetoric escalated:

Richard G. Lugar, a Republican senator from Indiana: "I strongly believe that Congress should abolish the income tax system in its entirety and begin anew."[38]

Sam Johnson, a Republican congressman from Texas: "I believe that the Sixteenth Amendment has created a system that is economically destructive, impossibly complex, overly intrusive, unprincipled, dishonest, unfair, and inefficient. Now is the time for us to restore freedom to the American taxpayer ... [and] repeal the Sixteenth Amendment."[39]

James A. Traficant Jr., a Democratic congressman from Ohio: "Our tax code sucks. It is time to abolish it and throw the IRS out with it."[40]

In the summer of 1998, the House, in a 219 to 209 vote, approved a bill to phase out the tax code and the IRS along with it by 2002. A similar measure deadlocked in the Senate, 49 to 49, reflecting a deep-seated antipathy to the tax in the upper house of Congress as well. Representative Steve Largent, the Oklahoma Republican who cosponsored the bill, called the House's action "a vote where common sense prevailed."[41] Similar legislation, the Tax Code Termination Act, was introduced in both houses in 1999.

Of all the income tax's critics, perhaps the most aggressive is Representative Bill Archer, the Houston Republican who is chairman of the House Ways and Means Committee, Congress's powerful tax-writing committee. Archer is the first chairman in Ways and Means history who is actively working to abolish the income tax. The current system, Archer says, "is flawed so badly that reforming it (again) won't work. It needs to be done away with entirely." The solution, he has said, is to "pull the income tax out by its roots and throw it away so it can never grow back."[42]

Archer has held congressional hearings to explore doing just that, sponsored retreats to plot strategy, and appointed aides who serve as "liaison to coalition groups as part of the Ways and Means Committee's effort to abolish the income tax."[43]

Archer has spent most of his political career pursuing that objective. He was elected to the Texas House of Representatives in 1966 as a Democrat, but he was a rock-ribbed Republican at heart, and as his low-tax, small-government views coalesced, he officially switched parties. In 1971, he was elected to Congress from Houston's 7th Congressional District and has been easily reelected ever since, so closely have his views dovetailed with those of his district's overwhelmingly conservative, affluent, and antitax voters. He joined Ways and Means in 1973 and became chairman in 1995.

With his constituency of wealthy residents who enjoy large salaries or substantial dividend, interest, and capital gains income — and in some cases all four — Archer could argue that in campaigning to repeal the income tax, he is only serving the interests of those who elected him. But those voters are not representative of the United States. And the policy Archer advocates would affect not only his wealthy Houston friends, but all Americans. While Archer did not seek reelection in 2000, his movement for repeal will live on in the Ways and Means Committee, where other members are equally committed to junking the income tax.

As determined as congressional critics are to repeal the income tax, they still lack the necessary numbers to pull it off. So they are doing the next best thing: They're undermining the IRS, sapping its enforcement capability, heaping disrespect on it, and stirring up discontent. In lieu of outright repeal, opponents are taking the income tax apart piece by piece, hoping it will one day collapse of its own unsupported weight. They may be right.

FAVORITISM FOR A FEW

Even before Congress launched wholesale attacks on the IRS in the 1990s, lawmakers were sowing the seeds among average Americans for a deeper distrust and disillusionment with the income tax. This was accomplished by stuffing tax bills with hidden special-interest provisions — carefully crafted amendments that give one taxpayer, or a small group of taxpayers, a break at the expense of all others. Called transition rules, rifle shots, and special tax bills, these passages stand out like blinking lights in the numbing jargon of the tax code, mocking Congress's incessant pronouncements about tax fairness.

The practice of surreptitiously inserting the custom-tailored tax breaks began innocently enough. In 1924, a Pennsylvania senator slipped in a clause enabling a wealthy Philadelphia nun to donate her entire annual income from stocks and bonds to charity without incurring any tax consequences. The "unlimited charitable deduction" was the first special-interest tax provision, and although it was prompted by the best of intentions, wealthy taxpayers soon found ways to corrupt it. Not so well intentioned was a clause that mysteriously appeared in the Revenue Act of 1951, which gave Hollywood movie mogul Louis B. Mayer a multimillion-dollar tax cut by converting income he received from deferred salary into a lower capital gains tax rate.

Specially crafted provisions benefiting tiny numbers of taxpayers continued to appear in tax bills occasionally until the 1970s. Since then, the volume has exploded. The new era of rampant special-interest tax breaks was defined by the Tax Reform Act of 1986. Amid blasts of rhetoric from lawmakers as to how they were routing special interests and making the tax code fairer for middle-class America, tax-law writers working behind the scenes crammed the legislation with hundreds of clauses benefiting a handful of taxpayers.

Dan Rostenkowski, the Illinois Democrat who chaired the House Ways and Means Committee, called the tax reform measure "a bill that reaches deep into our national sense of justice — and gives us back a trust in government that has slipped away in the maze of tax preferences for the rich and powerful."[44] Then Rostenkowski inserted dozens of special provisions, including one worth at least $150 million to the Commonwealth Edison Company, the utility serving Rostenkowski's native Chicago.

Bob Packwood, the Oregon Republican who headed the Senate Finance Committee, hailed the measure, saying, "[taxes] are about fairness, and this bill is fair."[45] Then Packwood slipped numerous special breaks into the bill, including one exempting an Oregon railcar leasing company from the repeal of two business tax breaks.

Daniel Patrick Moynihan, a Democratic senator from New York, was among the most ardent champions of tax reform, calling the legislation "a profound statement concerning the requirements of citizenship and the ethical basis of the American republic."[46] Before voting on the bill, Moynihan plugged in at least a half dozen custom-tailored tax breaks for favored taxpayers, including the following: "In the case of a taxpayer which was incorporated on Feb. 17, 1983, and the five largest shareholders of which are doctors of medicine, any royalties of such taxpayer from products resulting from medical research shall be treated in the same manner as royalties from computer software are treated."[47]

That cut the tax bills of five doctors who were the principal owners of a Rochester, New York, company that sold vaccines to pharmaceutical companies. Moynihan's favor exempted the doctors' company from certain taxes that were ordinarily imposed on royalties derived from such sales.

Opportunities for this kind of favoritism have flourished over the last two decades as Congress, which once enacted a tax bill every few years, began gradually to enact one every year and finally several in one year.* This constant rewriting of the tax code has wreaked havoc, adding complexity, instability, and uncertainty to

---

* There was the Economic Tax Act of 1981, the Tax Equity and Fiscal Responsibility Act of 1982, the Deficit Reduction Act of 1984, the Consolidated Omnibus Budget Reconciliation Act of 1985, the Tax Reform Act of 1986, the Omnibus Budget Reconciliation Act of 1987, the Technical and Miscellaneous Revenue Act of 1988, the Omnibus Budget Reconciliation Act of 1989, the Omnibus Budget Reconciliation Act of 1990, the Tax Extension Act of 1991, the Energy Policy Act of 1992, the Omnibus Budget Reconciliation Act of 1993, the Social Security Domestic Employment Reform Act of 1994, the Balanced Budget Reconciliation Act of 1995, the Taxpayer Bill of Rights in 1996, the Taxpayer Relief Act of 1997, and the Internal Revenue Service Restructuring and Reform Act of 1998. And there was the Taxpayer Refund and Relief Act of 1999, although it was later vetoed by President Clinton.

the entire system, making the income tax more difficult to enforce and creating anger and frustration among taxpayers. But to the tax-writers, the chaos has created a gold mine. The annual tax law derby has enabled them to turn the tax code into a cash register for campaign funds. The mere hint of possible changes by either the House Ways and Means Committee or the Senate Finance Committee brings a flood of special-interest money to committee members from those who want to be sure they'll have access to the committees when they get down to putting the final touches on the latest bill.

In the three election cycles from 1994 to 1998, members of the House and Senate tax-writing committees collected more than $200 million in campaign contributions from corporations, company executives, political action committees, and individuals. Most special interests spread the money around, giving to Democrats and Republicans. The insurance industry, for example, contributed $5.2 million to tax-writers of both parties in the House and Senate.

For many tax-writers, the tax code has become an annuity, with the same special interests donating to their war chests year in and out, Federal Election Commission records show. Lawyers and lobbyists gave Robert T. Matsui, a Democratic congressman from California, $73,000 in the 1994 election cycle, $64,000 in 1996, and $61,000 in 1998. Jennifer B. Dunn, a Republican congresswoman from Washington State, received $40,000 from the air transport industry in 1994, then $43,000 in 1996, and $49,000 in 1998. The health care industry gave William M. Thomas, a Republican congressman from California, $83,000 in 1994, $143,000 in 1996, and $136,000 in 1998.

On the Senate side, the pharmaceutical industry gave Senator Orrin G. Hatch, the Utah Republican, $268,000 in 1994, $277,000 in 1996, and $282,000 in 1998. The insurance industry gave Senator Chuck Grassley, the Iowa Republican, $166,000 in 1994, $183,000 in 1996, and $203,000 in 1998. Securities firms and investment bankers gave Senator Bob Kerrey, the Nebraska Democrat, $508,000 in 1994, $490,000 in 1996, and $421,000 in 1998. After Bob Graham, a Democratic senator from Florida, joined the Senate Finance Committee in 1995, the real estate industry contributed $168,000 in 1996 and $252,000 in 1998 to his campaigns.

Lawmakers have hit upon some ingenious ways to keep milking the cash cow. Rather than making certain changes in tax law permanent, they enact them for one- or two-year periods, after which the provisions expire. As the expiration date nears, special interests begin to lobby for an extension and invariably cough up more campaign funds.

This is exactly the scenario that's been played out since 1997 with banks, insurance companies, and financial institutions over an obscure definition of foreign income. Lobbyists for a coalition of financial interests approached the tax committees in 1997 to amend the law to let them classify some foreign earnings as "active financing income." This may not sound like much, but it was worth millions and was designed to shield an ever-greater amount of foreign-based earnings from U.S. taxes. The Treasury Department estimated that the provision would cost taxpayers about $300 million in its first year alone.

Congress went along, and approved the measure in 1997. But the deferral was only for one year, meaning that as soon as lawmakers reconvened in 1998, the lobbying would begin all over again for another extension, perhaps even a permanent one. Those pushing to extend the tax break were familiar names from the campaign of the year before, such as the global insurance giant American International Group Inc. (AIG). Like most others lobbying for the extension, AIG has been a hefty campaign contributor. In the 1997–98 election cycle, AIG and its officers contributed more than a half-million dollars to both political parties.[48]

When an omnibus budget bill cleared Congress in October 1998, a clause extending the "active financing income" provision cleared too. Better yet for the insurance companies and other supporters, the 1998 clause broadened the definition, meaning they could escape more taxes. As before, the extension was for only one year, but a trade journal reported that big insurers were "thrilled" by their victory and had hopes of one day making it permanent. "It would be very nice if this got off the extender bandwagon and could be made permanent," said one insurance lobbyist, "but once you're there, it's very tough to break out of that group."[49] Indeed so — especially when neither party wants to give up such a dependable source of cash.

Many GOP lawmakers have singled out complexity in the tax code as a dragon worth slaying, but after Republicans won control of Congress in 1994, the first two major tax bills crafted on their watch, in 1997 and 1998, were among the most complex ever enacted by any Congress. The 1997 bill, the ironically named Taxpayer Relief Act, was a nightmare for many taxpayers, with its multiple rates for calculating capital gains taxes and some 400 changes plugged in to the tax code on the eve of another filing year.

The magazine *Tax Notes,* the single most authoritative source on the intricacies of tax law, described the bill's provisions as "so complex, so onerous, so disjointed and confusing, that they will likely result in a Taxpayer Refund Relief Act of 1998. . . . This legislation should confirm the time-tested wisdom of always securing the best available financial guidance from trusted qualified advisors, preferably one's astrologer or bartender."[50]

What exactly do the campaign contributions buy? First of all, access. Then, if you're lucky, your own special tax law. Ask Richard M. DeVos.

DeVos is one of the founders and owners of the privately held Amway Corporation, the $5-billion-a-year global consumer-products giant in Ada, Michigan. Amway is one of the world's largest direct marketers of vitamins, home-care products, and personal-care items, many manufactured by the company.

Started by DeVos and Jay Van Andel in the basements of their Ada homes in 1959, Amway has grown into one of America's most controversial and secretive retail businesses. To sell hundreds of products from body powder to stain removers, Amway employs 12,000 and depends on a vast web of 3 million independent distributors in more than eighty countries and territories who all need each other to survive. Company operations resemble a pyramid scheme, but it has been structured in such a way as to be a perfectly legal one. Each person who signs up to sell Amway products is expected to recruit a friend or neighbor to do the same, who in turn is expected to recruit others. The approach has helped make DeVos and Van Andel two of the richest men in America. *Forbes* magazine put their combined net worth at $2.9 billion in 1998.

Amway gatherings often have the feeling of a religious revival, with inspirational tapes and motivational speeches celebrating God and free enterprise. Amwayites quote from the Scriptures, while at the same time celebrating the material rewards that can come from selling Amway products.

At the heart of the Amway credo is the belief that anyone who embraces the company's principles can become rich. Amway will get you started for $175, the cost of an "Opportunity Kit," containing Amway products, promotional material, and a company history. Amwayites have their own lingo: Someone who becomes an Amway distributor is first called a Pearl. At a certain level of sales, the distributor earns a Ruby pin, and then an Emerald. Those who really have the sales touch can win a Diamond pin. No one outside the company knows how many are diamonds, but there are enough to hold a convention each year in Hawaii.

A small number of distributors do quite well, earning up to $100,000 or more a year. But for the overwhelming majority, perhaps 90 percent or more, the job is part time. The income that it produces for them — a few hundred dollars, or maybe several thousand dollars — is intended to supplement their primary source of earnings. Most of those who practice the profession full time gross less than $25,000 a year.[51] Because of its unorthodox business practices, the company has been the target of regulatory investigations and lawsuits.

Politically, Amwayites are conservative and well connected. Godlessness, homosexuality, and affirmative action are denounced at Amway's pep rallies, and the company has powerful friends in Congress. Texas Republican Tom DeLay, the House majority whip, is a former Amway salesman, and four other Republican members of the House are Amway distributors. These alliances have helped the organization to become an increasingly potent political force. As *Mother Jones* magazine has noted: "This ever-growing network of Amway devotees, heavily influenced by the company's dual themes of Christian morality and free enterprise, donates money and operates like a private political army."[52]

Amway the corporation, and its owners, have been major supporters of the Republican Party. Indeed, Amway proudly proclaims that its "owners share the U.S. Republican Party's views on free enterprise, personal freedom, and personal responsibility. For decades, Amway's founders have consistently supported Republican initiatives."[53]

In 1994, Amway Corporation contributed $2.5 million for a new broadcast center at the Republican Party's national headquarters in Washington, D.C. And two years later it donated $1.3 million to support the Republican national convention in San Diego. During the 1997–98 election cycle, the company and its owners gave $1.3 million to the GOP. Richard DeVos and his wife, Helen, alone kicked in $1 million of that total. It paid off.

When Congress was set to pass the final version of the Taxpayer Relief Act in the summer of 1997, Amway's lobbyists scored a big win. For more than a year, they had been pushing for a special provision to allow a more liberal interpretation of international tax rules affecting two of the company's Asian affiliates. Initially, neither the House bill nor the Senate-passed version contained the tax concession. As the bill neared final passage, Amway's lobbyists, including J. Roger Mentz, who had been an assistant Treasury secretary in the Bush administration, sprang into action. Going straight to the top, they appealed to House Speaker Newt Gingrich and his Senate counterpart, Trent Lott, for a little help. And they got it. When the act became final, tucked away in the fine print was this nugget:

SEC. 1123. VALUATION OF ASSETS FOR PASSIVE FOREIGN INVESTMENT COMPANY DETERMINATION.

(a) IN GENERAL — Section 1297, as redesignated by section 1122, is amended by adding at the end the following new subsection . . .

(2) DETERMINATION USING ADJUSTED BASES — The determination under subsection (a)(2) shall be based on the adjusted bases (as determined for the purposes of computing earnings and profits) of the assets of a foreign corporation if such corporation is not described in paragraph (1)(A) and such corporation . . .

In language that only a tax lawyer would have a prayer of understanding, section 1123 set forth a complex, 221-word formula for "measuring assets" of certain foreign entities known as controlled foreign corporations. As complicated as the formula was, the result was simple: a tax break for two Amway subsidiaries — Amway Asia Pacific Ltd. and Amway Japan Limited.

Shortly before the House and Senate approved the final tax bill, Gingrich and Lott had the provision inserted during a closed-door conference session. No hearings had been held on the exception, and there was almost no time to debate it. But lawmakers went along. While the provision also benefited several other companies, it was worth millions of dollars to the Amway subsidiaries.

Of all the special-interest groups, the narrowest of them all may be the one that triumphed when Congress passed a health insurance act in 1996. Increasingly, lawmakers fold tax provisions into bills that have little or nothing to do with taxes, and so it was with the Health Insurance Portability and Accountability Act of

1996, which was to help workers maintain health benefits coverage when they change jobs. Tacked on to it was a section affecting a tiny group of folks who will never have to worry about medical coverage: rich Americans who have moved abroad to avoid paying taxes.

The legislation was prompted by a stream of news stories about wealthy Americans who had renounced their citizenship for tax reasons in the early 1990s. John (Ippy) Dorrance III, an heir to a Campbell Soup Company fortune, renounced his U.S. citizenship to live on an estate in Ireland. Michael Dingman, a former chairman of Wheelabrator-Frye Inc., emigrated to the Bahamas. Joseph Bogdanovich, then chairman of Star-Kist Foods, gave up his citizenship for an undisclosed foreign address.

Most Americans who renounced their citizenship continued to spend time in the United States. Kenneth Dart, heir to a billion-dollar fortune in Dart Container Corporation, gave up his citizenship in 1994 to become a citizen of Belize, the tiny Central American nation that hawks passports like souvenirs. Of course, Belize was just a post office box for Dart. His new base was actually in the Cayman Islands, where he built a $5 million compound overlooking the ocean. But even that address was misleading. Though no longer a U.S. citizen, Dart continued to spend time in the United States, principally in Sarasota, Florida, where his wife and children still lived and where the headquarters of Dart Container, the hugely private and enormously profitable company that makes half the plastic cups sold in America, are located.

A year after giving up his citizenship, Dart hatched a plan to live in Sarasota full time in 1995 without having to start paying U.S. income taxes again. This came to light after the Belize government applied to the U.S. State Department for permission to open a consular office in Sarasota. Initially, the department was puzzled by the request. Few Belizeans live in Sarasota, and the tiny country, with a population of only 236,000, already had a consulate in

Miami. Then it became clear: To run the Sarasota office with "special responsibilities in the area of trade and finance," Belize had just the right man: Ken Dart.[54] As a foreign diplomat, Dart could live on American soil tax free. This was too much for the State Department, which turned down the proposal.

With the number of rich Americans fleeing the country for tax reasons seemingly on the rise, Congress in 1995 tackled the question of whether to make expatriation less attractive. At the time, tax law stipulated that anyone who renounced citizenship to avoid taxes was liable for income taxes for ten years afterward. But the law had no teeth, and it was difficult for the IRS to prove that a taxpayer had renounced citizenship solely to avoid taxes.

To strengthen the law, Senator Daniel Patrick Moynihan proposed a tax on the assets of any wealthy individuals who expatriated, to be levied at the time they gave up citizenship — a kind of capital gains exit tax. Moynihan's proposal targeted only the well-off — those with assets exceeding $600,000 (or $1.2 million for couples). Although enacted by the Senate, the provision ran into trouble in the House. Bill Archer, the Ways and Means chairman, called the proposal "seriously flawed."[55] Representative Nancy L. Johnson, a Connecticut Republican, said it had "significant technical problems."[56] Other lawmakers said it would foment "class warfare." Still others claimed that the proposed tax was a "cheap political stunt."[57]

In the end, a House–Senate conference deleted the exit tax and substituted a measure that purported to get tough with expatriates but that was much less stringent. Under the new guidelines, anyone who gave up citizenship and who had assets of $500,000, or who paid $100,000 in income taxes was presumed to be expatriating for tax reasons, and became subject to income taxes for ten more years.

Although the new law sounded tough, it was filled with loopholes and has had little apparent effect on expatriation by the rich. *Forbes* magazine reported in July 1999 that wealthy Americans continue to "slip through the net" without being taxed, citing the case of Tara Getty, beneficiary of a $400 million inheritance, who renounced his citizenship the previous winter. Americans who leave the country for tax reasons are legally barred from reentering the United States. But, according to *Forbes*, Getty had no difficulty returning to America for a wedding.[58] One estate lawyer said the U.S. policy banning reentry by expatriates is meaningless because the government does not enforce it. "The tiger has no teeth," he said.[59]

The tiger would have teeth, of course, if the exit tax had been enacted. Instead, rich Americans, if they choose, can continue to thumb their nose at other taxpayers. Their numbers have never been great; fewer than 1,000 persons give up their citizenship in an average year. But the potential tax loss to the Treasury is significant. If the exit tax had been enacted, Treasury estimates it would have raised $1.4 billion in its first five years.

THE BEGINNING OF THE END

The triumph of wealthy special interests in Congress is now so complete that they are shaping government policies in ways they could only dream of even a few years ago. The extent of their influence is evident in the aggressive campaign to kill the estate tax, which, with few exceptions, affects only the most affluent Americans. Congress's handling of the estate tax could be a preview of the future of the income tax, because the tactics involved are identical to those being employed to undermine the income tax.

The death tax, as the estate tax is often called, was enacted in 1916 to limit the ability of rich families to pass on their wealth to succeeding generations. Ironically, while Republicans are leading the charge to eliminate it in the twenty-first century, another Republican, President Theodore Roosevelt, argued the case for it early in the last century. He maintained that "no advantage comes either to the country as a whole or to the individuals inheriting the money by permitting the transmission in their entirety of the enormous fortunes which would be affected by such a tax."[60]

Many powerful interests rejected Roosevelt's view, and in the decades that followed they mounted periodic campaigns to scrap or reduce the death tax. But their efforts never went far until 1999. That year, congressional Republicans put forth more than a dozen bills, some calling for increasing the exemption so the tax would touch fewer people; some proposing to phase out the tax over a decade; and some seeking its immediate repeal.

Representative Jennifer Dunn, the Washington State Republican who cosponsored the Death Tax Elimination Act, declared: "It's been said that only with our government are you given a 'certificate at birth, a license at marriage, and a bill at death.' [This act] . . . seeks to phase out the onerous death tax. . . . The death tax deserves to die."[61]

Representative Charles Joseph Scarborough, a Florida Republican, introduced the Death Tax Sunset Act to "put an end to the federal government's most outrageous form of taxation. . . . The thought that our government can take over half of a person's life savings when they die should sicken every American."[62]

Representative Charles Christopher Cox, a Republican from the wealthy enclave of Newport Beach, California, introduced the Family Heritage Preservation Act calling for instant repeal: "Hard-working American men and women spend a lifetime saving to provide for their children and grandchildren, paying taxes all the while. . . . When the purpose of that hard-earned saving is about to be achieved, families discover that between 37 percent and 55 percent of their after-tax savings is confiscated by Federal estate taxes."[63]

All the rhetoric would suggest that the heavy hand of the federal government is dipping deep into the pockets of Middle America, seizing more than half its hard-earned savings, and threatening to impoverish widows and orphans.

Not even close. In fact, the tax applies to few citizens, fewer still from Middle America. On this point, the statistics are overwhelming. In 1995, a total of 32,000 returns were filed on behalf of decedents who owed the estate tax. The number of taxable estate tax returns was a mere 1.4 percent of the adults who died that year. That was down from 3.7 percent in 1962. In short, the estate tax touches the tiniest number of people. That's because it does not take effect until assets go above $675,000 for a single person, or $1.35 million for a married couple. Under present law, those figures will rise to $1 million and $2 million in 2006.

Estate tax critics in Congress scoff at the notion that its repeal would be a windfall for the rich. As Representative George R. Nethercutt Jr., a Republican from Washington State, puts it: "The death tax started early in the twentieth century targeted at a few super-rich families. Most people still believe this is a 'soak the rich' law and that repeal would only benefit the rich."[64]

Actually, that's precisely who would benefit. In 1995, a total of 13,830 taxable returns were filed for estates valued between $600,000 and $1 million. Average tax paid: $47,083. All other returns listed estates of more than $1 million, a sum that hardly qualifies as "middle class." At the very top, 231 returns were filed for estates of more than $20 million. Average tax: $8.7 million.

To discredit the tax, lawmakers and special interests have mounted other equally bogus arguments. They contend repeal would benefit "millions of farmers and small-business owners," in the words of Senator Rod Grams, a Republican from Minnesota.[65] Not in your lifetime. Even assuming that every single return showing estate tax due was submitted by a farmer or small-business owner, it would take more than thirty years to reach even one million returns.

Others call the estate tax double taxation because it's a tax on money that has been taxed before. But this is true of most taxes. When you pay real estate or sales taxes, you've already paid federal, state, and local income tax on that money. Indeed, you pay federal income tax on money that you don't even see that's withheld for Social Security and Medicare taxes. Still other lawmakers insist the estate tax has harmed the economy. But given that the United States is in its longest period of sustained growth ever, that case is hard to make.

Most misleading of all is the claim that the law levies a 55 percent tax on some estates. "How can we justify taking 55 percent of Americans' life savings when they die?" asked Florida's Representative Scarborough.[66]

In truth, no one, including the richest of the rich, shells out 55 percent of his assets in estate taxes, just as no one pays the top income tax rate of 39.6 percent on all his earnings. Only a portion of any estate is taxed at the maximum rate of 55 percent. For the richest of the rich, those whose holdings exceeded $20 million at their death, the estate tax on returns filed in 1995 averaged just 16 percent of total assets.

To build support for repealing the estate tax, lawmakers and special interests use public opinion polls that are conducted in such a way as to produce answers that will support their views. As might be expected, these polls show that Americans overwhelmingly favor the repeal of the tax — a conclusion that will be invoked in Congress, will find its way to the evening news, and will be picked up by newspapers and magazines.

Consider a poll conducted for Americans Against Unfair Family Taxation (AAUFT), a name as warm and fuzzy as apple pie and motherhood. A coalition of family-owned businesses, the AAUFT is one of several special-interest groups that are trying to stir up grassroots opposition to the estate tax and to line up support to abolish it. Similar to polls financed by critics of the income tax, the AAUFT survey approached 1,000 adults in 1999 with questions calculated to generate responses highly critical of the estate tax. One sample question: "In your opinion, is it fair or unfair that the federal government taxes your income when you receive it, and then taxes your estate after you die?"

Implicit in the question is the suggestion that once money is taxed, it is never taxed again, and that everyone pays the estate tax. Both are false premises. As you might guess, a stunning 89 percent of those polled labeled the proposition "unfair."

Another question: "Do you think it is fair or unfair that under current law, the Internal Revenue Service, or IRS, can take up to 60%, which is more than half, of an individual's estate in taxes after death?" No matter that no one pays 60 percent — or anything close to it — in estate taxes, the question produced the desired result for opponents. An overwhelming 93 percent said it was "unfair."[67]

Those who have the most to gain from ending the estate tax are the wealthy, and some of them are working hard for repeal. Folks like the Koch (pronounced *coke*) brothers, Charles and David, who are two of the richest men in America. *Forbes* estimated that each had a net worth of $3.4 billion in 1999. The brothers own Koch Industries, the second-largest privately held company in America, a $30-billion-a-year oil, gas, chemical, and agribusiness behemoth based in Wichita, Kansas, that employs 16,000 persons worldwide. The company was founded by Charles and David's father, an early supporter of the conservative John Birch Society.

Charles, born in 1936, quietly runs the company's day-to-day operations from Wichita. David, three years younger, is a bit more social. He and his attractive wife, Julia, twenty-three years his junior, flit between homes in New York, Florida, Colorado, and France. David Koch made headlines in 1995 when he paid $9.5 million for the late Jacqueline Kennedy Onassis's Fifth Avenue apartment. A collector of fine wines and art, David hosts lavish New Year's Eve parties at his home in Aspen. Both brothers avoid publicity. Even less would be known of them had it not been for a bitter family feud that has pitted Charles and David against two other brothers, William and Frederick, who have claimed in a prolonged court battle that they were cheated out of part of their inheritance when Charles and David bought their shares of the company in 1983.

In recent years, Charles and David Koch have set their sights on eliminating the federal estate tax. Reports filed by lobbyists working for Koch Industries in Washington have targeted the estate tax as one of the company's specific lobbying goals. It's impossible to guess how much repeal would further enrich the family, but it would certainly add to their wealth.

In the past, the notion of abolishing the estate tax was just a millionaire's pipe dream. But no more. One of the 1999 bills to repeal it was incorporated into the omnibus tax bill Congress passed that year. Although the bill was vetoed by President Clinton, it was a major milestone. Never before had such a provision even survived to a House–Senate conference, let alone win approval by both houses and be sent to the White House. Without a big change in Congress, the death of the death tax may be only a matter of time. Will the income tax be far behind?

COLLAPSING OF ITS OWN WEIGHT

While members of Congress are employing the same tactics to kill the estate tax that they will use to do in the income tax, one other congressional practice will make it easier to achieve the latter goal. That's the lawmakers' penchant for making the tax code more complex every year.

Chronic additions, revisions, and clarifications have made the income tax bulky and bewildering. It isn't just the length of the code — 3,100 pages and an additional 46,900 pages of regulations, rulings, and explanatory material — that's the problem; it's the ambiguity arising from passages that defy understanding and complicate compliance and enforcement.

Financial publications often conduct surveys to see how well tax professionals understand the income tax. Periodically, *Money* magazine asks fifty tax-return preparers to complete a return for the same average family. Each time, no two preparers come up with the same numbers, and quite often the bottom lines are wildly at odds. In 1997, *Money* took its annual review a step further to conduct its own "audit" of the IRS and concluded that 8 million Americans receive incorrect bills or refunds because of IRS mistakes. Many of the errors were attributed to the impenetrability of the tax code. How does the U.S. government expect people to comply with the law if its sheriff doesn't know what's right or wrong?[68]

Railing about this confusion and the frustrating work it forces on taxpayers is an ever-more popular sport in Congress, where lawmakers compete with one another to denounce the complexity of the income tax as a reason to eliminate it — even though they are responsible for every bit of it.

"I thought we would go back a little ways and we would see the 1940 Tax Code, and I can still lift this one up," Representative Sam Brownback, a Kansas Republican, told his colleagues in April 1996. "I cannot pick up the current Tax Code of the United States. I guess I need to be lifting weights . . . it is a stack about 2½ feet tall of books. It contains 555 million words that control our lives."[69]

"The Tax Code of the United States in terms of its complexity, the cost to society, the cost to business, the frustration to citizens, the anger toward the Internal Revenue Service is truly a disgrace," Senator Pete V. Domenici, a New Mexico Republican, told colleagues in January 1995. "We have to make it simple and make it work."[70]

Steve Chabot, an Ohio Republican, linked the evils of the tax code to severe environmental consequences in a House address in April 1996: "We have to cut down 293,000 trees just to put together these forms that we send out to the American public and I personally think that we ought to leave a lot more of these trees standing and cut down the Tax Code substantially."[71]

Congress routinely holds hearings to decry complexity. The high-level study commission on IRS restructuring also cited complexity as one of the system's prime flaws. Critics in Congress blame the existence of the income tax itself, and, by extension the IRS, which must enforce it.

The IRS has certainly done its part to muddy tax law administration. After all, this is the agency that once came up with regulations calling for colored dyes to be injected into diesel fuels to differentiate between taxable and nontaxable fuel. But it was Congress, not the IRS, that added this section to tax law:

(1) Subpart A of part I of subchapter J of chapter 1 is amended by striking section 644 and by redesignating section 645 as section 644.
(2) Paragraph (5) of section 706(b) is amended by striking "section 645" and inserting "section 644".
(3) The table of sections for such subpart is amended by striking the last 2 items and inserting the following new item: "Sec. 644. Taxable year of trusts. ([[Page 111 STAT. 857]])."

And this one:

SEC. 1014. CERTAIN PREFERRED STOCK TREATED AS BOOT.
(a) Section 351. — Section 351 (relating to transfer to corporation controlled by transferor) is amended by redesignating subsection (g) as subsection (h) and by inserting after subsection (f) the following new subsection:
(g) Nonqualified Preferred Stock Not Treated as Stock. —
(1) In general. — In the case of a person who transfers property to a corporation and receives nonqualified preferred stock —
(A) subsection (a) shall not apply to such transferor,
(B) subsection (b) shall apply to such transferor, and
(C) such nonqualified preferred stock shall be treated as other property for purposes of applying subsection (b).

These provisions are part of the Taxpayer Relief Act of 1997, but every tax bill has similar gobbledygook. Congress treats tax code complexity as if it were a computer virus — a mysterious bug that has invaded the system from somewhere outside and that lawmakers are powerless to stop. But that's become part of the game on Capitol Hill: Complain vociferously about the income tax, while refusing to correct the problem.

Tax Notes magazine, which has been reporting on Congress's sorry record in this area for nearly three decades, put the matter in perspective in 1997:

> Complicating the tax code is like speeding on the Capital Beltway. Everybody knows it's wrong but everybody does it anyway. Anyone proposing strict enforcement of the speed limit would be considered a goody two-shoes idealist. Anybody proposing that taxwriters be prevented from increasing tax complexity would be laughed off the podium. Sissy! Wimp! Real men drive fast. Real men negotiate "historic" budget agreements. Only grandmas drive 55. Only junior staff spend time on simplification.[72]

So rather than simplifying the code, Congress continues to complicate it, feeding the growing national anger, cynicism, and frustration over the income tax, then cashing in on public discontent when taxpayers cry out for simplification. It's a perpetual-motion machine that critics in Congress hope to keep going until they can bring about repeal.

No one has played this game better than Bill Roth, the Delaware Republican who became the Senate ramrod for the IRS restructuring bill in 1998 that watered down IRS enforcement capabilities. Roth also wrote a book, *The Power to Destroy* (1999), about IRS abuses uncovered by his committee. Few have been more active in making tax law over the last two decades; dozens of bills have passed through the Finance Committee since he became a member in 1974.

Like his colleagues, Roth bemoans the bewildering tax law and calls for simplicity. Taxpayers, he says, are "flummoxed by the complexity of the tax code."[73] To solve that, Roth once promised to introduce legislation to "simplify some of the code's worst complexities."[74]

But few have done more to add to the tangled law than he has. His monument: Roth IRAs, the dizzyingly complicated individual retirement accounts that he pushed through Congress in 1997 and that bear his name.

Unlike traditional individual retirement accounts, which provide a tax deduction when a contribution is made, the Roth IRA gives taxpayers a deduction when earnings are withdrawn. The Roth IRA established a detailed set of phase-outs, phase-ins, and exceptions to rules that permitted early withdrawals because of death, disability, or the purchase of a first home. The law also let taxpayers convert a traditional IRA to a Roth, for those who could figure out whether it made sense to do so.

Of the new IRA, Roth said: "It will be a blessing to countless Americans as they prepare for the future."[75] If so, taxpayers certainly didn't know it. Most were baffled, not knowing whether to establish a new stand-alone Roth account or roll over an existing IRA into a Roth, or simply leave their existing retirement accounts in place. All this was good news for financial planners. *Practical Accountant* magazine described the tax law including the Roth as a "megadose of adrenaline for financial planning."[76]

But it was also bad tax policy. Daniel Halperin, former deputy assistant Treasury secretary from 1978 to 1981 and professor of taxation at Harvard Law School, called the Roth "the antithesis of sensible tax and budget policy,"[77] a program that gave us "numbing complexity for ordinary citizens and budget busting, without any policy justification."[78] Halperin added: "Creating two alternatives for IRA savings adds only complexity, which is bound to lead to numerous errors by ordinary folks."[79]

This intractable complexity places powerful ammunition in the hands of those who would kill the income tax. For all the talk of simplifying the code, more confusion and ambiguity were woven into it during the 1990s than in any other decade. It's almost as though the income tax's opponents in Congress are intentionally making the tax weaker and more intricate each session — in hopes it will strangle on its own red tape in the long run.

In the meantime, the tax system drifts. A New York tax lawyer sums it up: "It seems almost as though Congress and the White

House have decided the tax law is so unmanageable that they should not disturb the voters by trying to administer it."[80]

That's exactly what's happening, except for those unfortunate few who get caught up in the government's enforcement mill.

CHAPTER 5

PURSUING THE POWERLESS

TAX CHEATERS' LOTTERY

*I*f spring is approaching, it must be income tax indictment time. As surely as baseball players begin drifting toward Florida to prepare for another season, every February and March newspapers blossom with stories about people indicted for cheating on their income taxes. They are usually prominent individuals or hold highly visible positions, thereby guaranteeing bold display in hometown newspapers and on radio and television. Coming on the eve of the April 15 tax-filing deadline, the media attention serves as a warning to all citizens that they, too, may be prosecuted if they fail to fully report their income or if they claim unlawful deductions.

In February 1999, for example, the U.S. Attorney's office in New York City secured a sixty-six-count indictment for tax fraud against Albert J. Pirro Jr., a real estate lawyer, the highest paid lobbyist in the state, and a major fund-raiser for the Republican Party. He also happened to be the husband of the Westchester County district attorney, Jeanine F. Pirro, who at the time was a serious contender for the U.S. Senate seat in that state.

The *New York Times* devoted the top of its Metro page to a photo of the couple and this headline: "Westchester Prosecutor's Husband Is Indicted; U.S. Accuses Real Estate Lawyer of $1 Million in Improper Deductions."[1] The *New York Daily News, New York Post,* and local television and radio stations echoed the story. All recounted the charges that Pirro had written off $1 million of personal expenses as business deductions on company tax returns.

The *Times* reported that

> in November 1988, Mr. Pirro leased a Mercedes-Benz for his wife in the name of one of his companies, Ferris-Pirro Development Corporation. . . . The indictment said that from 1988 through 1997 Mr. Pirro routinely declared lavish personal purchases as the expenses of his law firm, real estate firm or other closely held companies. The salary of his family's domestic servant was paid for by a Pirro firm known as Suburban Messenger. A $3,700 awning for the Pirro's Italianate mansion in Harrison, New York, was assigned to a Pirro firm, AJP Management Group.
>
> Other family expenses assigned to his business or not declared on his joint personal tax returns included: a $123,000 Ferrari sports car; a leased Mercedes-Benz for his mother-in-law, and $10,000 worth of furnishings for a vacation home in West Palm Beach, Florida. The indictment said that Mr. Pirro even charged to his law practice the legal bills for a paternity suit in which he was named by an Indiana woman as the father of her fifteen-year-old daughter. DNA tests last year subsequently confirmed his paternity. If convicted on all charges, Mr. Pirro faces a maximum of five years in jail on a conspiracy count, five years in jail on each of four tax evasion counts, and three years in jail on each of 28 false tax return counts.[2]

Pirro denied the charges, and his prosecutor wife expressed her support at a news conference. "This has been an invasive and hostile process for my husband and for my family," an anxious Mrs. Pirro said, placed in the unusual role of championing a criminal defendant. "I am convinced of my husband's innocence and confident that he will be exonerated."[3]

Every year, in large cities and small towns across America, in the weeks leading up to April 15 similar stories appear in the local news media. Sometimes the amount of unpaid taxes is in the millions of dollars. Other times it's only a few thousand dollars, creating the impression that the IRS and U.S. Justice Department pursue tax-law violators with an even hand. And almost always, the news accounts recite the maximum penalties for the charges, suggesting that the accused could be hit with massive fines and spend many years, even decades, in prison. A sampling of such stories in recent years illustrates the practice.

- February 5, 1998, *St. Petersburg* (Florida) *Times.*
  A longtime North Florida lawmaker was indicted Wednesday on charges that he underpaid his federal income taxes for two years and plotted with his wife to hide his true income. . . . The couple faces a maximum of five years in prison and a $250,000 fine for the third count, conspiracy to defraud the federal government.

- March 15, 1997, *Central Maine Morning Sentinel,* Waterville.
  A Waterville jeweler on Thursday pleaded guilty in U.S. District Court to filing false income tax returns. Lionel M. Tardif, 49, of Oakland, faces a maximum prison sentence of three years, according to Assistant U.S. Attorney Gail Fisk Malone, who prosecuted the case.

- February 15, 1996, *Los Angeles Times.*
  A San Juan Capistrano man and former supervisor with the Internal Revenue Service was indicted Wednesday with his wife on charges that he lied to an IRS agent during an audit of his tax returns. . . . They could be sentenced to as many as 28 years in prison, but probably would receive a sentence "substantially less than that," said Marc C. Harris, the assistant U.S. attorney prosecuting the case.

- February 23, 1995, *Daily Oklahoman,* Oklahoma City.
  Prominent Oklahoma City attorney Michael Gassaway is facing prison time again after a federal grand jury on Wednesday alleged tax fraud and evasion in a seven-count criminal indictment. The charges carry penalties of up to 33 years in prison and $535,000 in fines if the criminal defense attorney is convicted.

The message from this yearly ritual is hard to miss: If you falsify your tax return, the IRS and Justice Department will come down on you with all the government's might, with the news media dutifully reporting every embarrassing detail. The IRS acknowledges the ritual. Following the indictment of eight Pennsylvanians in February 1997 for underpaying their taxes by several hundred thousand dollars, Joan Schafer, a spokeswoman for the Philadelphia IRS office, underscored the value of the timing. "It makes an excellent filing season message," she said. "This is the time of year when people are thinking about filing or not filing or not reporting all their income."[4]

The only problem is, the message is a hoax, one abetted by newspapers and magazines, radio and television stations, which all play along with the charade.

For the few who are singled out for prosecution, the image is an accurate one. But for every one person charged with income tax evasion or willful failure to file a return, tens of thousands get away with it.

In plain terms, tax cheating has become so common, so widespread, running through all levels of society, from the very poor to the very rich, that the United States could not build enough prisons to hold everyone who's doing it. Think Prohibition magnified many times over.

Call it the tax cheaters' lottery — the world's only lottery in which the overwhelming majority of players are winners. As far back as 1983, before tax dodging had reached its current epidemic state, and at a time when offshore tax evasion still was largely the exclusive province of the rich, an IRS official, questioned about the risk of prosecution faced by those who shipped their assets to tax havens, replied: "It would be an unfortunate happenstance if you were caught. You would be a very unlucky person."[5]

That's even truer today — for all varieties of tax fraud. As for the lottery's losers, they fall into two groups. One is the tiny number of tax-law violators, fewer than 1,000 a year, who are picked for prosecution and often notoriety. The other is all the honest taxpayers who in the end must make up the difference.

MORE FRAUD AND FEWER AUDITS

Evidence of America's disintegrating tax enforcement is in the statistics. IRS conducts two kinds of audits. One is at the district level, where auditors and revenue agents with a background in accounting deal with, as the GAO explains, "more complex issues, such as those on business or investment schedules that are attached to tax returns, usually through face-to-face meetings in an IRS office or a taxpayer's place of business."[6] The other audit, which is the most prevalent, is carried out through correspondence by examiners who handle simpler matters.

The face-to-face district audit numbers are the most revealing. In 1981, the IRS conducted 1.5 million of them. By 1998, that figure had plummeted by two-thirds, to 550,000. This at a time when the number of individual tax returns filed had climbed 29 percent, from 93 million to 120 million. More to the point, returns filed by people with incomes in excess of $200,000 had rocketed up 1,400 percent during the same period, from 120,000 to 1.8 million. Meanwhile, the number of revenue agents and auditors has plunged 20 percent, from a peak of 19,800 in 1989 to 15,800 in 1998.

Preliminary data show that this grim picture worsened still in 1999. District audits continued their downward spiral, falling to 380,000 — off 75 percent from 1981. The audit rate, that is, the number of returns examined out of the total number filed, plunged to its lowest level in modern history — under 1 percent. At the same time, individuals and families with incomes of less than $25,000 were more likely to be audited than those with incomes of more than $100,000.

A look at the correspondence audits offers further insight into the IRS's ailing enforcement program. From 1992 to 1997, the service conducted between 200,000 and 1.1 million each year. The 1.1 million audits occurred in 1995, when Congress directed the IRS to look at growing fraud involving the earned income tax credit. After the IRS stepped up audits in that area, it did indeed find widespread fraud and error. Of the 1.1 million returns checked, almost 800,000 had "missing or invalid Social Security numbers."[7]

Predictably, the audit blitz triggered an outcry in Congress. After all, most lawmakers have as much interest in ferreting out tax fraud as they do in restricting campaign contributions. After the IRS followed through on Congress's mandate to conduct the audits, lawmakers criticized the agency for picking on poor people. The IRS hastily pulled back and correspondence audits fell 500,000, which is why, you may recall, fraud is rampant in the earned income tax credit program.

You might think of correspondence audits as the McDonald's fast-food equivalent of tax return examinations. Personnel in one of the IRS's ten service centers around the country scan returns that have been classified as likely candidates for audit. They look for potential errors, usually involving income, deductions, exemptions, or credits. When they spot a questionable entry, which occurs in 50 to nearly 90 percent of the cases, a letter is sent to the filer asking for an explanation or documentation.

Letters sent to individuals who claim the earned income tax credit ask the filers to supply information concerning their children, such as Social Security numbers, birth dates, and school records, to verify the children exist and the filers are eligible for the credit. What happens next varies wildly from one section of the country to another.

A GAO investigation found that at least three of the ten IRS service centers certified EITC claims as legitimate "based on assurances from the taxpayers but without documentation or third-party verification."[8] In other words, the IRS examiners took the tax return filer's word that he or she was not cheating. No proof necessary, just a friendly "You can trust me."

Why, you might ask, were some individuals excused from supplying documents that others were compelled to furnish? According to the GAO, "Officials at one of the three service centers stated that the documentation requirements were eased because the center's tax examiner work force was inexperienced and unable to otherwise audit the large volume of returns within the prescribed time frames."[9]

Thus, meeting the IRS management goal of "auditing" a fixed number of returns was more important than assuring that those seeking refunds were entitled to them. As for the other seven service centers, they demanded "varying degrees of taxpayer and third-party justification." Only three of the ten "required taxpayers to submit documentation, such as birth certificates and Social Security cards or third-party residency verification from schools or day care providers."[10]

Overall, "more than 50 percent of the taxpayers" ignore the ominous-looking letters from the tax collector raising questions about their returns.[11] They throw them out with the other junk mail. When that happens, the IRS sends out a second notice, a proposed tax assessment based on the information that it has gathered from other sources. Between 1992 and 1997, the additional taxes assessed ranged from $1,300 to $2,800 on correspondence audits. And how do taxpayers respond to the notices telling them they owe more taxes?

From one-third to two-thirds ignore them.

As disturbing as those numbers are, it gets worse. The GAO study showed that

> in fiscal year 1996, the time between the filing of a return and the start of the correspondence audit averaged 10 months. It then took 11 more months before the IRS assessed any taxes that were recommended during the audits. As for the characteristics of these 1996 returns, an estimated 75 percent had reported adjusted gross incomes of less than $15,000. In part, this percentage reflects the correspondence audit's focus on simple tax issues and [the Earned Income Tax Credit].[12]

It took the IRS nearly two years to examine and assess additional taxes on the simplest returns filed by the people at the bottom of the economic pile. Just imagine how many man-hours would be required to pore over the returns of the people at the top, a group that is small when compared with the overall tax-filing population, but growing.

At the dawn of the 1990s, some 835,000 individuals and families filed returns reporting income of more than $200,000. By 1997, their ranks had more than doubled, to 1.8 million. But they don't have much to worry about from the IRS. During the same years, the IRS's workforce shrank from 112,000 to 101,700 — a consequence of congressional budget cutting.

The IRS is awash in similarly bleak statistics.

- The number of fraudulent returns detected under a program that focused on questionable refunds plunged 68 percent from 1993 to 1997, falling from 77,800 to 24,900. Similarly, the amount of fraudulent refund dollars detected fell 40 percent in that period, from $136.8 million to $82.5 million. Did taxpayers overall suddenly become more honest? Hardly. The reason for the decline was that IRS management slashed the staff assigned to the program by 31 percent.

- In 1995, the IRS identified 3.3 million paper returns claiming the earned income credit that had missing or invalid Social Security numbers. But the agency had only enough manpower to follow through on fewer than one-third of those returns. The vast majority received the credit whether they were entitled to it or not.

- About one-fifth of the tax returns audited at the examiner level in 1996 included complex business and investment schedules that should have been passed along to more experienced auditors. Few were, even though they included "business returns that deducted sizable expense amounts compared to the reported business income."[13] The result: Fraudulent or erroneous tax returns were closed without review.

- The IRS filed 168,000 liens against delinquent taxpayers in fiscal year 1999. That was down an unprecedented 88 percent from the 1.45 million liens recorded seven years earlier, in 1992. Similarly, levies on wages and bank accounts of delinquent taxpayers plummeted 84 percent, from 3.25 million in 1992 to 504,000 in 1999. And seizures fell off the charts, plunging 99 percent from 11,000 to 160 during the same period.

- The number of tax prosecutions in federal courts has been going steadily down. It peaked in 1987 at 1,550, according to court statistics compiled by Transactional Records Access Clearinghouse, a data-gathering and research center at Syracuse University. Prosecutions dipped below 1,000 in 1994 for the first time in years, and then continued a downward march, reaching 766 in 1998 — a falloff of 51 percent from the earlier decade.

This alarming picture has not gone unnoticed. As a few magazines and newspapers, most notably the New York Times, began to suggest that tax-law enforcement was on a precipitous decline, the IRS began to worry about its public image. Studies have shown that "the more tax evaders a taxpayer knows, the more likely he is to evade taxes himself."[14] Now the word was out that the IRS lacked the manpower and congressional support to pursue tax dodgers.

President Clinton, always one to latch on to an issue that appears to be heating up, responded accordingly. In his budget for 2001, he called for a 9 percent increase for the IRS to pay, in part, the salaries of 633 additional auditors. Treasury Secretary Lawrence H. Summers said the added manpower was needed "to maintain people's confidence that this is a tax system that works."[15]

In truth, Clinton's proposal was as phony as many of today's tax returns. Another 633 auditors would not make a dent in the avalanche of fraud.

To appreciate just how phony, let's return to the mid-1980s. Between 1986 and 1987, some 7 million children and parents disappeared in the United States — at least from tax returns. When Congress enacted the Tax Reform Act of 1986, which required Social Security numbers of children and other dependents to be reported, some 7 million exemptions vanished overnight. That represented the number of children and other dependents who had never existed but had been claimed as personal exemptions. Sort of like listing the pet goldfish as a dependent. But even back then, the IRS lacked the manpower to examine those 7 million returns. With Clinton's 633 new auditors, the IRS will have a smaller workforce than it did in 1987, when there were fewer tax returns and less fraud.

While Congress and the White House bear part of the responsibility for what has happened to enforcement, the IRS itself must also share some of the blame. Within the agency, upper management traditionally has set goals that encourage auditors and revenue agents to pursue the easy cases and ignore the tough ones, thereby discouraging talented investigators from going after big-time tax cheats. Furthermore, the agency generally has lacked the sophisticated personnel required in a world where global financial transactions are executed in seconds, rather than days or weeks, and where mountains of paperwork are generated by computers to conceal the movement of untaxed money. As one IRS veteran acknowledged when discussing the World Wide Web: "[Our] people aren't skilled enough to work on the Internet."[16]

Thus prosecutions come down disproportionately hard on average citizens whose tax misdeeds, measured on a scale of 1 to 10, are a 1 or a fraction thereof. On a much bigger scale, noncriminal audits to uncover underpayment of taxes are slanted even more against middle- and lower-income filers. When taking auditing time into account, affluent taxpayers receive a pass. "The IRS always seems to be after the little person," said Charles Grassley, the Republican senator from Iowa. "We even had testimony on this . . . one of the agents . . . said, 'We were told to go after the little guy. They do not have the resources to fight it.'"[17]

Although the public has long believed that the IRS administers two tax laws, one for the affluent and well connected, another for everyone else — and statistics confirm this perception — IRS employees provided firsthand evidence to that effect when they testified before the Senate Finance Committee in the spring of 1998.

They told of the agency's obsession with statistics, in effect pretending to audit a large number of tax returns rather than subjecting a smaller number to closer scrutiny. They told of how administrators refused to compromise when dealing with taxpayers who could not afford to hire someone to represent them, while at the same time cutting deals with wealthier taxpayers who were accompanied to audits by high-priced lawyers and accountants.

Among those who testified was Maureen O'Dwyer, a career IRS examiner in the New York district office. She described pressure by IRS supervisors to close cases within a set time frame to meet agency goals, even if it meant that taxpayers would be excused from paying what they owed. More significant was her account of the double standard applied by IRS managers.

If ordinary citizens refused to agree to the additional taxes imposed after an audit, the taxes were assessed automatically, along with penalties and interest. In short, these taxpayers were given no options. But affluent individuals, with much larger sums at stake, who were accompanied by lawyers and accountants, stonewalled requests for documents and information, and were permitted to drag out the process until their cases were closed. Sometimes no additional taxes were assessed. Sometimes the taxes were assessed, but penalties were waived.

During O'Dwyer's precise and lucid testimony, two incidents emerged that showed why the tax system is in trouble, and that Congress cares little about taxpayer fraud. The first involved the history of two audits. The second concerned the response to O'Dwyer's stories from influential members of the Senate Finance Committee. Let's begin with her audit stories:

The first taxpayer was very cooperative. He went through [the audit] alone, represented by neither an accountant nor lawyer. When it became apparent that there would be unreported income, the examiner asked him to bring in his accountant. The man declined. He was embarrassed and could not bear to have his accountant think that he had these charges leveled against him by the IRS. His tax deficiency without penalties for two years was about $45,000. With interest and penalties, especially the civil fraud penalty, this amount increased to over $100,000. The man had no bank account and no assets other than his cooperative apartment which he was arranging to sell in order to pay for this IRS assessment.

The examiner asked the manager to remove the fraud penalty. . . . The examiner also explained that if this man had representation, refused to agree, and his case went to appeal, that the civil fraud penalty would probably not be upheld. Deliberate intent would be difficult to prove, especially when assessing the character of this man. During the audit years, the man had successfully raised two children as a single parent, paid for medical expenses of friends who could not afford to do so, and had altruistically donated money to impersonal charities without thought of any personal gain. The manager simply responded, no, he's guilty. This taxpayer without an advocate was callously condemned.[18]

Next, O'Dwyer recounted the story of a second taxpayer, whose case was overseen by the same IRS manager. This taxpayer, O'Dwyer said,

never appeared for the audit. He was represented by a CPA attorney and also by a former IRS Criminal Investigation Division employee. . . . Both of his representatives were uncooperative, cited IRS harassment of their client, procrastinated, held back information, and consistently attempted to intimidate the examiner. Despite this, the examiner persisted and found substantially large deductions that were false. . . . The deficiency, not including penalties for this taxpayer, was $450,000. With civil fraud and other penalties as well as interest, it would be over $1 million.

The moment the examiner found these false deductions, the representatives changed their approach to the audit. Formerly hostile and aggressive, they now . . . cited the prestige of the taxpayer and [his standing in] the community . . . but they offered no explanation of the falsification and the repeated taking of personal deductions which had been previously disallowed. . . . In comparison to the first taxpayer, this man, considerably more wealthy, lived off his tax return. He deducted his designer clothes, the wages paid to his housekeeper, the furnishings and rent of his personal apartment as well as trips abroad for both him and his father. His charitable donations were to foundations in his own industry, always bearing his own name, and designed to enhance his career.

An examiner has no authority to remove a penalty. A manager does under certain conditions. When exhorted by the representative simply to be understanding and give a little to the taxpayer, the manager without hesitation removed the fraud penalty. When asked by the examiner why —[19]

Just as O'Dwyer was about to explain why an IRS manager canceled the penalties of an affluent taxpayer who was found to owe nearly a half-million dollars in taxes, while refusing to cancel the penalties of a taxpayer who failed to report all his income and owed $45,000, she was interrupted in mid-sentence by Daniel Patrick Moynihan, who had been a member of the Senate Finance Committee for more than two decades.

Moynihan was annoyed that he had not been given copies of O'Dwyer's prepared testimony and that she was exceeding the ten minutes normally allotted to witnesses. Speaking to committee chairman Bill Roth, Moynihan fumed: "Now, we gathered here at nine-thirty. It is now ten o'clock. And Mrs. O'Dwyer is still going on about people who are nauseatingly friendly having been whimpering and such. We do have rules, sir. And can we not keep to a ten-minute rule?"[20]

Bob Kerrey quickly chimed in, also expressing his concern for the committee rules. "I mean, not only do we have rules governing this committee and if there is going to be changes in the rules, we should vote on it. . . . I mean, we set the rules. Furthermore, there are standing rules of the Senate that govern the conduct of the committee. And that also makes clear that this testimony needs to be made available to everybody on the committee."[21]

The remarks by Moynihan, who was seemingly indifferent to the IRS's double standard in tax-law enforcement, sparked partisan wrangling among committee members. While O'Dwyer sat quietly at the witness table, the senators debated whether committee rules really required written testimony to be handed out the day before a hearing, whether witnesses could speak for more than ten minutes, whether the testimony of the IRS employees who had agreed to appear — at great personal risk to their careers — was intended to embarrass the Clinton administration.

As for suggestions of possible retribution, Moynihan gave his assurance to O'Dwyer and the other waiting witnesses that he personally would protect them. "If you feel under any threat to your life or position," assured Moynihan, who would be leaving office in two years, "you have the senior senator from New York State here to say that it will not happen."[22]

When the lawmakers finally ended their exchange over the fine points of procedural protocol, O'Dwyer, without skipping a beat, picked up where she left off:

> When asked by the examiner why he removed . . . a fraud penalty, the manager's response was, "If I didn't, the [taxpayer's] representative would lose him as a client."
>
> Why such an astounding and perverted response from an IRS manager? Because this was a manager who was always looking for a tax appointment outside the service. By this decision, he bonded a network with two men he saw as wealthy and powerful and in a position to recommend him for some future job opening.[23]

Lest anyone believe this particular decision to wipe out a portion of a wealthy taxpayer's bill was an aberration, O'Dwyer added: "This manager stands not alone in his behavior. Other even more senior level [administrators] and executives do the same. . . . They network and make friends in preparation for careers outside the service. Their sense of morality has been eclipsed by their personal ambition."[24]

The testimony and all the statistics paint a gloomy enough picture of IRS auditing efforts. But there's another piece of the agency's enforcement machinery — or more accurately, missing piece — that is even more depressing. In an era when the electronic highway spans the entire globe, reaching into distant villages in China and India, and millions of dollars are moved about with a computer keystroke, the IRS's vast computer system would be more properly at home in a museum. If this were an air war, the Pentagon would be waging it with the P-38 and the B-25. And there would be no missiles.

COMPUTER CRASH

At Martinsburg, West Virginia, a Civil War–era town in the rolling hills of the northeast corner of the state, sits a massive two-story, brick warehouselike structure, encircled by a forbidding fence topped with barbed wire and patrolled by armed guards. This is the Martinsburg Computing Center of the IRS. Through the efforts of Robert C. Byrd, the state's veteran Democratic senator, it has grown since 1961 from a modest rural outpost into the single largest computer entity in the IRS network. The center has expanded from 39,000 square feet to 400,000. Its computer rooms on the first and second levels house eleven mainframes in an area the size of two football fields. They operate round-the-clock, seven days a week, receiving tax return data from the agency's service centers and businesses, and constantly updating the IRS's master files. Once the home for a select number of tax documents, Martinsburg has become the repository for an electronic copy of every tax return filed by every American, and all information returns reporting income from wages, interest, and dividends. The staff has swelled to nearly 1,000, making it one of the largest employers in the West Virginia panhandle. Any way you look at it, Martinsburg is a stunning monument to Byrd's political clout.

Unfortunately, by the close of the twentieth century the Martinsburg Computing Center had also become a monument to an entirely different development: the IRS's failure to modernize its vast computer network so that it could keep pace with the volume and complexity of America's tax returns. Crippled by an outmoded system, Martinsburg is incapable of initiating the sophisticated audits necessary to monitor an ever more intricate tax structure. What's more, Martinsburg is not unique: the IRS's other national computer centers and its ten regional service centers are also behind the times. The obsolete computers have become a disgrace to the service and a hallmark of slipshod planning, poor decision making, clumsy execution, and wasted public funds.

Beyond the damage to the IRS's reputation, this technological failure has left the service woefully unprepared to enforce the tax code. More so than any other agency, the IRS is ideally suited to benefit from the electronic revolution. At the heart of tax enforcement is the task of comparing numbers, a classic function of computers. By matching financial data from multiple sources, state-of-the-art computers would enable the service to spot individuals who inflate deductions, who omit capital gains income, who underreport their earnings, or who simply don't bother to file a tax return at all.

While the IRS does perform some elementary matching, it has never come close to realizing the potential offered by modern technology. As matters stand now, it is lucky most years to get through the filing deadline without a major computer breakdown. Thus the government agency most in need of technological tools is the one that has done the least to acquire them.

Not that the IRS hasn't tried to keep pace. It has spent billions and billions on computers and software. The investment has produced a Rube Goldberg–like invention encompassing about 50 individual computer systems that require 19,000 separate software applications, plus minicomputers and desktop machines that run another 30,000 programs. The IRS says 62 million lines of program code are needed for these applications, which must be revised every time Congress changes the tax law. Thousands of technicians and programmers operate the network and constantly rewrite the software.

Since the late 1960s, billions of dollars have been wasted on a succession of programs aimed at converting the system to paperless tax returns. First came the "System of the Seventies" in 1969, followed by the "Tax Administration System" in 1976, followed by the "Equipment Replacement and Enhancement Program" in 1978, followed by "Tax Systems Redesign" in 1982, followed by

"Tax Systems Modernization" in 1986. All failed, or in some cases never even got off the ground.

Consequently, the IRS finds itself in the incredible position of having many aging computers — each the product of individual agency fiefdoms — that can't exchange information with one another. Many run on archaic software, written in an ancient computer language that young programmers are no longer taught. A career information specialist brought in to assess the IRS's technology woes threw up his hands in 1997. "We don't know what we don't know," he told one interviewer.[25]

How did this happen?

Slowly. But once the IRS veered off track, it's been impossible to get it back on again.

The computer glitches are all the more remarkable because the agency was once in the forefront of technological innovation. It was one of the first government bureaucracies to embrace large-scale computing as a way to reduce manpower and enhance its performance. In 1958, the IRS embarked on an ambitious program to automate the processing of tax returns. That year, authorities began inputting tax return data onto computer punch cards. After that, the information was transferred to magnetic tapes and then fed into high-speed computers that made it easier to keep track of a taxpayer's records and gave revenue agents a new tool to check on fraud and avoidance.

In 1962, IRS Commissioner Mortimer M. Caplin called the computer the "most revolutionary tool ever given a tax collector."[26] Caplin's $25 million "bloodhound," as *Business Week* described it, promised to be an "electronic nose that will sniff out with wondrous speed and precision the millions of taxpayers each year who stray from the path of righteousness."[27] By 1967, the new system was fully in place, opening the door to speedier processing and more precise monitoring. What no one knew was that year would mark the high point in the agency's record for technological innovation.

Shortly afterward, tax officials realized that the system they had just installed would soon be outmoded. They began planning for the next generation of high-speed technology and dubbed the effort the "Tax Administration System." This would allow any examiner with a terminal to obtain an instant readout on a taxpayer's records, just as a bank employee can provide customers with up-to-the-minute information on their accounts. At the time, it often took examiners weeks to retrieve a return and answer a taxpayer's question. But in the wake of Watergate disclosures that President Richard M. Nixon had used the IRS to compile an "enemies list" of citizens to be harassed with tax audits, Congress shied away from the IRS proposal. The agency was forced to jettison its ambitious plans and settle for overhauling the existing equipment. Even that proved difficult.

By 1982, with the old system becoming more outmoded with each passing day, planners went back to the drawing board and came up with "Tax Systems Redesign." A long-range effort to bring state-of-the-art computers and telecommunications technology into the IRS, the TSD program was also intended to provide faster access to all taxpayer information and automate manual and paper-intensive processes. As each modernization plan was unveiled, the IRS commissioner, whoever he or she happened to be, was invariably optimistic. Typical of the rosy view from the top was this speech from Roscoe L. Egger Jr., commissioner from 1981 to 1986:

> We at the IRS are moving ahead with plans to redesign our entire system of tax administration within the next ten years. We're already moving forward on a number of fronts. On this score, the IRS snapshot of the future is getting more and more definition with each passing day. . . .
> We're making some important inroads with optical scanning technology, with optical scanning of federal tax deposit cards and 1040-EZ tax forms. Scanning and information returns are already a dynamic duo. Matching information documents submitted on mag media is a tremendous plus. Optical scanning of paper information documents will close one very real compliance gap.[28]

In truth, the IRS was not doing well at all. A new generation of Sperry Univac mainframe computers was incompatible with older models. The conversion project was also plagued by a turnover in managers within the IRS. Instability characterized the entire program. A GAO official offered this critical assessment: "A commercial concern that handled a conversion that way would be out of business."[29]

As it happened, the IRS almost did go under in 1985. The tax-filing season that year was a nightmare — a period of such monumental technological breakdowns and public relations gaffes that some say the agency has never recovered. Because of inadequate trial runs on the new Sperry Univac, IRS computers began spewing out refund checks to taxpayers who were not entitled to them. A Philadelphia lawyer, owed nothing by the government, was stunned to receive a check for $32,426. A nine-year-old boy in Lancaster, Pennsylvania, awaiting an $11 refund, found a check for $16,072.40 in his family's mailbox. A Paoli, Pennsylvania, management consultant who thought he was square with the IRS received a $330 refund check. When he returned the mistaken payment, the IRS computers ran off yet another check for him — this one for $29,000.[30]

At the same time computers mailed checks to taxpayers who had no refunds coming, they failed to send checks to those who did. In the summer of 1985, millions of angry taxpayers jammed IRS switchboards demanding their refund checks; millions more never got through the clogged phone lines.

The computer collapse created chaos up and down the pipeline the IRS relies on to process returns. Huge backlogs developed. Embattled, overworked employees at the IRS service center in Philadelphia resorted to some novel ways of keeping up with the flow. They stuffed tax returns into trash containers, tried to flush them down toilets, hid them above ceiling tiles over their desks, and took armloads home for disposal, all to create the illusion they were keeping pace with filings.

A GAO audit later reported that a janitor at the Philadelphia office had found "envelopes containing unprocessed documents and remittances in a trash barrel on the loading dock" awaiting incineration.[31] Among the items slated to be burned were thirty-six individual tax returns, twenty-four estimated tax payments from individuals, and $333,440 in taxpayer payments to the IRS. At the height of the debacle, 1.6 million individual taxpayers and businesses were awaiting responses from the IRS over complaints about erroneous notices, lost tax payments, and disagreements over tax bills.

Chastened by the imbroglio, the IRS went back to the drawing board again. By 1986, it had roughed out plans for yet another grand overhaul, "Tax Systems Modernization." This was a ten-year, $20 billion program to phase in new processes and equipment. Approved by Congress, TSM was the agency's most far-reaching plan yet. It was a project, in the GAO's words, "much larger than most other organizations have ever undertaken."[32] TSM would cut costs and, more important, it would bolster enforcement. As before, IRS officials were enthusiastic.

"Tax Systems Modernization . . . is fundamentally changing the way we conduct business," Henry H. Philcox, the agency's chief information officer, wrote in 1990. "Processing time for an electronically filed return will be a matter of minutes. . . . Electronic management of compliance cases will usher in a new, more professional and timely era of tax enforcement. . . . Instead of waiting 24 hours, a week or months for an answer or explanation from us, you will be able to obtain it in a matter of seconds. Predictability will replace uncertainty."[33]

Once again, the IRS was kidding itself. Crucial components of the new system soon ran into serious trouble. Two large-scale scanning initiatives — one to feed paper returns into electronic readers and another to digitize tax returns — were plagued by technical snafus. The first program, SCRIPS, an optical character reader and scanner, performed at only a fraction of the speed the IRS had hoped, and the scanner could read only one side of a 1040 form. The IRS had expected that SCRIPS would pay for itself by reducing the staff needed to manually input data and by increasing the accuracy and speed with which the information was entered. SCRIPS failed to deliver, and the IRS couldn't even tell congressional auditors how much the system would cost taxpayers. The reason: "[The IRS] does not have an accurate cost accounting system."[34]

An even graver setback was the failure of the Document Processing System, a once highly touted program conceived in 1988 to digitize tax returns. The IRS used a succession of private contractors and spent $284 million trying to make the system work before abandoning it. These failures left the agency as dependent as ever on the 1960s-era computers that had been the backbone of the tax collection process for three decades.

By 1996, when the modernization plan should have been nearly complete, the entire effort was, well, nowhere. The GAO, which had been monitoring the $20 billion undertaking for years, had consistently given the IRS low marks because of cost overruns, sloppy procedures, and poorly conceived plans. The GAO warned that the program "was jeopardized by persistent and pervasive management and technical weaknesses."[35] Even a high-level Treasury Department official acknowledged that "TSM has gone off track." Lawrence H. Summers, then deputy Treasury secretary, told Congress that the failures "call into question the ability of the IRS to manage the modernization effort successfully."[36] Still, the service pushed ahead with TSM and announced plans to install a prototype scanner at its Austin, Texas, regional office.

The illusion within the IRS that TSM was still viable was finally shattered on the morning of January 30, 1997, by one of the agency's own. Arthur A. Gross, a highly respected information technology specialist who had been recruited by the service months before to try to rescue the floundering modernization plan, bluntly told the IRS restructuring commission that the billions the agency had spent to update its computers had essentially been wasted. The systems the agency had spent years developing, Gross said, "do not work in the real world." He added that as dysfunctional as some of the systems were, the IRS was "wholly dependent on them" to collect $1.4 trillion in taxes every year.[37] Gross also expressed doubt about the

IRS's capability to develop a modern system in house, saying the agency lacked the "intellectual capital" for the job.[38] He proposed that the task be turned over to a private vendor.

Although Gross subsequently resigned over differences with IRS Commissioner Charles O. Rossotti, the agency eventually took his advice. In December 1998, a fifteen-year, $5 billion contract to modernize the IRS's antiquated network was awarded to a consortium headed by Computer Sciences Corporation of Falls Church, Virginia. The company's assignment is to develop new software, replace old computers, and introduce new technologies to streamline the processing of tax returns.

In announcing the contract, Rossotti sounded a good deal like his predecessors of the last two decades: "This is a massive job we are about to undertake. People shouldn't expect to see changes from this project immediately. But for the long term, it will replace inefficient technology from the 1960s with systems that will improve service to the taxpayers and the nation."[39]

What that means is this: Even if everything comes on line as scheduled, and a world-class computer system is finally produced, the IRS still won't have this crucial piece of equipment to help with enforcement for at least ten years, and quite possibly longer. Thus, at a time of soaring taxpayer fraud, the agency is without the tools to combat it. That's especially good news for the exploding number of tax-law violators whose tactic of choice is the movement of cash and assets along the global electronic highway. But not to worry. There are so many more tax dodgers who are easier for the IRS to go after right here at home, even if the amount of lost revenue is insignificant by comparison.

OPERATION SLAM DUNK

September 12, 1994, a Monday, was D-day for teams of IRS investigators. The agency that sent Al Capone to prison for income tax evasion because no other law enforcement body could secure a conviction against the murderous Chicago mobster had mapped a coordinated attack against a new gang.

On that day, in cities across the country, more than a hundred IRS agents turned up on the doorsteps of a ring of some fifty suspected tax dodgers — all referees in the National Basketball Association. The agents read the referees their rights, advised them they were the targets of a criminal investigation, and questioned them about their part in a scheme to pocket fringe-benefit income and use frequent-flier miles to escape payment of income tax. Reduced to simplest terms, the referees were submitting phony expense accounts — originally with their employer's approval.

No single tax case in memory better illustrates the IRS's heavy-handed and misguided approach to tax-law enforcement, as well as its misallocation of resources and flawed audits, than the investigation dubbed "Operation Slam Dunk."

At a time when tens of thousands of wealthy individuals and a much larger number of merely affluent persons are investing and moving billions of untaxed dollars offshore, inflating deductions and writing off personal expenses as "business" deductions, or not even bothering to file returns, the IRS decided to devote five years and counting of investigative effort adding up to tens of thousands of man-hours to a criminal case against referees, some of whom escaped paying less than $4,000 a year.

This is not to suggest that the referees, whose salaries ranged between $70,000 and $180,000, had filed honest tax returns. They most assuredly had not. They had underreported their income and pocketed thousands of dollars without paying income tax on it. They had submitted bogus airline tickets to justify their expenses. No, the issue was not whether they had filed false tax returns. It was whether they were criminals. And if they were, so are many millions of other citizens, on a much grander scale.

A little background is in order. For NBA referees, their job is on the road. They travel nine months of the year, one night in Cleveland, the next in Seattle, on to Denver and Miami and finally home for a day or two in Philadelphia or Norfolk. Then it starts all over again. In the 1980s, the NBA and the referees' union incorporated certain travel benefits into their contracts. Under the terms, the

NBA paid its referees the cost of a first-class airline ticket for flights lasting longer than two hours and a full-fare coach ticket for travel under two hours. The referees, in turn, were permitted to exchange the tickets for cheaper seats and to keep the difference. This was considered one of their fringe benefits. By the government's own admission, "the right to downgrade first class airline tickets was a major employment inducement by which potential NBA referees were told they could supplement their salaries."[40] The NBA did not withhold taxes on this money, nor did it report the money to the IRS. The referees did not declare it as income on their tax returns, considering it an untaxed fringe benefit provided by their employer.

The practice was clearly improper. The money was taxable income and should have been included on individual tax returns. At the same time, the NBA itself furthered the tax-avoidance scheme by establishing a system that encouraged the illicit conduct and allowed it to submit W-2 forms to the IRS knowing the reported income was understated.

In any case, in 1989 the IRS issued new regulations that required employers to report such arrangements as income. But the NBA and the referees' association were locked in contentious bargaining over a new contract. During that period, the NBA changed the rules several times. In the end, it gave the referees a couple of options, including withholding. Most did not take it, continuing instead to collect the money without reporting it as income, insisting it was part of their collective-bargaining agreement.

In 1993 or early 1994, the IRS received a tip that the referees were not declaring the ticket money as income on their returns. That was the beginning of "Operation Slam Dunk."

From the outset, it was a curious investigation. The NBA, which in the early years had sanctioned the use of phony receipts and agreed in effect to provide illegal off-the-books income to its employees, was exempted from the probe. So, too, the referees' association, which negotiated the benefit, and the travel agents who provided the fictitious invoices for first-class travel — and in some instances actually devised the system. Only the referees were singled out.

Over the next four years, the investigation grew even curiouser. The cases of about twenty-five referees were turned over to the IRS civil division, where returns were audited and additional taxes, interest, and penalties assessed. This would have been normal procedure, since the amount of lost tax revenue involved did not reach IRS guidelines for criminal prosecution. Nonetheless, the Justice Department decided to indict twelve referees. As of early 2000, the investigation remained open on more than a dozen who still could be charged.

In the case of those indicted, what happened next was right out of the Kenneth Starr textbook on how to use the power of the U.S. government to intimidate people. The indicted referees were told that they could plead guilty and avoid a jail sentence. This, of course, would make the IRS and Justice Department case statistics look good. Or they could demand a trial. But if they were found guilty, they would go to prison and would be compelled to pay large fines.

A presiding judge joined in applying pressure in at least one instance. The case was that against Jesse Ray Kersey of Williamsburg, Virginia, at the time a fourteen-year veteran of the NBA. At a preliminary hearing in July 1997, with a trial date looming, U.S. District Court Judge Robert G. Doumar told the referee and his counsel that a jury probably would not believe that he didn't think he had to pay taxes on the money. "My suggestion is you get together with . . . [the assistant U.S. attorney] and make a deal," the judge told Kersey and his lawyers. "And I'm strongly suggesting that."[41]

Kersey and his attorneys got the message loud and clear. The choice was plain enough: Go to trial and risk prison, or plead guilty and stay out of prison. Kersey chose the latter.

Under the terms of an agreement with the U.S. Attorney's office, he pleaded guilty to filing a false income tax return and was sentenced to three years on probation and fined $20,000. He was also ordered to file accurate amended tax returns and pay all taxes, interest, and penalties owed.

Kersey and all the other referees who were charged had no criminal records. They were church members and highly regarded citizens. They were active in charitable and youth programs. Most had young children at home. Terrified by the possibility of a year or two in prison, eleven of the twelve pleaded guilty. All were put on probation. All were placed under house detention for varying periods. All now carry the stigma of being convicted felons. When they complete employment questionnaires or credit histories that inquire about a criminal record, they must answer yes. All lost their jobs as NBA referees following their indictments (although they continued to be paid pending the outcome of their trials). All were forced to resign after their guilty pleas (but subsequently were rehired). All piled up hefty legal bills.

At least one federal judge, who presided over the trial of referee George T. Toliver in Harrisonburg, Virginia, took note of the special treatment accorded the NBA and the referees' association by the Justice Department and the IRS. It was treatment that also was extended to the travel agencies that had made the bogus expense accounts possible. Said U.S. District Court Judge James P. Jones:

> I don't intend for one minute to take away from Mr. Toliver's culpability, but after listening to the evidence in the case, it does seem to me that the NBA and the referees association certainly share the blame to the extent of making this situation possible. And I was, frankly, dismayed, really, to learn of the facts . . . in regard to the situation that, in my view, provided a temptation to Mr. Toliver, and perhaps others, to engage in the activities which resulted in these charges.[42]

In fact, in Toliver's case a former travel agency representative told the court that it was the agency that suggested how he could obtain cheaper airline tickets. The agent testified that when Toliver first came into the office, he had a handful of tickets he had received from the NBA and she explained to him that he could "have them refunded and then purchase round trip tickets at lower fares."[43]

When Toliver went to trial, the possibility of being convicted and receiving the maximum sentence of three years in prison and a quarter-million-dollar fine weighed heavily on his mind. Midway through the proceedings, gripped by the fear of being separated from his two daughters, who were sixteen and eleven years old, he pleaded guilty to one count of filing a false tax return. He was confined to home detention for six months without electronic monitoring, placed on probation for two years, ordered to complete 100 hours of community service, make restitution to the U.S. government ($10,700), and pay the cost of prosecution ($20,500).

Only one referee, Steven M. Javie, who was married but had no children, chose to go to trial and see it through. As the criminal case unfolded in a federal courtroom in Philadelphia, the tax issue turned out to be murkier than the IRS had alleged. While Javie submitted receipts for first-class tickets and bought coach tickets, keeping the dollar difference, he nonetheless flew first class. He did so by using his frequent-flier miles to upgrade the coach seat. In his mind, the transaction was a wash. He took frequent-flier miles that he could have used for family vacations and instead applied them to travel for work.

The IRS rejected this argument, insisting that tax was due on the frequent-flier miles and that Javie had knowingly and intentionally defrauded the government. But as it turned out, the investigating agent was none too familiar with IRS policies on frequent-flier miles.

Listen to the exchange between Javie's lawyer, Gregory T. Magarity, and the IRS agent who conducted the investigation:

Magarity: Do you, sir, know what the IRS regulations are for when frequent-flier benefits are taxable or nontaxable?

IRS agent: No, I don't. No, I don't.

Magarity: Did you try to make a determination or find out before you determined what was going to be taxable income for Mr. Javie?

IRS agent: No, I did not.

Magarity: Do you know whether there are regulations with regard [to frequent-flier miles]?

IRS agent: I don't know, but I would hope there would be.[44]

In addition to not knowing government regulations, the IRS couldn't even do the math involved in the charges on which it was trying to send Steve Javie to jail. It failed to give him credit for flying between many cities. In doing so, the agency understated Javie's legitimate expenses and thereby falsely inflated the amount of income tax he owed. It would be like the IRS disallowing the mortgage-interest deduction on your tax return — even though you paid the interest — and saying that you owed taxes on that money. The sloppy arithmetic proved embarrassing for the IRS agent on the witness stand. As Magarity walked him through the records on which the case was built, he was forced to acknowledge the oversight time and again.

Magarity: Now, look at the ticket. Did you allow him the cost from Los Angeles to Denver or from Los Angeles to Philadelphia?

IRS agent: Wait a second. Philadelphia to Los Angeles, Philadelphia to Los Angeles, $627, allowed cost, Los Angeles to Denver to — no, I didn't.

Magarity: Okay. So you missed that one, right?

IRS agent: Missed that one.[45]

Next, Magarity questioned the agent's math that allowed Javie credit for a flight from Philadelphia to Portland, but no return trip.

Magarity: You don't have an American Express [receipt] for the trip Portland to Philadelphia, do you?

IRS agent: I don't have the return trip to Philadelphia on that one.

Magarity: Okay. So did you miss that one, too?

IRS agent: Missed that one.[46]

And then there was the time Javie refereed a game in Portland one night, in Sacramento the next, and then back in Portland.

Magarity: The receipt you're looking at gets him from Sacramento to Portland to the game on the 16th. Your summary says —

IRS agent: Right.

Magarity: — he then went from Portland to Sacramento.

IRS agent: That's correct.

Magarity: Well, where is the receipt showing he goes from Portland to Sacramento?

IRS agent: That's one leg I missed.[47]

And on and on it went.

Magarity: Then what did you credit him for Dallas to Philadelphia?

IRS agent: Nothing, absolutely nothing. . . .

Magarity: Under your methodology, under your stated methodology, should he be credited for the $714?

IRS agent: "I should have, but I didn't.[48]

In reconstructing income and expenses, which is all about adding and subtracting, the IRS did neither correctly. And the consequences of this particular audit could be not just having to pay additional taxes, but doing jail time.

Not too surprisingly, the ten-man, two-woman jury acquitted Javie of tax evasion. Some of the jurors were aghast at the errors in the government's case. They also didn't think the amount of taxes owed warranted a criminal action, and they especially had problems with the notion of sending someone to jail over frequent-flier miles.

Howard Pearl, general counsel for the referees' union, spoke for many when he said: "I think that the acquittal of Steve Javie proved, as we have known all along, that no reasonable person would consider this conduct to be criminal. The problem is that the resources, emotional and financial, that are required to fight the government are more than most people possess."[49]

It's important to remember that Javie was the only one of twelve indicted referees to receive an impartial hearing from a jury. His was the only case in which the government's evidence was subjected to a line-by-line cross-examination and public inspection. All the other defendants were pressured into pleading guilty.

To be fair to the IRS, it should be noted that the final decision to bring criminal charges against anyone for tax-law violations rests with the Justice Department. The IRS can only recommend prosecutions.

Perhaps the person most outraged by the government's decision to initiate a criminal action against Javie and the other referees was his attorney, Greg Magarity. A relentless interrogator with a keen sense of fairness, he understands the extraordinary power that government can wield for good or ill when it decides to pursue someone suspected of wrongdoing. He had spent seven years in the U.S. Attorney's office in Philadelphia, rising to become first assistant U.S. Attorney before leaving for private practice. During those years, he had prosecuted many criminal cases, but none like Javie's.

With a few exceptions, Magarity said, selective prosecution "is not a defense to criminal charges and triggers no governmental discovery obligation. In most cases, the motivation and rationale behind a criminal investigation are clear without disclosure, if not at the beginning, then at the end. Not so here. The incongruity of this investigation at the outset grew to irrationality in its conclusions."[50]

Worse, Magarity said, was the IRS's failure to explain why some referees were singled out for criminal prosecution while others, who engaged in the same acts, were subjected to traditional civil audits. He observed: "Notification from the IRS criminal division that your case has been transferred to the civil division for resolution is the white-collar equivalent of receiving an HIV-negative lab report. The transfer means that your case will now be handled like a typical IRS audit — they assess tax, interest, and penalty; you pay; end of story."[51]

Worse still, the IRS dragged out the investigation for more than four years after it first notified the referees they were targets of a criminal probe. For the referees, Magarity said, it was like living in "a POW camp. Fear, uncertainty, humiliation, loss of face and control . . . dominated their daily existence."[52]

Listen to George Toliver on why he decided to plead guilty: "The most important thing to me is that when I go to bed at night, I sleep ten feet away from my daughters. . . . I didn't want to be behind a wall somewhere while they were growing up. I didn't want to roll the dice."[53]

The justice system itself is rigged against those who would exercise their constitutional right to a trial. Federal sentencing guidelines are determined by the amount of tax loss due to fraud, with an offense score increased or decreased by other factors. Two points are subtracted, for example, if the defendant pleads guilty.

"The alleged tax loss in each of the referee cases was far below the norm in criminal tax prosecutions," Magarity said, adding that "with only a small tax loss and a two-point reduction for a guilty plea, [the] referees could virtually choose to avoid prison, if they gave up their right to trial."[54]

To summarize "Operation Slam Dunk": In September 1994, the IRS advised more than fifty NBA referees that they were subjects of a criminal tax investigation. By the end of 1999, the cases of more than half had been transferred to the IRS civil division. A dozen cases were still open. And twelve referees had been indicted. The Justice Department secured guilty pleas from eleven of the twelve defendants, lost the only case that went to trial, all over an average tax owed of about $8,000 a year.

Why would the IRS mount a multimillion-dollar investigation for such a small return? Publicity. Indictments of NBA referees guaranteed widespread media coverage. Newspapers predictably availed themselves of the opportunities for wordplay the story presented: "NBA Referees Are Charged With Traveling Violations" (*Washington Post*). "Refs' Tax Charges Put NBA In Foul Predicament" (*Chicago Tribune*). "Feds Blow The Whistle On Two NBA Referees" (*Portland Oregonian*).

THE BIG FISH WHO GET AWAY

The criminal prosecution of the referees illustrates the failed tax-law enforcement policies of both the IRS and Justice Department. And it confirms the stories of IRS agents who say the agency stalks small-time tax cases while ignoring big ones.

Think about it for a minute. Every member of an industry, in this instance the referees of the NBA, was targeted for criminal prosecution. Ultimately, twelve people were indicted. When was the last time that you read about indictments of a dozen Hollywood entertainers — who work in an industry that holds the patent on creative accounting — for tax fraud? That's an industry, by the way, where individual tax fraud may be counted in the millions of dollars, not in the thousands. When was the last time you read about the indictments of twelve Wall Street traders? Or twelve Washington lobbyists? Or twelve investors who move money and assets around the globe, concealing their true ownership? Actually, you can forget the latter group. The IRS does not have a clue as to the identity of these people. It doesn't have either the manpower or the expertise to mount anything more than a few token investigations.

Again, don't blame the IRS for laxity. In addition to Congress, which refuses to provide adequate funding, the executive branch, namely the president via the Justice Department and State Depart-

ment, also discourages tax investigations involving offshore entities as well as powerful financial institutions within the United
States. Ask Robert M. Morgenthau, the blunt-spoken, longtime
Manhattan district attorney, about what federal law enforcement
agencies are doing to track offshore money, and he replies suc-
cinctly: "Nobody's doing a thing."[55] A veteran IRS agent concurs.
"They are missing the boat. . . . They just aren't looking."[56]

Which is not to say the federal government is *incapable* of looking — it just doesn't want to. For example, at the most sophisticated level, the federal government could, if it chose, track every
electronic transaction to and from any country in the world. In
other words, if it were so inclined, it could determine which international banks and other financial institutions are helping individuals and corporations hide money and assets.

But someone, somewhere, has to assign manpower to follow
the electronic transactions. As one former government agent puts
it: "The FBI, like Al Haig, always says 'We're in charge.' But in
charge of what?"[57]

This same indifferent attitude runs through all federal law
enforcement agencies when it comes to tracking and arresting tax
fugitives. Now, you might think a government that can mount a
relentless investigation of NBA referees and bring pressure to bear
on them to plead guilty would use the same resources to hunt
down those people who have been indicted and fled the country.
But you would be wrong.

Meet Jay Picon, who with his wife, Pamella, has built what the
couple describes as "the most beautiful and comfortable resort
in Belize," the Mopan River Resort.[58] Actually, Jay Picon is the
assumed name of Joseph R. Ross, a former Tulsa, Oklahoma, businessman and multimillionaire community pillar who's now a tax
fugitive in Central America.

Ross is the true poster boy for tax filing day: someone who
doesn't pay his taxes and has never gotten caught. Unlike the hap-
less NBA referees who were hotly pursued over a few thousand

dollars, Ross has gotten away with much, much more, without so much as having to sit through an uncomfortable interview with a revenue agent. Indeed, the one time agents got close, Ross had an option that just doesn't exist for the average person — he skipped the country.

A onetime flight engineer for Pan American Airways, Ross went into business after World War II training pilots for commercial airlines. He founded Ross Aviation Inc. in Tulsa in 1947 and gradually expanded to four more cities around the nation. By 1965, he claimed that he ran the largest flight training school in the world. When the Vietnam War came along, Ross instructed hundreds of pilots who saw action in Southeast Asia. In Tulsa, his success landed him a directorship on the board of one of the city's banks.

No doubt it was an impressive story of an enterprising businessman seeing an opportunity and seizing it. But Ross had help. U.S. taxpayers funded all sorts of government contracts that fueled his business and personal fortune. He trained pilots for the Army and Air Force. He picked up business from the Immigration and Naturalization Service instructing foreign pilots. He had contracts with the post office. He also served as a consultant or adviser to other federal agencies, including the Civil Aeronautics Board and the Atomic Energy Commission.

In 1971, Ross was one of fifteen American businessmen chosen by the U.S. Department of Transportation to serve on a committee to offer advice on security matters affecting air travel. He flew to Washington twice a month for meetings with several agencies, including the FBI, to discuss cargo thefts and airplane hijackings. Ross never tried to conceal the source of his burgeoning fortune. He once told a *Tulsa World* reporter that 100 percent of the $4-million-a-year business was in government contracts.[59]

At the same time he was cultivating his reputation as a successful entrepreneur and community figure with close ties to government agencies, Ross was up to something else: establishing secret foreign bank accounts. With the help of a Mexican accountant, he first funneled assets to a Mexican bank, and then later to a secret trust in the Channel Islands, a British tax haven.

Sometime in the 1980s, a relative tipped off federal agents about Ross's financial dealings. Ross got wind of the investigation and liquidated his assets. Just as law enforcement authorities were preparing to indict him for his failure to disclose his interest in $500,000 in foreign bank accounts, he fled the country.

In a letter published later by the *Tulsa World,* Ross said that when he discovered the feds were aware of his offshore doings, he knew he would be indicted. Ross said he briefly weighed what to do, then decided to flee.

"I had all the ingredients — that is, money, travel knowledge and a great wife to make it all worthwhile," he said.[60] The Rosses went to Mexico, and then on to several other nations before settling in Belize in the late 1980s, where they became citizens.

Like many offshore centers, Belize will sell you a passport and make you a citizen for a price. In 1999, the going rate was $65,000. But just because the Rosses became Belizeans didn't mean they had to live in that country. Their new passport was really a ticket back to North America. In the late 1980s, they settled in Vancouver, British Columbia, using the names Gilberto and Pamella Picon. The name came from the Mexican accountant who had once established Ross's secret foreign accounts.[61]

In Vancouver, the gregarious, outgoing couple established themselves as popular members of the city's social circuit, attending black-tie events, patronizing the opera, donating to local charities, and throwing parties in their spectacular high-rise condo overlooking the Vancouver skyline. They summered in France near Mont Blanc or in the waters off British Columbia, aboard their yacht, *No Refund$.*[62]

Their social calendar filled up even more after Pamella Picon was appointed consul general of Belize in 1994. If nothing else, it was a mark of their close ties to the Belize government. She was at the time that country's only diplomatic representative in Canada. But then again, the Rosses had turned to top Belizean government officials to establish trusts and oversee their real estate holdings.

Ross's carefree, tax-free lifestyle almost came to an end in 1997. Acting on a tip, the IRS alerted the Royal Canadian Mounted Police that Gilberto Picon was actually Joseph Ross and wanted on tax charges in the United States. On December 20, 1997, he was arrested by the Mounties in Vancouver. A hearing was set on whether to extradite him to the United States.

A Vancouver judge allowed him to post $50,000 bail and ordered him to surrender his passport. The Canadian prosecutor handling the case saw nothing to worry about. "I don't have reason to think he won't attend the . . . hearing as required," he told the *Tulsa World* on January 2, 1997. "So far, he has complied with reporting."[63] Less than two weeks later, Ross reverted to form. He slipped out of Canada and made his way back to Belize, once again beyond the reach of U.S. authorities. Like many countries, Belize will not extradite over tax offenses.

Back in their adopted homeland, the Rosses picked up pretty much where they had left off in Vancouver — living the good life. They created their own foundation, the Picon Foundation for the Promotion of Belize, to extol the wonders of the tiny nation, which is smaller than Massachusetts, to investors and tourists. They founded a tour company to bring in visitors from around the world. They began publishing a tourist guide, the *Belize Report,* which they describe as an "in-depth traveler's guide to lodging, restaurants, sights, adventure and travel tips; plus immigration, investment and retirement information."[64] It also provides a capsule summary of how you can buy a Belize passport and become a citizen.

The guide is distributed in hotels, restaurants, and other public places. It even has its own page on the World Wide Web. In bold letters for all to see under the guide's masthead is the name of the editor: Pamella G. Picon.

But the couple's most ambitious venture has been the construction of a lavish resort in western Belize. On the banks of the scenic Mopan River about an hour's drive from Belize City, the expatriate couple set out to create the country's most beautiful resort.

Carved out of the jungle in a region of spectacular natural beauty and archaeological renown, the Mopan River Resort is in an area abounding with waterfalls, caves, birdlife, tropical forests, and Mayan ruins. Guests stay in individual thatched-roof cabanas along a riverbank that can be reached only by custom-built ferries.

"The river setting is its most unique aspect," says the Rosses' Web page. "The gentle nature of the Mopan allows us to build much closer to the water than resorts on other rivers in Belize. The only access to our resort is by crossing the river, so the feeling of seclusion is there, but the cultural flavor and sleepy village life of Benque Viejo is close at hand."[65]

Guests are invited to "relax on the shady veranda of your cabana, and watch the gentle waters of the Mopan flow along the grass-covered riverbank." Or to while away the time in the resort's garden "amongst the existing mature coconut, avocado, mango, citrus and cedar trees." Or to take in the birdlife — "herons, king-fishers, toucans, parrots, jays, warblers and hummingbirds."[66]

If you think that fleeing the United States to escape payment of taxes requires you to maintain a low profile, think of the Rosses. On the Web page promoting their resort is a photograph of the couple, using the Mexican surname that has been their cover for a decade: "Your hosts, Pamella and Jay Picon, have traveled to almost 40 countries around the world, and visited numerous facilities in Belize. This gives us a good feel for what is needed for comfort and enjoyment, without having to charge our guests a fortune. Our emphasis is on the whole experience, which includes comfort, uniqueness, adventure, and enjoyment at a fair price."[67]

For Ross, the good times roll on, vindication of his decision to slip away from the United States. As he wrote in the letter to a friend intercepted by U.S. authorities in 1994: "When you know you are guilty, why would someone want to stay around and arm wrestle with the long arm of the government when there is no doubt that you are going to lose?"

No doubt about it. Ross didn't lose.

Officially, Ross has been a tax fugitive since June 30, 1986. That's the day his indictment was filed in U.S. District Court in Tulsa. He was charged with failing to disclose his interest in a foreign bank account. Two superseding indictments, returned later in 1986 and in June 1987, expanded the charges to include filing false tax returns and fraud.[68] Ross has been living safely beyond the taxman ever since.

But Ross isn't alone. Another accused tax cheat who fled the United States rather than stand trial has remained safely at large for seventeen years. Interestingly, some of his money has found its way back into the American political system — albeit indirectly — in the form of campaign contributions to President Clinton and the Democratic Party.

THE GOOD LIFE ON THE RUN

Marc Rich is a billionaire investor who divides his time between Switzerland and the coast of Spain, where he has a luxurious castle overlooking the Mediterranean, with a swimming pool carved into the side of the mountain. A former New York commodities trader, Rich packed up his business — one of the world's largest and most profitable — and moved to Switzerland after he was indicted in 1983 on tax fraud and racketeering charges. Rich, two colleagues, and two of his companies, Marc Rich & Co. A.G. and Clarendon A.G. Ltd., were charged with filing false tax returns, failing to report more than $100 million in income, using phony invoices and sham transactions to claim tens of millions of dollars worth of improper deductions, moving tens of millions of dollars into offshore accounts, and engaging in illegal oil-pricing schemes.

Rich and his associates were also accused of buying oil from the Iranian government in 1980, violating a ban imposed by President

Jimmy Carter on doing business with that country. More point-edly, Rich was charged with trading oil and wiring money to Iran at the same time that fifty-three Americans were being held hostage for more than fourteen months in the U.S. embassy in Tehran, thereby personally profiting from their captivity. Rich later ignored a worldwide embargo against South Africa, imposed by the United Nations to protest apartheid, and sold oil to that country.

To continue doing business, Rich's companies subsequently pleaded guilty to some of the charges and paid $172 million in taxes and penalties in what was described at the time as "the largest tax fraud uncovered in U.S. history."[69] Rich, unwilling to risk a trial, conviction, and a maximum prison sentence of 300 years, fled the United States with his family and set up operations in Zug, Switzerland. There he has been doing business ever since and con-tinues to rank among the world's top commodity traders, dealing in crude oil, soybeans, magnesium, grain, copper, nickel, sugar, electricity, zinc, chrome, coal, and just about anything else you can think of.

Incredibly, for many years, at least up until the early 1990s, Rich also did a substantial business with the U.S. government. Clarendon, which he continued to control, sold millions of dol-lars' worth of copper and nickel to the U.S. Mint to make pennies and nickels. The mint is part of the same Treasury Department that was, in theory, seeking to arrest him as a fugitive. He sold U.S. wheat to other countries through American-taxpayer-subsidized agricultural programs. In all these dealings, Rich wrote the text-book for the twenty-first-century businessman who chooses to conduct his affairs in cyberspace, beyond the laws that people liv-ing within the United States must abide by.

When the fugitive financier's business dealings with the U.S. government were recounted by the authors in the *Philadelphia Inquirer* in 1991, members of Congress were deluged with letters from angry constituents. Lawmakers forwarded the mail to Treasury.

In one response, dated February 13, 1992, the Treasury's assistant commissioner for criminal investigation wrote that privacy laws prevented him from discussing Marc Rich, "who allegedly resides in either Spain or Switzerland." Nevertheless, he continued: "Let me assure you that the apprehension of fugitives charged with criminal violations of the Internal Revenue Code, whether they are within the United States or abroad, is one of our highest priorities. . . . Please be assured that we diligently pursue our fugitives and few escape."[70]

Another year passed before Treasury got around to severing its business ties with Rich. But as for "diligently" pursuing Rich, well, Treasury hasn't been too diligent. He continues to roam freely across Europe, a reminder of the existence of one tax law for the wealthy and another for everyone else. (Remember the referees?) During his early years in exile, Rich and his wife at the time, the former Denise Eisenberg of Worcester, Massachusetts, were regulars in the Swiss and Spanish social whirls, throwing and attending all the best parties. She had followed Rich to Europe with the couple's three young daughters, later telling one publication that "it was like, 'It's my husband. I'm his wife. This is life,' you know. . . . It was like shit happens."[71] But in 1991, angered and embarrassed by her husband's philandering, Denise Rich, who had never been accused of a crime, returned to the United States and eventually filed for divorce.

This would be the end of her story as it relates to tax fugitive Marc Rich except for this: In one transaction alone, Denise received $150 million from her husband after they split. Since then, she has become a major campaign contributor to President Clinton and the Democratic Party, thereby earning a mention in internal White House memoranda that identified her as one of the "top supporters of the administration and the Democratic National Committee."[72]

By the late 1990s, Denise had become a fixture on the New York celebrity-socialite scene, throwing memorable parties at her Fifth

Avenue penthouse, where in winters she had the terrace covered with ice so that hors d'oeuvres could be passed by waiters on skates and "scantily clad women in fluorescent wigs" could whirl about.[73] At other times, she is photographed with Henry Kissinger and Barbara Walters and Alec Baldwin and Diahann Carroll and Dan Rather and Luther Vandross and Sarah Ferguson (the Duchess of York) and her pals Bill and Hillary Rodham Clinton. Then she's riding in a stretch limousine, bound for Harlem with hip-hop star Foxy Brown, or observed "picking up close to $1 million in diamond and ruby jewelry for the holidays at the new Piranesi Boutique on Madison Avenue."[74]

Her parties are endless. Birthday bashes for Kelsey Grammer and Patti LaBelle and Natalie Cole; a Millennium New Year's Eve fete at her estate in Aspen, where Michael Douglas and Catherine Zeta-Jones cuddled before announcing their engagement.

And then there are all the charity affairs for AIDS and cancer, notably the G&P Charitable Foundation that she created to promote cancer research after her twenty-seven-year-old daughter died of leukemia. The foundation, established in 1996, threw its first big fund-raiser in October 1998, a star-studded gala attended by 1,500 at a Manhattan hotel. The guest speaker: the president himself. Gossip columns blossomed with tributes to the foundation's good deeds.

During a later appearance on CNN, Denise Rich reported that "we raised close to $3 million" and noted that President Clinton "was honorary chairman" of the event.[75]

But her bookkeeping was not quite what it seemed. According to a tax return filed with the IRS by the G&P foundation, the big party generated $2.4 million in contributions, but $1.1 million of that — nearly half the money — was paid out in expenses. This is not unusual for celebrity fund-raisers, which spend as much or more on the party as they distribute to their charitable causes. In the foundation's first three years, the tax returns showed total income of $2.5 million and expenses of $1.2 million. The returns through 1998 show no charitable grants were made during those years, although the news media reported that the foundation distributed $1.4 million in grants to medical researchers in December 1999.

About the time Denise Rich joined the New York social and celebrity set, she also became a major political donor. In 1993, she gave more than $100,000, mostly to the Democratic National Committee. That was followed by another $100,000-plus in 1994 and a total of $200,000 in 1995 and 1996. From 1993 to 1999, she poured more than $800,000 into Democratic coffers, with most of the money going to the Democratic National Committee.

In September 1998, she hit the big time, hosting a $50,000-a-couple lunch at her apartment for President Clinton. About a hundred people dined on grilled sea bass, including the president and first lady; Vice President Al Gore and Tipper, and Democratic congressmen like Richard A. Gephardt of Missouri and Charles B. Rangel of New York. Incidentally, it was less than a month later that the president was back in New York to be the keynote speaker at the fund-raiser for Denise's foundation. Denise also contributed $10,000 — the maximum amount allowable — to the Clinton Legal Expense Trust to help cover the president's legal bills in the Monica Lewinsky affair.

Denise Rich has maintained that the money she contributes to the Democratic Party is all hers, that she's a successful songwriter and comes from a wealthy family. But documents filed in a lawsuit in New York County Supreme Court in connection with the value of her holdings in Marc Rich's companies suggest that many — if not most — of her millions came from her then-husband, the tax fugitive. In an affidavit, Denise stated that she owned stock in a collection of her husband's companies, including Clarendon and Marc Rich & Co. Holding A.G. The affidavit included this interesting clause: "I understand that this statement may be disclosed by the Corporation to the United States Internal Revenue Service and that I could be punishable by fine, imprisonment or both if I have made any false statements herein."[76]

The documents show that in 1990 Marc Rich and his trusted lieutenants planned to cash out a portion of their shares in Marc Rich & Co. Holding A.G., a firm in which Denise owned about 14 percent of the stock. The court papers include letters between attorneys seeking a way to transfer to Denise the proceeds from the stock sale to allow her to legally pay the least amount of taxes. As one internal memorandum between Marc Rich's headquarters in Switzerland and lawyers in New York handling the matter put it: "All measures shall be taken to grant [Denise Rich] the lowest possible taxation, especially full tax credit against U.S. tax and the best possible cash planning."[77]

At one point, nearly a dozen New York lawyers were at work arranging the transfer to Denise from her expatriate husband and dealing with its tax consequences and other matters. When complaints about the size of her legal bill — it reached $140,000 — surfaced several years later, one of the attorneys replied in a court filing: "While this is a substantial amount, it is not unusual in view of the fact that Mrs. Rich received over $150 million in the 1990 redemption and required extensive, sophisticated legal assistance to minimize her tax exposure."[78]

Indeed so. At the height of the negotiations, one of the tax lawyers was on the telephone five times in eight weeks to IRS officials in Washington, seeking their advice on Denise Rich's complex tax situation.

The $150 million was only part of Marc Rich's assets that were channeled to Denise. She also received stock from him, the value of which is not publicly known. It could have been worth a few million dollars. Or a few hundred million.

However much she received, it is clear that at least $150 million from a fugitive the government says it wants to apprehend ended up with his then-wife, who in turn has parceled out three-quarters of a million dollars to the Democratic Party and its candidates and has hosted a fund-raiser in her home attended by the president of the United States.

Whatever this says about the efforts of the U.S. government to reel in a major tax fugitive after seventeen years, there is an even more ominous threat looming on the tax-law-enforcement horizon. This one may be the most confounding of all.

CHAPTER 6

A CULTURE OF DECEIT

CUTTING CORNERS

With so many opportunities to cheat, is it any wonder that income tax compliance is crumbling? Growing hordes of tax dodgers deduct expenses they're not entitled to, hide assets, underreport what they owe, or don't even file a return at all. Once, any of those actions would have cost average citizens at least a few sleepless nights. But today, why worry? Congress has made sure the IRS no longer has the resources to catch tax cheats. And policymakers don't want them to in any event. The message coming out of Washington is loud and clear: It's okay to cut corners on your taxes. As you might expect, with so much temptation, more and more people are doing just that.

But are people inherently more dishonest than they once were? Unfortunately, the answer is yes. The willingness to cheat and the decline in tax compliance reflect a wider trend in American society: plummeting ethical and moral standards. They're the catalyst that has ignited the explosion of anonymous corporations and trusts in the Caribbean; the use of the Internet to conceal assets; the sale of the tax code by members of Congress in exchange for campaign contributions; the dramatic increase in corporations that pay little or no taxes and thus shift the cost of government to powerless individuals; law enforcement agencies that wink when the influential violate the law at the same time they prosecute the helpless; and banks that look the other way when they process cash from suspect sources. The end result of these and similar trends: runaway tax fraud.

The erosion of ethical standards is most noticeable in two areas of daily life: in the institutions where standards once were quite high, like schools, colleges, and universities, and in the everyday language of public officials, lawyers, university professors, accountants, and plain ordinary citizens. People are using words to suggest one thing when they mean quite another, or are interpreting a word or a phrase in a way that is most advantageous to them — at the expense of everyone else, and of the truth.

While the reasons for this decline in values are many and varied, the evidence that it's happening is everywhere. Children seize the assets of their ailing parents and then shift responsibility for their nursing home care to other taxpayers. Phony automobile insurance claims are so common that auto body shops post signs saying it's unlawful to inflate repair bills. Homeowners' insurance claims are similarly doctored. Gainfully employed workers collect unemployment benefits. Healthy workers collect worker's compensation payments for nonexistent injuries. State employees accept bribes to fabricate identification cards. Health care companies pad invoices. Sports figures openly acknowledge that they violate the rules of the game. Perhaps most disturbing of all, generations of Americans are being taught that it's socially acceptable to cheat. In fact, the learning process begins in elementary school and continues through high school and college.

Each year, the federal government pays billions of dollars to people who knowingly file phony claims under the Supplemental Security Income (SSI) program of Social Security. The claims are submitted by a cross-section of citizens, among them parents who encourage their elementary-school-age children to fake learning disabilities or psychiatric disorders to collect a federal check.

Listen to Wayne Parker, area manager for the Louisiana Disability Determinations Service, talk about how teachers spend much of their time filling out forms so that parents can collect monthly SSI payments, or "crazy checks," on behalf of their children:

> Several teachers have reported overhearing their students discuss what you have to do to receive a crazy check. One teacher reported that a child told her that his mother had promised him a Nintendo if he would fail and get expelled from school.
>
> A first grade student from Riverside Elementary in Simmsport, Louisiana, asked her teacher if she was crazy. When the teacher asked her why she asked such a question, the little girl replied, "My Mama said I had to be crazy so she could get a check. . . ."
>
> The principal of South Side Elementary in Lake Providence reported being called from his office to see a student who was rolling around in the hall yelling, "They are after me." When he arrived, he found nothing wrong with her, but one of the teachers said, "We'll be getting the forms on her pretty soon." They received the forms five days later. . . .
>
> Some parents have even demanded that their child be placed in a special education classroom when the child was performing well in school. A preschool child from East Carroll Parish told a school psychologist that he saw balloons coming out of the walls. When questioned about the statement, he said, "Oh, I forgot, Mama said say blood was coming out of the wall."[1]

For many students, the cheating they're involved with as youngsters is merely a prelude to what they'll do through high school, college, and graduate school.

In a 1998 poll of more than 3,000 students who appear in the *Who's Who Among American High School Students* — the best and the brightest of the nation's secondary schools — 80 percent admitted they had cheated. More than half dismissed their actions as "no big deal." A full 95 percent were never caught. And 97 percent planned to go to college.[2]

Given that background, it should come as little surprise that college students feel the same way. In surveys of 7,000 students at small and medium-size colleges, almost 80 percent of undergraduates "reported one or more incidents of cheating."[3]

In the spring of 1999, two dozen students at San Diego State University, including seniors about to graduate, were caught cheating. They had obtained answers to a test that had been given earlier in an evening session. The class? Business Ethics. Acting on a tip, the professor rearranged the order of the questions for the day class. When the papers were turned in, twenty-five students had provided the answers in the sequence of the earlier evening test.

Not only is cheating widespread, few students see much wrong with it. "Students are a lot less embarrassed to admit they're doing it now," a spokesman for Duke University's Center for Academic Integrity said in 1999. "They say everyone in society cheats now."[4] A *U.S. News & World Report* poll in 1999 found that "84 percent of college students believe they need to cheat to get ahead in the world today" and 90 percent said "cheaters never pay the price."[5]

Whether in high school or college, students are now afforded unparalleled opportunities for obtaining the answers to tests ahead of time and substituting the work of others for their own. To be sure, old term papers and tests have always been available on college campuses for the student willing to go in search of them. But cyberspace does for cheating students what it does for cheating taxpayers: It provides the ready vehicle, instant access, an unmatched selection, and complete anonymity.

Need a term paper on the Renaissance, the pyramids of Egypt, the Great Wall of China, anabolic steroids, Keynesian and supply-side economics, or the influence of Islam on Malcolm X? How about a report on Virginia in the seventeenth century, the symbolism in Hemingway's short stories, the survival methods of Australia's Aborigines, Sigmund Freud's theory of the origins of sacrifice, or a case study of the Procter & Gamble Company?

For the student faced with a looming deadline for a term paper or book report, the Internet offers more options than Starbucks does flavors of coffee. Dozens of Web sites peddle their wares to the ethically impaired, using the same marketing techniques that sell everything from lingerie to used cars, all accompanied by the fine-print disclaimers found in sweepstakes advertisements.

A+ Papers targets students who are interested in, well, an A grade. "With over 3,000 papers in our archives, we will have the paper for you! And these papers are actual college papers done by professionals or by fellow college students . . . that received an A+. Go down to the topic you need, and find that A+ paper!" Prices vary from $9.99 for 300 words on "Nationalism in Europe after 1848" to $119 for 3,200 words on "The Media and Privacy: Commercial Interests versus Privacy Interests." The Web site carries the obligatory warning: "The intended purpose of our papers is that they be used as models to assist you in the preparation of your own. In accordance with NJ Statutes 2A:17-77.16-18 and similar statutes that exist in other states, A+papers.com will never distribute papers to ANY student giving us ANY reason to believe that (s)he will submit our work, either in whole or part, for academic credit at any institution in their own name."[6] Right.

Jungle Page — "if we can't help you, no one can!" — appeals to students seeking original work by offering "professional pre-written essays, only $19.97 each." It boasts that "our papers are NOT submitted by students . . . they are written by our team of professional writers." It also offers an assortment of other services, including college entrance essays: "OK, so you've gone through school, completed all your assignments on time and never missed a class . . . now it's time to get into the next level. College? Graduate School? We'll even help you out if you want to be a lawyer. . . . A great application essay can help you stand out from among the thousands of other applications similar to yours. We can help you create the perfect essay." The first two pages are $79.95. Each additional page is $15.[7]

Essayworld takes this one step further by providing hints on "how to cheat" and testimonials from satisfied customers. One suggestion for getting a perfect grade in a science or math test where calculators are allowed: "Just about any graphing calculator will work. In the program section, you can type in formulas, examples, notes, and even answers. . . . Be sure to get a calculator such as the TI-86 with its 96k of ram and hide the notes in with real programs. . . . During the test, if the teacher sees you, he'd think you are just working on some question on the test." Visitors to the Web site expressed their appreciation for the cheating tips and canned essays. "Cool site," said an Illinois student. "I really like some of those ideas for cheating." A Texas student offered: "Amazing cheat site. I'm passing this year." An enthusiastic Connecticut student wrote: "I think this is a kick ass site for people like me and every other person which hates to write essay's [sic]. Keep up the good work." From a Virginia student: "This is a cool website. I made an A in all of my classes because of this!!" An Oklahoma student commented: "THIS IS THE BEST SITE. YOU GONNA PASS MY FRESHMAN COMP CLASS FOR ME. THANKS!!"

Then there's School Sucks — "download your workload" — where the "students are students, and the teachers are nervous" — and the term papers are free.[8] Cyber Essays bills itself as a "one-stop source for free, high-quality term papers, essays, and reports on all subjects" and is a "completely free service that relies on students to submit their own papers in order to keep this site expanding."[9] A1-Termpaper is a sort of Yellow Pages of term papers that offers "approximately 20,000 pre-written term papers for your research requirements." Credit cards accepted — Visa, MasterCard, American Express, and Discover.[10] Lazy Students caters to those who loathe reading and libraries by providing "research services so that writing your paper is as painless as possible."[11] And Downcrap — "a great place to get your homework done if your kids forgot to do it" — targets parents who don't have a problem buying the answers for children who don't do their homework.[12]

Finally, there's the aptly named Web site Cheats, not to be confused with the Evil House of Cheat and the Cheat Factory, two competitors. Cheats offers papers on subjects from Archimedes to Sumerian Life, at lengths from as few as 225 words to more than 4,000. The Web page provides a description of each report, the number of words, and a critique and starred rating system similar to capsule film reviews found in newspapers and magazines. A 589-word report on Moses, Mendelssohn, and Samson Rafael Hirsch earns only one star and this caustic comment: "The most boring, worst, report I've ever seen . . . on this page because it's the only report I could find on Moses, Mendelssohn and Samson Rafael Hirsch."

On the other hand, a 2,460-word report on the Auschwitz concentration camp garners five stars: "An absolutely great report. This would get anyone an A+. Everything you've ever needed to know about the concentration camp in Outwits [sic]."[13]

The Web site, of course, carries a stern warning against plagiarism:

> These reports are to be used solely for the purposes of learning about something, or for research. Use of these papers for anything else is not my responsibility. By downloading any of these reports, you are stating that you will not treat these reports as your own, and you will not hold the owner of this page responsible for anything that is done with the report. Plagiarism is a serious offense, and it is in no way condoned by the owner of this page.[14]

For students who put such warnings in a class with other Internet admonitions that say, "You must be eighteen years old to enter this site," the Web page operator adds this friendly request: "If you do happen to turn one of these reports in as your own, let me know how it goes, and I can adjust the ratings a little bit."[15]

Whose advertisements appear on some of these Web sites from time to time? Just your everyday companies like Amazon.com, the

Internet bookseller; the Money Store, which specializes in loans to homeowners with less-than-perfect credit; BellSouth Mobility, the wireless communications provider; Dow Jones & Company Inc., publisher of the *Wall Street Journal;* Discover Loan Center, a business unit of Morgan Stanley Dean Witter & Co.; and Microsoft Corporation, the ubiquitous software company that powers computer life.

But before you come down too hard on students who turn to cheating, consider their mentors. All too often the lesson that it's okay to break the rules is one they learned in elementary school.

Schools are under increasing pressure to improve standardized-test results, to show that their students are making serious academic progress. With all attention focused on that goal, teachers, principals, and superintendents are encouraged to manipulate the testing process as well as the scores to produce the most favorable results. Sometimes they even selectively throw tests out.

Such was the case in Austin, Texas, where in April 1999 the Austin Independent School District and a deputy superintendent were indicted on charges of tampering with a state achievement test for elementary school pupils. It marked the first time in Texas history that criminal charges were lodged against a school district for cheating. The district and the administrator were accused of switching sixteen student identification and Social Security numbers to eliminate their tests from school scores and thereby raise the performance level at three schools.

Later in 1999 in New York City, several dozen elementary and middle school teachers and two principals were accused of giving answers to students taking standardized reading and mathematics tests. For five years, according to investigators, "teachers and principals let students mark their answers on scrap or notebook paper, then told them which answers to correct when they filled in the bubbles in the official test booklets." They also "directed students to erase incorrect answers, or even changed the answers themselves."[16]

While these may be extreme examples of educators promoting cheating, another dishonest practice is much more prevalent and can be found in schools throughout the country. It's called grade inflation — the practice of handing out A grades to pupils who do B work or less; Bs to pupils whose work is worth a C or less, and Cs to those who are barely passing or are failing.

How widespread is this phenomenon? Look no further than the profiles of students who complete the college-board tests administered annually. They show that as high school grades have gone up, test scores have gone down. From 1987 to 1997, the proportion of students taking the SAT who had grade averages of A+, A, or A- climbed "from 28 percent to a record 37 percent." During that same period, verbal SAT scores fell an average of 13 points, and math scores dropped 1 point.[17]

But don't be too critical of high school teachers who pass out inflated grades. They are merely emulating their counterparts on college campuses, where it all began.

Of all grades assigned by faculty members at Princeton University from 1992 to 1997, a whopping 83 percent were between A+ and B-. That compared with 69 percent during a comparable five-year period from 1973 to 1977. A's and A minuses accounted for 46 percent of the grades handed out by Harvard professors during 1996–97. That was more than double the 22 percent three decades earlier, in 1966–67. At Brown, the number of A grades climbed from 30 percent in 1986–87 to 40 percent in 1996–97.

In years past, 3 to 4 percent of a senior class at a private university would graduate with outstanding honors. Now at the University of Pennsylvania, "fully 20 percent of graduating students qualify for highest graduation honors."[18]

Some academics justify what they are doing by saying that lower grades would reflect unfavorably on the college or university, and besides, students are under pressure to get into ever more competitive graduate programs. As one professor put it: "We don't want to handicap our students."[19]

So it is that the college degree has become just another consumer product, like bottled water or Spandex shorts. The marketplace rules. The consumer pays $120,000 to a private university — $30,000 to a state university — and in return receives the degree of choice, with little regard for academic achievement. The high grades and honors that come with it are an entitlement, tarnishing the process for the truly deserving.

It's a case of giving the customers what they want. For colleges and universities, which now function like any other business, there is little choice. If one college does not, another will. An official at Bucknell University in Lewisburg, Pennsylvania, explained: "It would be suicide, in an economic-business sense. The university is a business. In the same way [Bucknell] is competing with other schools' tuition levels, they're also competing for grade distribution. If we're known as a school where the average grade point average is 2.8 and everywhere else is 3.2, we're going to lose out."[20]

Other academics want to avoid confrontations. Like the chairman of a department at Boston University who amended a student's grade from failing to passing even though the student had scored just 32 of a possible 105 points. His reasoning: "Both of his parents are lawyers."[21]

As a consequence of grade inflation, nearly two generations of students have grown up to believe they are entitled to good marks for poor work, or honors distinction for a pedestrian effort. Some even insist that low grades do not exist.

Alvin Kernan, a long-time distinguished scholar, professor, and administrator at Yale and Princeton, now retired, recalls the daughter of a famous movie star who came to see him "to complain about a grade of C that I had given her terrible essay, on the grounds that 'there is no such grade as C.' I showed her the registrar's official list of grades, and she still didn't believe it."[22]

The chairman of Princeton's English department described the reaction of a daughter of a prominent intellectual when she received her B- grade: "She threw down the paper on my desk and said, 'This is not the Princeton way.'"[23]

Obviously, this trend in education does not bode well for income tax compliance. After all, very little ground separates people who believe they are entitled to good grades regardless of their performance from people who believe they are entitled to keep a larger portion of their income tax free regardless of what the law requires. A longtime IRS auditor says that in years gone by, a taxpayer who made a "mistake" on his or her return was often genuinely embarrassed. No more. "Now they think they have the right to get away with it and they are annoyed when they don't."[24]

THE FRAUD INDUSTRY

This erosion of ethical values in education, where cheating was once an aberration, can be found in other fields as well. While dishonesty, fraud, and unethical behavior have always been a part of the nation's culture, for the most part they involved the ethical lapses of the few. Now, just as in education, they involve the many. They have become as much a part of daily life as the sport utility vehicle and the cell phone.

Insurance fraud costs an estimated $125 billion yearly. Workers who claim to have suffered injuries on the job collect worker's compensation benefits at the same time they are receiving paychecks while laboring for another employer. Employers, in turn, "misrepresent their payroll or the type of work carried out by their employees," thereby paying artificially low insurance premiums.[25]

In a 1997 poll conducted by the Insurance Research Council, 28 percent of the people said "it was all right to pad a claim to make up for the deductible that they would have to pay."[26] Almost 25 percent thought it was acceptable to inflate claims to recover premiums paid in years when they had no losses. Ordinary people do all of that and more. They stage phony accidents to collect damages. They have their cars stolen. They deliberately create water or fire damage in their homes to obtain new furniture and decor. They drive unlawfully without insurance and, when involved in an accident, force the honest person with insurance to pick up the tab.

Physicians, hospitals, home health agencies, laboratories, and other medical facilities collected from the government's Medicare program an estimated $43 billion in 1996 and 1997 to which they were not entitled. They charged for services that were unnecessary or not covered by the program. In other cases, health care contractors alter their records to cover up poor performance and keep the Medicare dollars flowing.

Fraud and dishonest business practices run through the entire health care industry. Insurance companies routinely refuse to pay legitimate medical claims, trusting that a certain percentage of the patients will pay for the care out of their own pockets or the physicians will waive payment. In other instances, insurance companies refuse to authorize treatment when it is clearly eligible, hoping that patients and doctors alike will fail to pursue the requests. Physicians file claim forms with false codes, knowing the procedures actually performed are not covered by an insurance policy.

More billions are paid out in fraudulent claims under the Social Security Administration's disability insurance program, which is to protect people who are unable to work because of injury, illness, or disease. Between 1990 and 1997, the number of such beneficiaries shot up 50 percent, from 3 million to 4.5 million. Many claimants feigned their disabilities. During the comparable period in the 1980s, the number of beneficiaries actually declined 3 percent, from 2.9 million to 2.8 million. Most telling, the number of disability claimants as a percentage of the population between ages 16 and 64 has gone up each year in the last decade, climbing from 1.9 percent in 1990 to 2.7 percent in 1997. One of every four claimants says they suffer from anxiety or some other mental disorder. One out of five is under the age of 40. Benefits paid out have also risen sharply, surging $21 billion between 1990 and 1997, compared with a $5 billion increase during the comparable period in the 1980s. Disability-insurance payments are often coupled with

Supplemental Security Income benefits, so those bilking the system are double dipping.

In California, scores of clerks in the State Department of Motor Vehicles were fired because they accepted bribes to issue illegal driver's licenses; 80 percent of the cases involved illegal immigrants who were not entitled to receive a license.

In exchange for cash payments of $125 to $500, government-authorized naturalization mills distribute answers to the questions on the naturalization test, allow the test takers to compare answers, and correct answers that are wrong. They then falsely certify that the immigrants "could read and write English and had knowledge and understanding of the history and form of American government," and thereby qualified to be naturalized.[27]

Each year, millions of noncustodial parents, mostly fathers, fail to pay about $40 billion in support they owe for their minor children. Of 19 million child-support cases, more than half involve families on welfare. To avoid attachment of their paychecks, some noncustodial parents cross state lines, some move across the country, some move into the cash economy.

Between September 1990 and September 1996, delinquent student loans soared 94 percent, from $9.9 billion to $19.2 billion, as a generation of college students walked away from their debts. When the U.S. Department of Education sent out 3 million delinquency notices, about 662,000 — or 23 percent — "were returned by the U.S. Postal Service as undeliverable."[28]

Proprietors of organizations charged with ensuring that "children and senior citizens in day care facilities receive nutritious meals" divert tens of millions of taxpayer dollars to their personal use.[29] They collect federal money for meals never served, for fictitious children and adults, and for day-care facilities that do not exist. They exaggerate the number of meals served and create phony invoices to support the sham figures. The organizations include nonprofits and church affiliates, some of which siphon off food money to pay inflated salaries and to cover the personal expenses of employees.

Governments at all levels invite dishonesty. Consider the "enterprise zones" established by the federal government to lure businesses to depressed areas. As part of this program, local governments waive sales taxes on steel, cement, lumber, and other construction materials used to erect buildings in the zone. To be eligible for the break, suppliers must be located within the enterprise zone. They seldom are. So dummy corporations are established in the zone to process paperwork for the building supplies and to pocket the waived sales tax. No one bothers to police the arrangements.

Cheating at the state and local level, though, pales alongside the unethical behavior found in some federal agencies. Immigration programs are administered in such a way that immigrants get the unmistakable message that the way to get ahead in the United States is to circumvent the law.

Beef-, poultry-, and hog-packing plants and other labor-intensive industries in the South and Midwest employ tens of thousands of illegal immigrants because companies are unable to attract enough U.S. workers. The reason: low pay, no benefits, and harsh working conditions. Although these plants brim with violators, the Immigration and Naturalization Service rarely raids them because Congress has refused to provide sufficient enforcement funds. On days when raids are carried out, some illegal workers are warned in advance by supervisors, who suggest that it might be a good time to take a day or two off. Others, who are not working up to expectations, receive no such warning. They are arrested, carted off, and deported. It's an informal system that allows companies to use the federal government to get rid of employees who fail to keep pace with a fast-moving assembly line. The message to newly arrived immigrants is that the government itself rewards dishonest behavior.

Even those immigrants who arrive "legally" are prompted to skirt the law to win permanent residency. Remember the software programmers recruited from India who work at America's largest companies and pay no income tax? Before leaving India, they signed affidavits stating they would return and would not seek U.S. citizenship. But those who have been questioned about the process have foggy memories concerning what they signed. Witness the following exchange between an attorney and an Indian programmer:

Attorney: Prior to being [sent] to the United States . . . did you have to sign an affidavit that said you wouldn't change your non-immigrant status?

Programmer: . . . If you mean this form, well, that's my signature on it.

Attorney: Did you sign that form?

Programmer: I did sign it but I'm not real sure that I read it.

Attorney: That's a different question. But you did sign it, that's your signature?

Programmer: Yes.[30]

In May 1999, an INS official testified before a House Judiciary subcommittee about growing fraud in the H-1B program. William R. Yates, acting deputy executive associate commissioner of the INS, told lawmakers that "anecdotal reports by INS Service Centers indicate that INS has seen an increase in fraudulent attempts to obtain benefits in this category."[31]

Yates testified the agency had discovered two primary types of fraud: one involving the hiring company, the other committed by the immigrant seeking employment. The hiring company, he said, may be nonexistent, or it may operate from a post office box or residence. "Often the requesting company acts as an employment agency, petitions for the foreign workers, but then attempts to find them other jobs, with associated additional fees, paid for by the intending company," Yates said. "In some cases, an existing company petitions for employees, but terminates them on arrival, enabling an otherwise ineligible person to enter into the United States."[32]

As for those seeking to come to America, Yates said they often fabricate the educational and professional papers needed for entry. "These documents are easily falsified," he said.[33] At one especially busy American consulate in India, Yates said, officials estimated that almost all the H-1B petitioners "were misrepresenting their academic or professional credentials."[34]

A sweeping investigation by the Office of Inspector General in the U.S. Department of Labor concluded that yet another program, the Permanent Labor Certification Program, is "being manipulated and abused. For the most part, employers use the program to obtain permanent resident visas for aliens who already work for them, some illegally. Others use the program to obtain the green card for friends or relatives for jobs that may or may not actually exist."[35]

Because this fraud is so widespread, federal law enforcement agencies merely look the other way. About a half-million foreign workers were certified during the 1990s — most of them unlawfully. As one government worker responsible for administering the program puts it: "Aliens who commit fraud to get here do not suddenly become upright Americans. Why should they? The United States government has showed them that lying, cheating and perjuring themselves is the way to get what they want."[36]

EVERYONE'S DOING IT

Low moral and ethical standards have become so ingrained in everyday life that they are accepted. With each passing year, there are fewer Americans who know that such conduct and conditions used to be rare or did not exist, and that people caught engaging in improper behavior were truly embarrassed by it. This new population includes millions of recent arrivals from countries like Russia, where there was no income tax and where citizens were compelled for generations to deceive their government as a matter of survival, to Mexico and other Latin American nations, where tax evasion has long been part of the culture.

In all, more than 150 million Americans — close to 60 percent of the population — have never known a time when students who earned poor grades actually received them; when cars did not come equipped with alarms; when fans who attended sporting events behaved as guests; when storefronts were not covered with steel grates; when amateur and professional athletes did not take performance-enhancing drugs; when stores did not have anti-theft devices; and when most citizens believed that government served a critical function in a civilized and democratic society. More to the point, they have never known a time when the overwhelming majority of Americans faithfully reported their income and paid the taxes they owed.

Just two generations ago, state driver's licenses were issued on paper, because forgeries and duplications were rare. Today, phony licenses are so common that they can be found in high schools, on college campuses, and in the neighborhood bars that surround them, as well as in the possession of those whose driving privileges have been suspended or revoked. In the escalating war to deter forgery, states moved first to licenses with photos and then to holograms. But it's done nothing to stem the tide of fraudulent licenses.

Not so long ago, to get a birth certificate you had to be a newborn; to get a passport you had to submit a lengthy form to the State Department. Today, bogus birth certificates and passports can be ordered over the World Wide Web — you can create an identity of your own choosing. A college degree, reporter's credentials, a passport from another country are all available for the asking.

Two generations ago, it was possible to walk freely through county, state, and federal courthouses without encountering a security guard. Today, you most likely will be required to sign in, walk through a metal detector, and in some cases obtain a building pass.

Once, amateur athletes did not have to submit to drug tests after participating in sporting events. Today, drug use is so popular that kits are sold that will allow the athlete to fake his or her urine test.

Two generations ago, there were no surveillance cameras in public and private buildings; no clerks monitoring the door of a clothing store dressing room to assure that the person trying on clothes did not leave wearing more than when he or she arrived.

And finally, two generations ago there was no Sensormatic Electronics Corporation. You may not recognize the name, but you know its products. The Boca Raton, Florida, company designs, manufactures, and markets the electronic tags and labels placed on wearing apparel sold in most clothing stores in America, as well as on a variety of other retail items, from disposable razors to power drills.

Not so many years ago, companies like Sensormatic weren't needed. But that was before the epidemic of shoplifting hit stores, supermarkets, drugstores, and other retail outlets. Store theft costs retailers $9 billion a year, and Sensormatic has grown right along with it into a $1-billion-a-year company with 5,000 employees installing antitheft products across the nation.

Yet, in another sign of the times, this company whose business it is to make certain that people don't engage in unlawful acts engaged in some itself. In March 1998, the Securities and Exchange Commission accused Sensormatic and its top officers of violating "the antifraud, reporting, internal controls, and books and records provisions of the federal securities laws in connection with its manipulation of its quarterly revenue and earnings in order to reach its earnings goals and thereby meet analysts' quarterly earnings projections."[37] In plain English, the company cooked the books to pump up its stock price.

Without either admitting or denying any wrongdoing, Sensormatic settled the SEC fraud charges by agreeing that it would not violate securities laws in the future.

But Sensormatic is an isolated case, right? Sadly, no. A 1998 survey of chief financial officers showed that 12 percent had misrepresented their company's financial results and a stunning 55 percent had been asked by their superiors to play with the numbers but said they resisted.

Whether in business or the professions, this sort of dishonesty has become commonplace. Attitudes toward it range from indifference to benign acceptance. After all, everyone's doing it. That was the justification put forth by Webster Hubbell, the Clinton administration official caught up in independent prosecutor Kenneth Starr's net. When he was indicted on charges of income tax evasion growing out of the overbilling of clients of his Arkansas law practice, Hubbell — a onetime chief justice of the Arkansas Supreme Court — claimed that the real beneficiaries were his law partners. As he explained to his wife Suzanna in a tape-recorded telephone conversation: "Where I have a contract with the client for time and the over-bill was a markup of the bill, the beneficiary is the firm."

She responded, "You didn't actually do that, did you, mark up time for the client, did you?"

"Yes, I did," her husband replied. "So does every lawyer in the country."[38]

Anyone who has ever pored over the endless pages accounting for every minute of a lawyer's time might be excused if they wholeheartedly subscribed to Hubbell's assessment. Susan P. Knoiak, a law professor at Boston University, summed up Hubbell's attitude this way: "It demonstrates how the old excuse of 'everybody does it' has found new life as a moral argument — if others do it (particularly adversaries or competitors), it's not wrong for me to do it, too. It is a theme that dominates our public and private morality, not just in law firms. We are in the age of lowest-common-denominator morality. So long as someone else is doing it, we, too, are free to indulge."[39]

The "everybody's doing it" excuse is also invoked in sports, where competitors try to secure an advantage by violating the rules of the game without getting caught. Football linemen perfect the ability to hold unseen. Basketball players routinely block illegally. Pitchers alter baseballs with foreign substances. Batters use corked bats. Athletes in every field consume performance-enhancing drugs. All to gain the extra edge.

Briana Scurry, the goalkeeper who preserved her U.S. women's soccer team's 5-to-4 victory margin over China in the 1999 World Cup championship when she blocked a penalty kick, tersely expressed the sentiment. Acknowledging that she had indeed moved forward a few steps to secure a better angle, a violation that went unchallenged, Scurry told reporters: "Everybody does it. It's only cheating if you get caught."[40]

Newspaper editorial page pundits, once the monitors of public morals, endorsed the logic. "The problem was not what Scurry did," opined the *Philadelphia Daily News,* "the problem was what she said. . . . Soccer isn't a math test, where it surely is cheating to copy the answers even if you don't get caught doing it. In sports, it is different. Cheating is doctoring the ball or using drugs. It isn't looking for, and taking, the winning edge, as Scurry did."[41]

That was the view voiced about the same time by Sterling Marlin, the race car driver, after NASCAR officials discovered a piece of improper equipment on his vehicle before the start of a race in Daytona: "Sometimes you try to get some things by. Everybody tries it."

With such practices rampant, it's no surprise the nation is awash in people who define words like *income* and *deductions* and *expenses* in the most creative way to escape the taxes they owe. Word games reached a zenith in the Clinton administration, when the country was led for eight years by a president who parsed words such as *is* and *sex,* which allowed him to glare steely-eyed into a television camera and tell millions of viewers, with burning sincerity: "I want you to listen to me. I'm going to say this again. I did not have sexual relations with that woman, Miss Lewinsky."[42]

The president's press secretary, Michael D. McCurry, in trying to put the best spin on the president's spin, told reporters: "I think every American that heard him knows exactly what he meant. . . . He didn't leave any ambiguity . . . whatsoever."[43]

As everyone now knows, the twenty-four-word statement was bloated with ambiguity.

In this, President Clinton was little different from the typical tax dodger who says, with equal sincerity and conviction, that the write-off on his tax return for meals he eats at fine restaurants represents a legitimate "business expense" because he is conducting research for a book on fine dining. This even though he has no contract to produce a book, and has never written or published anything.

Whether it's the president or the average tax evader, such word games enjoy the stamp of approval from no less an authority than the U.S. Supreme Court. In 1973, the court unanimously endorsed the practice in a case involving Samuel Bronston, the Hollywood producer who in the late 1950s set up a huge studio in Madrid, where he turned out such historical epics as *The Fall of the Roman Empire, King of Kings,* and *El Cid.*

Bronston operated on the grand scale. For *El Cid,* starring Charlton Heston and Sophia Loren, he built cities peopled by vast crowds supplied by the Spanish army, and he flooded rivers. For *The Fall of the Roman Empire,* he hired more than a thousand workmen, who toiled for seven months to rebuild the Forum.

As the impresario of such monumental undertakings, Bronston was in almost constant money trouble. He made and lost millions. His company had dozens of bank accounts in at least five countries. Legend has it that when Charlton Heston learned "that his chauffeur had not been paid he complained to Bronston, who opened a drawer and took out a bundle of dollar bills," which may explain why Bronston once was described as looking "like a man who had become accustomed to leaving by the back door."[44]

Bronston's production company finally sought protection in U.S. Bankruptcy Court in 1964. Two years later, a lawyer for creditors trying to track down his assets questioned Bronston during a hearing:

Lawyer: Do you have any bank accounts in Swiss banks, Mr. Bronston?

Bronston: No, sir.

Lawyer: Have you ever?

Bronston: The company had an account there for about six months, in Zurich.

Lawyer: Have you any nominees who have bank accounts in Swiss banks?

Bronston: No, sir.

Lawyer: Have you ever?

Bronston: No, sir.[45]

In fact, between October 1959 and June 1964, Bronston "had a personal bank account at the International Credit Bank in Geneva, Switzerland, into which he made deposits and upon which he drew checks."[46]

Bronston was charged with perjury. A jury later found him guilty of lying under oath, in that he gave an answer "not literally false but when considered in the context in which it was given, nevertheless constitute[d] a false statement."[47]

Bronston appealed, arguing that he could not be guilty of perjury if his answers were truthful, no matter how unresponsive they may have been. The Supreme Court agreed, thereby certifying the concept of the legally accurate and perfectly acceptable lie. In overturning the conviction, Chief Justice Warren Burger wrote: "It should come as no surprise that a participant in a bankruptcy proceeding may have something to conceal and consciously tries to do so. . . . It is the responsibility of the lawyer to probe. . . . If a witness evades, it is the lawyer's responsibility to recognize the evasion and to bring the witness back to the mark, to flush out the whole truth."[48]

Now project this line of reasoning to the more than 120 million people who file tax returns. Some of them, too, may have something to conceal and are reluctant to provide the requested information. How many auditors would it take to peel away the nuances of income and deductions and expenses? It's precisely that kind of word game that in part has eaten away at the very foundation of the income tax — the voluntary assessment system.

HIGH-PROFILE DODGERS

One of the consequences of ethical erosion is the ease with which people in public life now justify looking the other way when the law is broken. A situation that would have triggered an ethical alarm in the past does not even register a blip on the moral radar screen today.

Such was the case in January 1993, when the incoming Clinton administration stumbled into a minefield, setting off one explosion after another by tripping over a tax law that is widely ignored. That's the requirement that people who hire child-care or other household help pay Social Security and Medicare taxes on their workers' wages.

President Clinton, determined to be the first president to choose a woman to head the Department of Justice, nominated Zoe Baird for attorney general. A forty-year-old corporate lawyer, Baird had served in the Justice Department and the White House during the Carter administration. After leaving her Carter job, she had joined a Washington, D.C., law firm, then moved on to the post of counselor and staff executive at the General Electric Company. In 1990 she became senior vice president and general counsel for Aetna Life & Casualty, overseeing the work of 120 lawyers at its Hartford, Connecticut, headquarters.

As with all prospective Cabinet nominees, Clinton aides quizzed Baird prior to her formal nomination by the president. She gave details about her professional background and also disclosed that she and her husband, Paul D. Gewirtz, a constitutional law professor at Yale Law School, had employed a Peruvian couple who were illegal immigrants to look after their young son and perform certain chores at their New Haven home. She also informed the staff that she and her husband had failed to pay the couple's Social Security and Medicare taxes. (Baird and her husband did cough up $12,000 shortly after she was proposed for attorney general.)

By employing illegal aliens and failing to pay certain taxes, Baird and her husband had violated both immigration and tax laws. That should have been a red flag for the Clinton administration. After all, is it wise to have the Justice Department — which prosecutes violators of tax and immigration laws — headed by a person who had violated both? But neither the president nor his aides was the least bit troubled by that prospect, and they forwarded Baird's nomination to Congress.

During the opening day of her confirmation hearing, Baird told the Senate Judiciary Committee that in the summer of 1990 she and her husband "had been looking for almost two months to try to find a suitable person to take care of our son," who at the time was eight months old. Finally, they employed a couple from Peru through an employment agency, knowing that "it was illegal to hire them," but also knowing that the law was not enforced.[49]

They paid the woman $5.96 an hour, or $12,400 a year for a forty-hour week. According to an employment agreement, her duties included "preparing meals, feeding, dressing and bathing child, maintaining his clothing and room and attending to his physical and emotional needs in our absence. Light housekeeping duties as needed."[50] They paid the woman's husband a similar wage to perform odd jobs and drive Baird on her daily one-hour trip between home and office. In addition to the two salaries totaling about $24,800, Baird and her husband also provided free room and board.

Baird testified that before employing the couple, "my husband consulted with immigration lawyers in Connecticut who informed him that the immigration laws have employer sanctions for hiring someone not authorized to work in the United States, but the lawyers advised that the Immigration and Naturalization Service (INS) did not appear to view this as an enforcement matter."[51]

As for the unpaid Social Security taxes, Baird told the committee: "We believed that Social Security taxes needed to be paid and we tried to find a way to pay them, even though they [the household workers] didn't have Social Security numbers. We talked to the lawyer several times about this. . . . He told my husband that it was not possible to pay the taxes until they had the Social Security numbers."[52]

In truth, the advice was incorrect. Baird and her husband — two very high-powered lawyers themselves — seem to have relied on tax advice from an immigration lawyer, rather than a tax expert. That's akin to a cardiologist with a brain tumor seeking treatment from a dermatologist.

At Baird's Senate confirmation hearing, Hank Brown, then a Republican senator from Colorado, questioned her about whatever conversations she had with her household workers concerning taxes.

Brown: Did you ever advise them about their responsibility to pay Social Security taxes and income taxes?

Baird: . . . I don't know what conversations there were about their income tax.

Brown: You personally never advised them of their responsibility to pay income tax?

Baird: No.

Brown: Were you aware that the couple did not pay federal income tax in 1990 and 1991?

Baird: I can't tell you that I thought about it, although, on reflection, I would have assumed that, without the Social Security number, they probably didn't.[53]

In fact, Baird and her husband never provided a W-2 form, the document showing wages paid that every employer must give to an employee and file with the IRS. In the Baird case, the income of the two household workers was about $24,800 in 1991. That year, 42 million individuals and families with incomes below $25,000 filed returns and paid $42 billion in income tax. Those with incomes between $20,000 and $25,000 paid an average of $1,900 each.

Still more millions of people who received income from a job did not earn enough to pay income tax, but did pay Social Security and Medicare taxes. In all, 54 million individuals and families making less than $25,000 a year paid an estimated $13 billion in Social Security and Medicare taxes.

From the money left over after taxes, these 54 million people paid their food, housing, and other living expenses. The Baird employees, on the other hand, not only lived the tax-free life but enjoyed free room and board.

When Senator Brown asked about her failure to furnish a W-2 form, Baird replied: "Again, I didn't monitor that and I didn't, you know, I can only say I didn't pay attention to that."[54]

The Clinton administration believed that Baird's violations were minor, akin to parking illegally or littering. As Dee Dee Myers, the president's press secretary, put it at the time, "[The matter] was fully disclosed. He considered it and did not think it was a problem."[55]

The top-ranking Republican on the Senate Judiciary Committee agreed, seemingly smoothing the way for quick confirmation. "It's no big deal," said Orrin G. Hatch of Utah. "No one is above the law, but people make honest mistakes, and that should not deprive her [of] serving her country."[56]

A lot of people, it turned out, thought otherwise. Within days after the twin violations became public, support for Baird melted away in the Senate. Baird did not help her cause during the first day of the confirmation hearings when she sought to justify her failure to pay taxes by saying, "Quite honestly, I was acting at that time really more as a mother than as someone who would be sitting here designated to be attorney general."[57]

That brought an acid response from Joseph R. Biden Jr., the Delaware Democrat who headed the Judiciary Committee: "There are tens of thousands, millions of Americans out there who have trouble taking care of their children, both couples required to work or single parents, with one-fiftieth the income that you and your husband have, and they do not violate the law."[58]

Senate offices were flooded with critical calls. The mood was similar on radio talk shows across the country — callers were angered by Baird's belated decision to own up to her misdeeds only because she wanted a high-level government job. They were furious that a $500,000-a-year corporate attorney with a net worth of more than $2 million would invoke motherhood to justify breaking the law.

With members of his own party warning the president that Baird had less than a fifty-fifty chance of winning confirmation, the White House breathed a sigh of relief when she asked that her nomination be withdrawn.

While Baird quickly faded from view, the tax avoidance tale her nomination had showcased took on a life of its own. Articles appeared in newspapers around the country indicating that employing illegal immigrants and not paying taxes for them was a common, widely accepted practice — millions of mostly affluent families were doing it. In the following months, political figures in both parties lined up to confess similar sins.

Christine Todd Whitman, who planned to seek the Republican gubernatorial nomination in New Jersey, announced that she had sent a check for $14,000 to the IRS to cover taxes owed on a pair of illegal nannies who looked after her children.

Bobby Ray Inman, a retired Navy admiral, former director of the super-secret National Security Agency, and onetime deputy director of the Central Intelligence Agency, was selected by Clinton to become Secretary of Defense. He quickly sent a check for $6,000 to the IRS for taxes owed on a housekeeper, and later withdrew his nomination for other reasons.

Charles F. C. Ruff, former Watergate special prosecutor and U.S. Attorney for the District of Columbia, was dropped as a candidate for the No. 2 job in the Justice Department after it was disclosed that he had failed to pay Social Security taxes on a household worker. Ruff said he thought that because the woman was over retirement age he did not owe the taxes. He did. Everyone who works must pay taxes, regardless of age. In 1997 Ruff became Clinton's White House counsel, a position that did not require Senate confirmation.

Stephen G. Breyer, chief judge of the U.S. First Circuit Court of Appeals, sent a check to the IRS for his housekeeper's taxes after he was put on the short list to fill a vacancy on the U.S. Supreme Court. Like Ruff, he said he didn't think he owed the taxes because the worker was over retirement age. Having learned nothing from the Zoe Baird experience, the White House once again expressed its optimism. Said an aide to President Clinton: "He does not have a Zoe Baird problem. . . . This is not disqualifying."[59] He did and it was — at least for the moment. President Clinton, fearful of being accused of having a double standard if he pushed Breyer's nomination when he made no similar effort for Zoe Baird, appointed Ruth Bader Ginsburg instead. A year later, after the furor over unpaid taxes had died down, Breyer's nomination to the Supreme Court sailed through the Senate by a vote of 87 to 9.

Ronald H. Brown, named by Clinton to be his Secretary of Commerce, disclosed that he had only recently sent a check to the IRS for a household worker. So, too, did Paul Coverdell, Republican senator from Georgia. And Eleanor Dean Acheson, a Clinton-Gore fundraiser and granddaughter of Dean Acheson, Secretary of State during the Truman administration; she was appointed an assistant attorney general. And Mary Jo Bane, a former Harvard professor who was named an assistant secretary in the Department of Health and Human Services.

Most of the offenders were lawyers, and some mounted one of the most discredited legal defenses of all: "I didn't know it was the law." Ignorance of the law, as lawyers have advised nonlawyers for an eternity, is never an excuse.

More novel was the Baird defense offered by Alan M. Dershowitz, the Harvard Law School professor, who put forth a variation of the "everyone-does-it" excuse that if applied to income taxes could lead to the immediate collapse of the system. If government doesn't enforce a law, went Dershowitz's thinking, then people should not be held accountable for disobeying it. He wrote in a newspaper column in January 1993:

> The reason that honest and decent people like Zoe Baird and her law professor husband sometimes break laws like the ones prohibiting the employment of undocumented aliens is that some laws were made to be broken. They fall into a large category of rules, regulations and statutes that are so rarely enforced that many lawyers advise their clients to ignore them. . . . If a law is important enough to be on the books, it should be enforced. [60]

But the U.S. tax system rests wholly on the principle of *voluntary* compliance. It depends on citizens reporting their income honestly and paying the taxes they owe — not on an army of agents meticulously examining every return filed and scouring the nation to make certain that everyone who should have filed did so.

The legal advice that Baird had received concerning employment of people in the country illegally was quite similar to that given in tax situations by lawyers and accountants all the time. Although usually carefully worded, when stripped of the legalese and reduced to simplest terms it is this:

What you plan to do (hire an illegal immigrant or write off a personal expense as a business expense) violates the law.

The government does not have enough resources to investigate most cases of this type.

Therefore, the chances that you will be caught are slim to none.

If you are caught, the penalties will be inconsequential.

Ever more people are playing the game — in taxes it's called the audit lottery — especially wealthy individuals and families who should know what the law says and who have the money to comply with it. Corporations, too, through their executives, are playing the game with a vengeance. It's one more sign of the erosion of ethical standards across society, one more reason the tax system is withering away.

CHAPTER 7

CONGRESS'S PLAN TO RAISE YOUR TAXES

A SHIFTING BURDEN

S ome things are always with us. Death. Taxes. And the eternal quest to come up with a system that forces you to pay more in taxes than your neighbors, even though they earn a great deal more than you do, and are far wealthier than you are. Cordell Hull, the Democratic lawmaker from Tennessee who served twenty-four years in the House and Senate and who wrote the original income tax law, described this enduring struggle during a 1916 debate on the estate tax. Said Hull: "An irrepressible conflict has been raging for a thousand years between the strong and the weak, [with] the former always trying to keep the chief tax burdens upon the latter."[1]

Lest you think that Hull, who went on to serve as Secretary of State during the administration of Franklin D. Roosevelt, was given to exaggeration, consider this: In 1222 in Hungary, King Andreas II signed a proclamation that excused all the nobles from paying taxes. This decision created an unbridgeable economic gulf between the nobles and the common people, "who came to be known as *misera plebs contribuens,* miserable tax-paying people."[2] This tax immunity for the rich continued until the mid-1800s.

Nearly eight hundred years after King Andreas's decree, and eighty-plus years after Hull's warning, the conflict rages on. Once again, the strong are on the verge of achieving a great victory. After systematically reducing their tax load over the last two decades, they are poised to drive a stake through the heart of the progressive income tax and replace it with a system that will give them their smallest tax burden since the robber baron era.

Why is this happening? Simply put, a range of forces have come together, much like the critical mass that produces an atomic explosion, that will obliterate the income tax. By now, you know these forces well.

Congress deliberately weakened the IRS. It slashed the agency's workforce and withheld necessary funding. At the same time, lawmakers focused public attention on the agency's excesses — some of which were indeed outrageous — while ignoring the need for vigorous enforcement to maintain voluntary compliance.

With a weakened IRS, with declining ethical standards across society, with a mounting number of new Americans from countries where tax cheating is a way of life, and with the emergence of the Internet, tax fraud is growing faster than ever. So, too, the practice of tax avoidance by lawyers and accountants who file returns for clients that they know are questionable at best.

Add to this mix members of Congress who increasingly fall into one of three camps and sometimes all three: those who cater to the affluent — in no small part because they supply the cash to run political campaigns; those who are indifferent to the plight of ordinary working folks, and those who sincerely believe that the rich should be lightly taxed.

So when's Critical Mass Day?

Barring some dramatic reversal in Washington, it will come early in this new century, when the existing tax system, if left unattended, collapses from indifference and abuse.

It will be an unfortunate end to what has been a democratic experiment that has served the country well. For all the disenchantment today over the income tax's real or perceived ills, it is worth noting that it was not always so. While never perfect, the tax code that was in place from the 1940s to the 1960s was relatively free of loopholes and tax shelters. Special-interest provisions were inserted far less frequently, and the code favored comparatively few citizens. Income tax rates were much higher. As income increased during those earlier years, so, too, did the multiple tax rates. They began at 20 percent and rose to 91 percent on incomes over $400,000. This was the progressive structure that worked to moderate the income gap between the nation's richest and poorest citizens.

At the time, this limitation on huge incomes was crucial in fostering the growth of a healthy society. Europe and Japan were still recovering from World War II. The United States was the only significant economic force around. Absent the restraints of higher tax rates, the great American middle class might never have emerged on the scale that it did.

But beginning in the 1960s, and then continuing through the 1970s, 1980s, and 1990s, a succession of Congresses and presidents slashed rates and amended and revised the tax code interminably, rendering it deformed and unintelligible, most noteworthy for its exceptions and exclusions. In other words, the real problem is not the tax code. It's Congress and the White House, where a series of occupants, Democrats and Republicans, either shared Congress's disdain for the income tax (President Reagan) or lacked any commitment to it (President Clinton).

Now, rather than reform the existing system by eliminating special-interest provisions and reducing complexity, lawmakers, playing off the disenchantment they have created, are drumming up support for the abolition of the income tax. In doing so, they are spreading misinformation, citing mythical statistics, and misleading voters to build public sentiment for their cause. They are creating the false impression that the federal income tax has never been higher and that its burden has never been greater. Neither is true.*

Washington abounds with the mathematically impaired when it comes to taxes, and Rod Grams, a Republican senator from Minnesota, is fairly typical.

"Since 1993, Federal taxes have increased by 50 percent," Grams told the Senate in March 1999. "They have grown twice as much as Government spending and as a result, Americans today have the largest tax burden since World War II, and it is still growing."[3]

IRS tax data paint an entirely different picture. For 1993 they show that individuals and families with incomes between $30,000 and $40,000 paid an average of $3,521 in income tax. By 1997, their tax bill had fallen $174, to $3,347. That amounted to a tax cut of 5 percent. Individuals and families with incomes between $40,000 and $50,000 paid an average of $4,813 in income tax in 1993. By 1997, their tax bill had edged down $17, to $4,796, a tax cut of one-third of 1 percent. And finally, those in the $50,000-to-$75,000 bracket saw their taxes fall $167, from $7,454 in 1993 to $7,287 in 1997, a tax reduction of 2 percent. In other words, the heart of Middle America saw its taxes go down — not up by 50 percent, as Grams claimed.

Yet critics continue to claim that the federal tax burden is now much heavier. "The income tax burden in the 1950s was 5 percent,"

---

* Critics would have you believe that the rich are already overtaxed. You have heard the statistics, notably that the top 1 percent of income earners account for one-third of total federal income tax collections. What the critics neglect to mention is that one reason for the large dollar amount of taxes paid collectively by those at the top is that's where all the money is, more so than ever before. But more significantly, the average tax bill of upper-income individuals and families is quite low by historical standards. In 1954, all those with incomes of more than $1 million paid on average $1.1 million in income tax. Their effective tax rate: 55 percent. (This group includes people who earned from $1 million to $100 milion or more. The taxes paid are an average for all those individuals and families.) By 1996, persons in that income class paid on average $875,000 in income tax — or $225,000 less than the earlier generation. Their effective tax rate: 32 percent. If the 1954 tax rates had been in place in 1996, the top income earners would have paid an additional $625,000 in income tax. But wait, you say, $1 million in 1996 did not go as far as it did in 1954. True. But neither did $25,000. Yet the combined income and Social Security tax burden on that lower-paid group fell less than on the richest of the rich over the four decades. It's also important to keep in mind that in 1954 the income of most middle-class families was derived from one working spouse. Now it's two.

Jack Kingston, a Republican congressman from Georgia, told the House in March 1999. "In the 1970s when we were growing up, most of us in this room, it was 16 percent. Today it is 24 percent."[4]

Wrong again. In 1954, median family income was $4,167. That year, people filing returns with incomes from $4,000 to $4,500 paid an average of $376 in income tax. That was an effective rate of 9 percent. By way of contrast, in 1997, when median family income was $44,568, individuals and families with incomes from $40,000 to $50,000 paid $4,796 in income tax, for an 11 percent rate. Thus the income tax burden on middle-income families grew by just 2 percentage points between the decades — not by the 19 points asserted by Kingston, who came up with his fictitious tax burden by understating the rates of the 1950s and grossly overstating those of the 1990s.

Not to be outdone, Senator Paul Coverdell, a Georgia Republican, said flatly in September 1999 that "American workers are paying at the highest tax level they have paid since World War II." That isn't remotely true.

In the 1950s, the maximum rate was 91 percent. Under current law, it's 39.6 percent. As recently as 1980, individuals and families with incomes of more than $1 million — that's everyone who earned anywhere from $1 million to $100 million — paid, on average, $999,944 in income tax. Seventeen years later, they paid $810,728. Thus, the top-income-earning families in America have enjoyed a 19 percent tax cut, for a savings of $189,216. Not only was the tax rate on millionaires higher in 1980 than in 1997, not only did those individuals and families pay out more in income tax than those who came later, they did so on smaller incomes. The effective tax rate for millionaires in 1980 was 48 percent. In 1997, it was 30 percent.

Overall, the tax burden has increased for average Americans, but only if you look at all taxes — federal, state, and local — combined. As we have seen, the federal income tax burden has actually gone down. But the federal Social Security and Medicare tax bill has soared. So too state and local taxes, as Washington shifts more of the cost of services to the state and local levels.

Much like the child who murdered his parents and then asked the court for leniency because he was an orphan, members of Congress complain that the tax code is riddled with loopholes and unintelligible language. They, of course, are responsible for that.

To understand the games lawmakers play, look no further than the marriage tax penalty. For fifty years, Congress has amended and revised the tax code to deal with it. Sometimes a law change eased the penalty; other times it increased it. Sometimes it increased the marriage bonus; other times it lowered it. And sometimes it penalized single people more than married couples. The only constant has been Congress's refusal to come up with a permanent remedy.

Instead, the lingering presence of the penalty, which levies more taxes on some couples for being married than if they filed as single persons, gives lawmakers a chance to vent righteous indignation over this injustice.

In a speech typical of what you hear in many sessions of Congress, Gerald C. Weller, an Illinois Republican, delivered the standard speech on the floor of the House in June 1999: "The marriage tax is not only unfair, it is wrong. . . . Do Americans feel that it is fair that 28 million married working couples pay on average $1,400 more in higher taxes just because they are married?"[5]

What Weller and other lawmakers neglect to mention is that Congress put the penalty there. It comes and goes as an issue, periodically providing new generations of lawmakers with a reliable subject they can rant about to demonstrate they are looking out for their constituents' best interest. Except they aren't. They always "fix" the penalty with a temporary patch, guaranteeing the issue will resurface in a few years and make wonderful political fodder all over again. Sometimes, the lawmakers themselves remove the patch.

The penalty arises out of the interplay between multiple tax rates and filing schedules, and it's highest in those situations where both incomes are about equal. As a result, many married couples who file a joint return, with each spouse reporting income, pay more in tax than if they had filed individual returns. Yet not everyone is a loser. Congress long ago fashioned a kind of marriage tax lottery in which some people lose but more people win. They get a marriage bonus. That is, they pay less in tax by filing a joint return than they would if they filed individually.

The Congressional Budget Office estimated that in 1996 the marriage penalty cost 20.9 million families — 42 percent of couples — $28.8 billion. At the same time, another 25.3 million families — 51 percent of couples — enjoyed a marriage bonus worth $32.9 billion. On average, the losers paid a penalty of $1,380. The winners pocketed a bonus of $1,300.

Reacting to outcry over the penalty in 1981, Congress wrote a two-earner deduction into the Economic Recovery Tax Act of that year. The provision allowed a married couple to deduct up to $3,000 from the income of the lower-earning spouse. While the deduction did not eliminate the penalty, it eased it. Five years later, in the Tax Reform Act of 1986, Congress took it back. With only two tax rates — 15 and 28 percent — four-fifths of the taxpaying population would be in the lower bracket. The marriage penalty was seen of little consequence.

But as Congress is wont to do, a few years later it tinkered with the system again, adding some more rates and exacerbating the penalty, prompting yet another outcry and another round of congressional handwringing, triggered in large part by the news accounts of people who said they were divorcing to save money or delaying marriage to avoid the penalty. A typical article, published in 1998 by *USA Today,* told of a young Indiana couple who were postponing their wedding after their accountant informed them being married would increase their tax bill.

"That put the brakes on it," the man said. "We love each other, but we just can't afford to be married."[6]

Congress rewrote the marriage tax clause and inserted it into the 1999 tax bill. President Clinton later vetoed the overall bill, but the marriage tax was resurrected again in 2000.

While most of the income tax's outspoken critics are Republicans, you shouldn't read too much into that. Many Democrats are closet supporters of the GOP campaign to kill the income tax. And this, too, spells trouble for the tax's future. The party that was the staunch defender of the income tax in the 1950s is now, with occasional exceptions, eerily silent. There are no ringing defenses, no stirring debates over fixing what Congress has broken.

So what does Congress have in mind to replace the progressive income tax? Two alternatives have captured center stage: the flat tax and a national sales tax. The flat tax would be an across-the-board income tax on most citizens at the same rate, while a sales tax would be a tax on goods and services at the point of purchase. Proponents of the two taxes are promoting each plan for similar reasons.

The public is assured that either would simplify the tax system, eliminate burdensome record keeping, cut everyone's taxes, send special interests packing, and stimulate the economy. In truth, neither tax would do anything of the sort. They would, however, have the same common result: a hefty tax cut for the nation's wealthiest taxpayers and a greater tax burden on everyone else.

It may seem difficult to understand why elected officials would reduce the tax burden for a few at the expense of the many. But in Washington, when the subject is taxes, the wealthy and powerful usually get their way.

THE FLAT TAX

Proposed in one form or another from time to time since shortly after the progressive income tax was enacted in 1913, the flat tax has always been shot down. But, as frustration with the current complex tax code has escalated, as special interests have had their way with lawmakers, and as Americans have become increasingly disillusioned with the way the code has been manipulated, interest in the flat tax has flared anew. On the surface, it has great appeal. There would be only one rate. There would be no deductions and thus no record keeping. The tax return would be the size of a post-card. It sounds too good to be true. And it is.

When the flat tax was first proposed in the 1920s, its biggest advocate was Andrew W. Mellon, the Secretary of the Treasury from 1921 to 1932. Had there been a Forbes 400 list of richest Americans at the time, Mellon, a conservative Republican from Pittsburgh, would have ranked in the top half-dozen. He had made his fortune in banking, oil, coal, aluminum, and a slew of other businesses. When he took over at Treasury in 1921, the top tax rate was 73 percent on taxable income over $1 million.

In those years, the tax applied to few people. In 1928, only 4.1 million individuals and families out of a population of 120 million filed returns. And just 1 percent of the filers — 43,200 people — paid 78 percent of the income tax collected.

Like many others of his class, Mellon resented the progressive rates. In 1924, he paid $1.2 million in income tax. He was instrumental in persuading Congress to lower the maximum rate from 73 percent to 25 percent during his eleven years in office, but he never achieved his main goal of a flat tax, which he envisioned this way: "It is not too much to hope that some day we may get back on a tax basis of 10 percent, the old Hebrew tithe, which was always considered a fairly heavy tax."[7]

When Mellon left office in 1932, the flat tax lost its most public and vocal supporter. But by decade's end, the idea had resurfaced. With the country mired in the Great Depression, the top rate that Mellon had lowered to 25 percent rocketed back up to 79 percent on taxable income over $5 million. Once again, those at the top were distressed, and they appealed to sympathetic members of Congress for relief.

In January 1939, Representative Emanuel Celler, a liberal New York Democrat, introduced a resolution calling for a constitutional amendment to cap the top tax rate at 25 percent. Sounding a lot like Republican Mellon, Democrat Celler said that "it does not make sense to perpetuate tax laws and to impose tax rates which discourage risk taking by those who have this type of capital to invest in productive enterprises."[8]

With the world on the brink of war and the country still suffering from the Depression, Celler could muster little enthusiasm among his colleagues for what became known as "the millionaires' amendment." So its patrons tried a backdoor approach. They sought to persuade two-thirds of the states to petition Congress to amend the Constitution.

To wage the campaign, they formed a tax-exempt organization called the Committee for Constitutional Government. The committee was a forerunner of similar groups that flourish in our time. It was headed by Frank E. Gannett, a New York newspaper owner whose company would later become the Gannett Company Inc., publisher of *USA Today.*

After some initial successes, the campaign rapidly lost steam after World War II started, even though rates climbed ever higher and the income tax, for the first time, became a mass tax. The top rate went to 88 percent on taxable income over $200,000, and the tax was expanded to cover all working individuals through withholding.

In the postwar period, with the tax-limitation drive languishing at the state level, the action shifted back to Congress, where new legislation was introduced to cap the income tax at 25 percent. Once again, the movement attracted little popular support and within two years the campaign was dead, killed off by critics in and out of Congress.

One of the movement's most prominent opponents, Erwin N. Griswold, dean of Harvard Law School, spoke out on behalf of the progressive income tax and warned of the harm that would befall American society if the tax was fixed at one rate. In 1952 he wrote:

It is very clear that the benefits of such a change would redound to the relatively rich, and the burdens would have to be borne by the relatively poor. Not only would the change in effect eliminate progressive income and estate taxation . . . but it would confer the financial benefits almost exclusively on persons of very large incomes. . . .

For more than half a century, we have imposed taxes in this country in accordance with ability to pay. Progressive taxation has not merely been accepted, but has been widely hailed as a sound and constructive economic policy.[9]

Another thirty years went by before the flat-tax idea was revived in the early days of President Reagan's first term. In the end, Reagan and Congress settled on two rates in the Tax Reform Act of 1986. About four-fifths of the taxpaying population would be taxed at a 15 percent rate; the rest at 28 percent. What followed? The tax bills of the nation's wealthiest individuals and families plummeted and the income gap widened — not just between rich and poor, but between the rich and the middle class.

Today the flat tax is back. Of the several proposals trotted out during the late 1990s, the most popular is the one advanced by Senator Richard C. Shelby, an Alabama Republican, and Representative Richard K. Armey, a Texas Republican who became the House majority leader in 1995. They labeled their bill the Freedom and Fairness Restoration Act of 1999. Here is how they describe it:

The Armey-Shelby flat tax (H.R. 1040) scraps the entire income tax code and replaces it with a flat-rate income tax that treats all Americans the same. This plan would simplify the tax code, promote economic opportunity, and restore fairness and integrity to the tax system. The flat rate would be phased in over a three-year period, with a 19 percent rate for the first two years and a 17 percent rate for subsequent years.

Individuals and businesses would pay the same rate. The plan eliminates all deductions and credits. The only income not subject to tax would be a generous personal exemption that every American would receive. For a family of four, the first $35,400 in income would be exempt from tax. There are no breaks for special interests. No loopholes for powerful lobbies. Just a simple tax system that treats every American the same. . . .

No matter how much money you make, what kind of business you're in, whether or not you have a lobbyist in Washington, you will be taxed at the same rate as every other taxpayer. Individuals pay 17 percent of all wages, salaries, and pensions, after subtracting allowances. In 2001, when fully phased in, the family allowances [would] be $12,200 for a single person, $24,400 for a married couple filing jointly, and $5,500 for each dependent child.[10]

Armey and Shelby found a receptive audience. For several years, sentiment had been building in favor of a flat tax, as one lawmaker after another expressed support for the concept. Representative David J. Weldon, a Florida Republican, said it would "reduce the tax burden on working Americans and make the process of paying taxes much simpler."[11] Senator Larry E. Craig, an Idaho Republican, said it would "reward work, promote savings and economic growth."[12] Senator Connie Mack III, the Florida Republican, said a flat tax would "radically reduce the tax compliance burden currently imposed on every individual and business."[13] In what may have been the most grandiose vision of all, Representative Merrill Cook, a Utah Republican, contended a "flat tax can reform our entire political system."[14]

Even the Joint Economic Committee of Congress touted the benefits, noting that "levying a flat tax is not a radical idea. In fact, except for the income tax, flat taxes abound."[15] The committee pointed to Social Security and Medicare taxes as examples.

Actually, only Medicare is a true flat tax, with the 1.45 percent rate applied to all wage and salary income. Social Security, on the other hand, is the harshest of all regressive taxes in that the 6.2 percent rate is only applied to income up to a certain level. In 2000, earnings above $76,200 were not taxed. As a result, the more money a person earns, the lower the real tax rate. This is why Social Security and Medicare taxes fall far harder on middle- and lower-income families.

In 1954, a median-income family whose earnings came exclusively from wages paid $72 in Social Security tax. The effective tax rate was 1.73 percent. There was no disability insurance tax or Medicare tax. By 1998, the middle-income family paid $3,575 in Social Security and Medicare taxes based on a rate of 7.65 percent. From 1954 to 1998, a middle-class family's Social Security and Medicare tax bill jumped a staggering 4,865 percent. If median family income had gone up at the same pace, the average American family today would earn $207,000. As for those at the top, the family with an income of, say, $2 million pays Social Security and Medicare taxes at a rate of 1.66 percent. That means the median-income family's tax rate is four and a half times higher than the rich family's, but the rich family's income is forty-three times greater.

As for a flat income tax, it's nothing like what its backers have made it out to be. Let's look at some of the consequences of the Armey-Shelby flat tax, or any other version of a flat tax:

- On the individual side, the 17 percent rate would produce about $300 billion less revenue than the existing tax code. That's because many people from the upper middle class to the top would pay far less, and some income that is taxed now, like capital gains, would be exempt. Corporate tax collections also would fall well below the present level because the rate would be cut in half.
- To offset the large reduction in revenue, and the massive deficits that would follow, Congress could slash government spending dramatically, thereby shifting the cost of essential programs to the state and local levels. These taxes already hit middle- and lower-income people the hardest.
- If lawmakers could not bring themselves to make the draconian cuts — cuts that would reduce the United States to a second-rate country — they would be forced to raise the one, simple tax rate from 17 percent to 30 percent or more.

For the last word on the flat tax, let's turn to former senator Russell B. Long, the Louisiana Democrat and longtime chairman of the Senate Finance Committee who served thirty-eight years in the Senate before retiring in 1987. Once asked about the merits of a flat tax, Long said: "If you are rich, you'll love it. If you are not rich, look out. . . . The fact is that just about any flat tax system would give a big tax cut to the rich and finance it with a substantial tax increase on lower- and middle-income Americans."[16]

THE NATIONAL SALES TAX

If the flat tax would give the nation's rich an awesome tax cut, the other alternative being touted to replace the income tax — a national sales tax — would be an even greater windfall for them. As is the case with the flat tax, there are several different proposals, but all call for the tax to be levied on both goods and services.

Typical is one put forth in 1999 by Representative Wilbert J. (Billy) Tauzin of Louisiana, a strident opponent of the income tax, who started his political life in Congress as a Democrat but switched sides in 1995. Tauzin's proposed National Retail Sales Tax Act, which calls for a tax rate of 15 percent, has attracted a large following on Capitol Hill. It would eliminate the individual income tax, the corporate income tax, estate and gift taxes, capital gains taxes, and most excise taxes. It also would abolish the IRS. So what would life then look like?

Just about everything you buy would be taxed under Tauzin's plan. Imagine that you and your family are in the market for a new home, and you have found one that everyone loves. The price is $150,000. Tack on another $22,500 in sales tax. But don't worry; you won't have to deliver the cash up front. Just add $94 — plus interest — to your monthly mortgage payment for the next twenty years. Naturally, you will need carpets, furniture, and appliances — let's say $15,000 worth. Add $2,250. (If you pay for the items over forty-eight months, add an extra $47 a month plus interest to cover the sales tax.) What if you and the family want to rent rather than buy property? No problem. Add the 15 percent sales tax to your monthly rent. Instead of paying $800 a month, now it's $920.

Since your car has just passed the 125,000-mile mark, you replace it with a fully loaded Ford Taurus. So add another $3,000 to the $20,000 selling price. Again, though, you need not pay it all immediately. Just add $63 to your monthly car loan payment over the next four years. Plus interest. Of course, you could lease the Taurus. But the 15 percent will be added to the monthly lease payment.

Need back-to-school clothes and sneakers for the kids? Add 15 percent to the bill. The same for school supplies and books. Toys at Christmas? That's right, 15 percent. Same for the batteries to run the electronic games. Likewise your daily newspaper and magazines. Visit the neighborhood bar? Add 15 percent to the price of a beer. So, too, your morning coffee and bottled water. Want to take the family out for dinner at your favorite restaurant? Add 15 percent. Do the same when you make your weekly trip to the grocery store. Buy a computer and printer? Add 15 percent.

Next comes the tax never before tried — a 15 percent sales tax on services. Well, that's not entirely accurate. Florida enacted a 5 percent tax on services that took effect on July 1, 1987 — and then the fun began. National advertisers boycotted the state. Corporations canceled their Florida meetings. Conventions moved to other states. Hotels and restaurants, radio and television stations, real estate agents and homebuilders, the advertising industry and newspapers mounted a massive antitax lobbying campaign that fueled public outrage. In the words of one reporter, members of the state legislature "saw their political futures flash before their eyes."[17] As one lawmaker described the situation: "When you have a coalition of national advertisers and piano teachers, you're in trouble."[18] Legislators acted predictably. The tax that was approved in the summer was repealed by winter.

Members of Congress see no such problem with a federal sales tax on services. After all, the tax will apply to services in all states. No one will be able to escape it. Wherever you may live, when you send in the check for the homeowner's insurance covering the family home, add 15 percent. Ditto the car insurance, family life insurance policies, and the monthly utility bills — telephone, heating oil, natural gas, electricity, and water. Add another 15 percent to the bills for garbage collection, cable television, the cell phone, the Internet connection. Drop the young children off at a day-care center? You got it: Add 15 percent. The same when you get your clothes dry-cleaned. If your car breaks down and needs to be towed, add 15 percent.

When you visit the barber, hair stylist, or manicurist, add 15 percent. Want to go to the movies? Add 15 percent. Watch a video at home? Add 15 percent. Go to the health club? Add 15 percent. Join a weight loss club? Add 15 percent. Tack on an extra 15 percent to the price of tickets for baseball, football, basketball, hockey, and soccer games, and for the theater, opera, and symphony. Tap the ATM machine? Add 15 percent to the bank fee. Call in an electrician to fix the wiring in your house? Add 15 percent. Take the family pet for grooming and boarding? Add 15 percent. Get the yard landscaped or tended by a lawn service company? Add 15 percent. Install a home security system? Add 15 percent to the monthly charge. Hire a plumber, roofer, or house painter? Add 15 percent to their bills. File for divorce? Add 15 percent to the legal charges. Bury your parents? That's right, 15 percent on the funeral bill. Same for the tombstone.

Buy plane tickets for a visit to Disney World? Add 15 percent. Rent a car when you get to Orlando? Add 15 percent. Your admission tickets to Disney World? Another 15 percent. How about a trip to Las Vegas instead? Add 15 percent to all the money you put in the slot machines or wager at the blackjack tables. Add 15 percent to your hotel bill and cab fares.

As you can see, the sales-and-service tax piles up quickly. Every time you open your wallet or purse and take out money, every time you write a check, add 15 percent. But that's good, in the judgment of many in Congress. Under this system, they say, you can see exactly how much you are paying in tax. This will help you to make more prudent decisions as a consumer. You will save your money. That's the view of Representative John E. Linder, a Republican congressman from Georgia, a onetime dentist and enthusiastic supporter of a national sales tax:

> It's possible that people will spend every penny they have. They'll have a considerable increase in take-home pay [with the end of withholding]. But we can't tell you how to spend your money. You'll have more incentive to save because you won't be taxed on savings, you won't be taxed on capital gains or any investments. But if you choose to spend more money, you'll pay more taxes, and I think that's fair. You're making this decision, though, entirely by yourself. It's a voluntary decision. You'll pay as much taxes as you want, when you want to pay up.[19]

It's your call. No longer will money be withheld from your paycheck. You don't want to pay the sales tax? Simple. Don't buy anything or go anywhere. Don't buy the new house or the new car. Or eat out once a week. Or go to the movies once a month. Or take the kids to a sporting event. Or buy all those groceries and clothing. Of course, if enough people make that decision, then the tax rate would have to be raised to compensate for the reduced spending. And this brings us to the truly bad news. The real-world tax rate would be much higher than the 15 percent proposed in the Tauzin bill. It would be in the 20-to-30-percent range. Here's the math.

In 1998, spendable personal income in the United States totaled about $6.4 trillion. If every dollar were spent — and there were no additional savings — the 15 percent sales tax would generate $960 billion in revenue. While that may sound like a lot of money, it's not nearly as much as the existing tax system produces. Individual income tax collections alone in 1998 totaled $829 billion. The corporate income tax yielded another $189 billion. Estate and gift taxes produced $24 billion. Excise taxes, $22 billion. Total tax collections: $1.1 trillion. That means a 15 percent sales tax would leave the U.S. government with a deficit of $140 billion. But that's only the beginning.

Any sales tax will have to provide a floor so that the nation's poorest people are not taxed on life's necessities: food, clothing, and shelter. Everyone would receive this basic exemption, similar to the standard deduction in the current income tax. Subtract another $100 billion or so from the sales tax revenue. This brings the shortfall to $240 billion.

Another potential massive drain: the Internet. Many members of Congress are pushing legislation to make the Internet tax free. If they succeed, add many more tens of billions of dollars to the deficit.

Next, consider one of the major components of personal spending: health care. Are members of Congress really going to impose a 15 percent tax on the hospital and doctor bills of patients undergoing heart surgery or chemotherapy? Are members of Congress really going to add a 15 percent tax on the prescription bills of diabetics taking insulin or the dialysis treatment of kidney patients? Are members of Congress really going to add 15 percent to the medical bills of a woman having a baby or a person injured in a car accident?

Not likely. Even Florida didn't try to do that. So remove more tens of billions of dollars from the sales tax revenue pool, bringing the total deficit close to $300 billion. Remember, that's for one year. It means that every four years the U.S. government would pile another trillion dollars on the national debt.

Since a deficit of that magnitude would be intolerable, the sales tax rate would have to go up. The more likely rate: between 20 and 25 percent. Let's assume the lower figure. Now the $150,000 house costs $180,000. The $20,000 car costs $24,000. The $15,000 home furnishings cost $18,000.

Beyond the rate, there is the question of how a sales tax would be administered. Members of Congress who support it are also intent on killing both the income tax and the IRS in order to, as they put it, stop intrusive federal agents from prying into your personal finances. Nearly 100,000 jobs would disappear in Washington. Who, then, collects the national sales tax?

The Tauzin bill assigns that responsibility to state governments under the theory that nearly all have been collecting similar levies for many years. The states obviously would be compelled to hire additional staff. For taking on the hugely expanded workload, the states could keep a portion of the federal sales taxes they collect — 1 to 2 percent at a minimum — and then forward the balance to the U.S. Treasury. That would add another $10-plus billion to the federal sales tax deficit.

But ponder the mechanics of all this. The tax will be assessed by individual merchants at the point of sale. They will get to keep one-half of 1 percent of the tax collections for their efforts. Add another $5 billion to the deficit. But how will anyone know the amount of a business's true sales? Will all this take place on the honor system? Or will there be intrusive state government agents looking over the books to determine whether the tax owed was actually paid? Which brings up another issue — fraud. Opportunities for tax evasion under a sales tax system would be endless, so add more tens of billions of dollars to the deficit.

Advocates of the sales tax say that one of its big selling points is simplicity. No more complicated Internal Revenue Code or arcane government regulations. James A. Traficant Jr., a Democratic representative from Ohio, said he supported Tauzin's bill because "the only way to ensure sustained economic growth in America is to abolish the income tax and the IRS, and replace it with a system that is simple and fair."[20] Over in the Senate, Rod Grams of Minnesota said he supported a national sales tax because it would be "fairer (and) more simple."[21]

Simple?

Most states do indeed have sales taxes. Most states, even Florida, also exclude a number of items, like food. If a federal sales tax were instituted, would the states amend their laws and tax food and all the other goods currently exempt? Or would they impose the federal sales tax on groceries and the other items, but no local tax? How do casinos in Las Vegas impose a 15 percent sales tax on people playing slot machines? Is it levied whenever anyone buys a roll of quarters or silver dollars? Is it imposed with each hand played at the blackjack table, or with each wager at the baccarat table? Who is responsible for the tax when a consumer buys a product and charges it on a credit card? Do the credit card companies pay the tax? What happens if the merchant fails to include the tax? Are the credit card companies still liable? Will they charge interest on the sales tax?

While it's true that most states have sales taxes, most states and many cities also derive a portion of their revenue from income taxes that are keyed to federal reporting rules. If the federal income tax were abolished, would they set up their own income tax structure? Or would they compensate with a new sales tax of their own? If that happened, the overall tax rate would reach into the 30-percent range. That assumes a federal rate of at least 20 percent, a combined state and city rate that exceeds 8 percent in some areas, and several more percentage points to replace the lost state income tax revenue.

Further complicating the picture is that with few exceptions, states do not tax services. That decision was made long ago on the theory that evasion would be rampant and too difficult to detect. Under the proposed federal sales tax, states would be obliged to set up a new bureaucracy with agents trained in detecting service tax fraud. It would require an army every bit as large as the IRS. The reason: no obvious paper trail. How do sales tax collectors know that you hired an attorney to write a will? How do they know you ride in a cab daily? How do they know you hired a plumber to fix the toilet? How do they know you get your nails done every week?

Of course, they could implement regulations requiring service providers to keep meticulous records and file detailed, multipage tax forms. Or they could set up elaborate surveillance networks to monitor individual transactions. Or they could conduct random intensive audits. But how do they know the true billings of manicurists and lawyers and couriers and Web page designers and dance instructors and locksmiths and employment agencies and accountants and piano teachers and caterers and carpenters and photographers and carpet cleaners and personal trainers and hair stylists?

Lawmakers who advocate a national sales tax because it would be simpler and easier to administer than the income tax are at best disingenuous. It would be every bit as byzantine as the current Internal Revenue Code. It would be riddled with exceptions and exemptions. It would spawn as many special-interest groups as the income tax. It would be even more intrusive.

Special interests would lobby for rebates or partial exclusions. Indeed, the sales tax would begin its life with exceptions. Buy a car and pay an extra 15 percent or 20 percent. Buy stock and pay no tax. That's an investment. It doesn't count as an expenditure. Thus, if you have enough money to play in the stock market, you pay no tax. If you make only enough to live on — which is the case with about four-fifths of the population — you pay the tax on everything. Hence, the lobbies. The homebuilding industry would seek a full or at least partial exemption, just as it did in Florida. So, too, the insurance industry. Utilities, car manufacturers, banks, credit card companies, the gaming industry — all would seek special treatment. Politicians representing poor areas would lobby for tax-free zones exempt from the sales tax, just like the enterprise zones of today. When the economy takes a downward turn, as it always does in time, businesses hit hardest would demand tax relief to stimulate sales of their goods and services. With each exception, the tax rate would rise.

Another major exemption built into the proposed system from the beginning would cover businesses large and small. They would be exempt. They would pay no sales tax on the goods and services they buy. You would pay tax on water. They wouldn't. You would pay tax on electricity. They wouldn't. You would pay tax on a car. They wouldn't. You would pay tax on insurance. They wouldn't. You would pay tax on a telephone. They wouldn't. In fact, with the demise of the income tax, they would pay little or no tax at all. They would be able to enjoy all the services and protective benefits of government free of charge — you may recall the chief beneficiary of America's military presence in Kuwait was the U.S. oil industry, not the average American.

Although its backers invariably call the sales tax the "fairest tax," it is anything but that. To see why, let's use a variation of the concept of Tax Freedom Day — that day when Americans have paid all the taxes they owe for the year, based on their gross income. Observe what would happen if a national sales tax were the federal government's only source of revenue.

Let's compare a middle-income family, the Joe Average Family, with Mr. Wall Street Speculator, who collects $50 million in investment income in 2001. Assume the $50 million is his total income and that he decides to build a $10 million home. The 15 percent sales tax totals $1.5 million. Mr. Speculator will pay off the sales tax in eight days, assuming a five-day work week, fifty-two weeks a year. That means Tax Freedom Day for him falls on January 11, 2001.

Now suppose the Joe Average Family, with an income of $50,000, decides to buy a $150,000 home. At 15 percent, the sales tax comes to $22,500. The family will be required to work 117 days to pay it. For the Joe Average Family, Tax Freedom Day falls on June 13. In other words, the middle-income family must work fifteen times as long as Mr. Speculator to pay the tax on their house. To add to the disparity, Mr. Speculator's home is worth 67 times more than theirs. And if the sales tax rate were 20 percent? He would pay it in 10 days, the average family in 156 days.

What about the necessities of life? Like food? Suppose the Joe Average Family, two adults and one child, spends $150 a week on groceries. That brings the yearly food bill to $7,800. At 15 percent, the tax amounts to $1,170. The family works six days to pay the yearly tax on its food.

As for Mr. Speculator, let's assume he eats on a grander scale and spends five times as much for food, or $39,000 a year. His tax totals $5,850, which means it takes him a mere fifteen minutes of work to pay for the tax on his food. Looked at another way, the average family would be required to work 192 times as long as Mr. Speculator to pay the sales tax on their food. Of course, if he spent no more on food than the average family did, he would work just three minutes to pay the tax.

Perhaps it's a bit clearer now as to who would benefit the most from a sales tax. One other statistic may help you decide whether or not it's "fair."

IRS tax return data show that for 1997, a total of 263,178 individuals and families reported incomes between $500,000 and $1 million. The average income in that range: $672,854. If these people spent every penny on goods and services, a 15 percent sales tax would cost them $100,928. How does that compare with the income tax they paid? It represents a 49 percent cut from their average income tax payment of $196,610. In short, replacing the income tax with a 15 percent sales tax will allow them to pocket an extra $95,682.

Now look at how people with incomes of $40,000 to $50,000 would fare, again using the 1997 tax return data. A total of 9,768,567 individuals and families reported an average income of $44,713. If they spent every penny on goods and services, a 15 percent sales tax would cost them $6,707. Subtract a base exemption of about $2,000 that a family of three would receive and they would pay $4,707. How much of a tax cut would that mean? Sorry. Essentially none. That's because they paid $4,796 in income tax. Where the picture turns nasty is when the sales tax rate hits 20 percent. That would mean a 45 percent tax increase for the middle-income family.

As you can see, the people who will profit handsomely under a sales tax are the nation's wealthiest citizens. For the 1997 tax year, 142,556 returns were filed by individuals and families reporting incomes of more than $1 million. The average income of this group was $2,902,758. What would they pay under a 15 percent federal sales tax? If they spent every penny of their income (a seeming impossibility), their federal tax bill would be $435,414. A lot of money? Not really. Their average income tax payment in 1997 was $856,721. Thus a 15 percent sales tax would allow them to slash their federal tax bill by 49 percent, giving them an extra $421,307.

But wait. A sales tax is meant to encourage Americans to save. Besides, all those millionaires are not going to spend every cent they earn. So let's assume they invest 20 percent of their income. Now the 15 percent sales tax would cost them just $348,331. That would amount to a whopping tax cut of 59 percent, giving them an extra $508,390.

As bad as Tauzin's 15 percent tax would be, there's another sales tax proposal in Congress that is even worse. It would not only eliminate the individual income tax, corporate income tax, capital gains tax, estate tax and the IRS, it would cancel Social Security and Medicare taxes. It would also repeal the Sixteenth Amendment, which authorized the income tax.

The cleverly named "FairTax" was introduced in the summer of 1999 by Representatives John Linder, a Georgia Republican, and Collin C. Peterson, a Minnesota Democrat. The Linder-Peterson proposal, which provides for a sales tax of 23 percent on all goods and services, was devised by a Houston group called Americans for Fair Taxation.

Linder and Peterson spent the summer of 1999 crisscrossing the country, appearing on talk shows and at town hall gatherings, meeting with newspaper editors and like-minded citizens, pushing their basic one-tax-does-it-all concept and espousing the end of the IRS and its agents who, they say, pry into the most personal secrets of individuals.

"There's something wrong with the tax code," Linder says. "It can't be fixed. We have an intrusive and corrosive tax code. Since the 1986 tax reform there have been 6,200 more changes. The fair tax is less intrusive. You would get 100 percent of your paycheck and you wouldn't have to report on everything you do.... It would eliminate the IRS in 2005."[22]

Linder and Peterson are banking on a groundswell of public support to make their tax a reality. "The American people are way ahead of the politicians on this," says Linder. "The system that we have is unworkable. It's unfair; it's counterproductive; it's punitive. Our system is entirely voluntary."[23] The two lawmakers already have won the hearts and minds of some newspaper editors. In an editorial headlined "A FAIR PROPOSAL: National sales tax deserves support," an *Atlanta Journal and Constitution* editorialist wrote:

> Under their Fair Tax proposal, which warrants serious attention, you'd never file a tax return. The IRS wouldn't need 110,000 employees with the power to bring you to your financial knees. There wouldn't even be much need for the IRS.
>
> Best of all, you would receive your gross pay. No payroll tax, excise tax, Medicare tax, confiscatory death tax or levies on income, savings, investments, capital gains. The government would no longer tax productive activity while giving big breaks to special interests.
>
> The income tax would die a joyful death, and in its place would be a 23 percent national sales tax. Buy a loaf of bread, and you'd be taxed 23 percent. Actually, you'd have to buy more than a loaf of bread, because the government would grant an exemption for basic necessities. . . .
>
> It's simple. Buy a product or service, pay a tax. Save and invest, pay no tax. And best of all, Uncle Sam would no longer penalize Americans for working, as if that is a bad thing.[24]

But if it would take a tax rate of 20 percent or more to generate enough money to run the government and provide basic services, what would happen with a 23 percent tax rate that also eliminates Social Security and Medicare taxes?

The short answer is gargantuan deficits of more than a third-of-a-trillion dollars every year — a sum that would swell to upwards of a half-trillion dollars when the Baby Boomers retire. That assumes that proponents of the 23 percent rate intend to preserve Social Security and that their plan is not a hidden agenda to kill it.

As is the case with the 20 percent or even 15 percent rate, everyone at the top of the income ladder would enjoy a hefty tax cut. The tax bills of everyone in the middle and at the bottom would soar.

LOBBYING FOR THE RICH

As history always does, and most assuredly when it comes to taxes, it is repeating itself. Just as grassroots organizations sprang to life in the 1940s to support the idea of a 25 percent flat tax, so, too, have similar groups grown up to back both a national sales tax and the current version of the flat tax. Like their predecessors, they are tax-exempt organizations — they pay no taxes but seek to influence what you will pay. And as before, their funding has come overwhelmingly from the affluent.

These well-financed, powerful groups are bankrolling advertising campaigns, sponsoring town meetings, placing articles in newspapers, and molding public opinion through their press agents to create the impression of a spontaneous growth of support for overthrowing the income tax.

The group that perhaps best defines these forces is Americans for Fair Taxation (AFT), the organization that sponsored the nationwide speaking tour and town meetings of Congressmen Linder and Peterson to promote a national sales tax.

AFT's ingeniously named "FairTax" program is unlike earlier campaigns against the income tax. AFT avoids the class-warfare rhetoric that has been the stock-in-trade of those who criticize the income tax for penalizing success. Instead, AFT is trying to reach out to all Americans with its message that life would be simpler and better if only the nation would rid itself of the burdensome income tax.

AFT's feel-good Web page is a masterly testament to the power of propaganda. Its most striking image is a color photograph of an attractive young couple outdoors, gazing fondly at the smiling infant between them, an image that embodies the hopes and dreams of all families who want nothing more than a good life for themselves and their children. This greeting-card-style message is superimposed on the photo:

> Imagine . . .
> April 15th in the future . . .

Beside the photo, AFT has sketched out its own hopes for the future:

> No income taxes to pay.
> No individual tax forms to fill out.
> No federal deductions from your paycheck.
> A normal day, no different than April 14th or 16th. . . .
> With the FairTax it could all come true.

It sounds straightforward enough, and it's quite appealing if you don't do the numbers. And AFT is banking on just that — an emotional response to its inviting message, rather than a detailed analysis of the proposal.

AFT was organized in 1995 by a group of wealthy Houstonians, led by Leo E. Linbeck Jr., a construction industry executive, and Jack E. Trotter, an investor and former bank chairman. Both are longtime friends of income tax foe Bill Archer, the Republican chairman of the House Ways and Means Committee. The pair recruited other prosperous sponsors, including Kenneth L. Lay, the chief executive officer of Enron Corporation; Hugh McColl Jr., chief executive of NationsBank; Robert McNair, chairman of Cogen Technologies Inc.; Jack Valenti, head of the Motion Picture Association of America; and Grover Jackson, former general counsel for the Coca-Cola Company.

In its first year, AFT began to build a multimillion-dollar war chest to launch the assault on the income tax. To lend credibility to its campaign for a national sales tax, the group recruited academics from such prestigious universities as Harvard, Boston, and

Stanford. Dale W. Jorgenson, professor of economics at Harvard, was especially outspoken on behalf of the FairTax. "The investments the nation makes are taxed at hefty rates," he claimed. "We want those rates to go to zero, so that there would be a massive incentive to invest in plants and equipment and productivity."[25]

In 1997, AFT began to take its case public. Jack Valenti turned out to be an impassioned advocate, declaring in an article for Cox News Service that appeared under his byline:

> Our income tax system sinks under the weight of more than 1,200 pages of impenetrable prose that no living human being has fully read or understands.
>
> It is choking with dense arithmetic and a bewildering maze of obscurities. Abuses grow, an underground economy flourishes, avoidance is common, evasion increases, investment is punished and savings penalized. No other country in the world relies on such cluttered, messy tax rules which are both contradictory and abrasive.
>
> We need a tax system that is simple, easy to obey, easy to enforce, and most of all, open and fair to all. The one plan that fits these specifications like a silken glove is a national sales tax.[26]

In addition to placing articles such as Valenti's, AFT became adept at garnering endorsements for its national campaign. Whenever a group or public figure spoke favorably of the FairTax, AFT promptly issued a press release declaring another convert had climbed aboard the national sales tax bandwagon. The effect of all this has been to create the illusion that a populist movement is building. But the evidence suggests that this well-orchestrated campaign is being underwritten by a few wealthy benefactors.

Perhaps the best indication of the movement's small membership and deep pockets can be found in the records of a similar group, Citizens for a Sound Economy (CSE), that is also trying to kill the progressive income tax. CSE, based in Washington, has made overturning the current tax code a top priority. In 1998, CSE sponsored a nationwide "Scrap the Code" tour by Congressmen Tauzin and Armey, who went to thirty cities to discuss replacing the income tax with a national sales tax or a flat tax.

CSE and its affiliated foundation call themselves the "voice of consumers for free enterprise" in Washington. CSE claims to have 250,000 members, but a review of the organization's annual IRS returns indicates that whatever its total membership, a handful of wealthy supporters underwrite most of its work. From 1994 through 1997 nine contributors donated $9.2 million, or 61 percent of the organization's total contributions of $15 million during that four-year period.[27]

While the names of the big contributors are not listed, a foundation associated with the Koch brothers of Wichita, Kansas, the billionaire owners of Koch Industries, has long been identified as a major supporter of CSE, and one of the Koch brothers, David H., served as chairman of the CSE Foundation in 1998.

The CSE crowd would probably settle for anything that got rid of the progressive income tax, but it favors the flat tax to restore "honesty and decency to the tax code."[28] To join its campaign, CSE asks people to download two copies of Form 1040 from its Web page, scrawl the words "Scrap the Code" across them, and then mail them to leaders of the House and Senate: "Now is the time to send a message to Washington that enough is enough."[29]

No one disputes that the current income tax system needs an overhaul. And that Washington is responsible for the mess. "No sane individual, if asked to start from scratch, would come up with the current tax code in a million years," Todd Tiahrt, a Kansas Republican, noted on the House floor in 1999. "The tax code is baffling even to the experts."[30]

But it is misleading to suggest, as proponents of the flat tax and sales tax do, that those levies alone would somehow make the system simpler and easier for everyone. The truth is, both taxes would be subject to the same pressures and special-interest lobbying that have had a field day with the progressive income tax. Not to mention what adoption of either tax would do to the nation's social fabric.

So what to do?

As it happens, there is a way out. And it's simpler than anything being bandied about in Washington today.

STARTING OVER

The accusations are leveled all the time by critics of the income tax. They say that people who want a progressive rate structure are envious, that they want to punish the successful, that they want to promote class warfare, and that they want to redistribute money from those who work to those who don't.

Not true.

Throughout history, bad policies have flowed from government decision makers who failed to identify the real problems and hence asked the wrong questions. In the case of America's tax system, there's only one critical question, and all others grow out of it:

Can a democratic society survive when there is not just a gap, but an unbridgeable chasm, between the have-mores and the have-lesses, when one person has more money left over after paying taxes on income from one day of work than others will earn in their entire lifetime, when the wealth of one exceeds the wealth of millions?

If the answer to that question is yes, then it matters not what kind of tax Washington enacts. If the answer is no, then there's only one tax — the progressive income tax — that can at least limit the gaps in income and wealth.

Listen to Barry Bluestone, professor of political economy at Northeastern University in Boston: "When the gap gets bigger, it's harder for the rich to empathize with the poor and vice versa. You go from having a class economy to a caste economy. What I fear is that we will have a rending of the social fabric. It will be very difficult to bring everyone in society together."[1]

A century ago, the Progressives and the Populists saw this situation up close. Their solution was the income tax.

But, you ask, what about all those charges by members of Congress that the existing tax code — and by inference the progressive income tax — is too complicated, that what's needed is a "simple" flat tax or sales tax?

Nonsense. Any tax can be as simple or as complex as Washington wants.

Regardless of the kind of tax system, the IRS, reeling from years of congressional attacks, budget cutbacks, and reorganizations, needs to be recast one final time.

It should be divided into two separate and distinct agencies: one that is service oriented, to answer questions and help taxpayers with their returns; the other to enforce the tax law vigorously but fairly. No individual or government agency should be expected to behave like Mr. Rogers one day and Hulk Hogan the next.

As for the tax system itself, its critics are correct on one point: The existing Internal Revenue Code should be scrapped. Then the tax-writers should start over, crafting a fresh, simplified progressive tax based on the principle that a tax system is intended solely to raise revenue to run the government, not to encourage behavior, whether to buy a home or to give money to charity.

The basic elements:

1. Eliminate all credits and deductions — including write-offs for charitable contributions, medical expenses, state and local taxes, gambling losses, and mortgage interest payments.
2. Treat all income the same, whether from wages or capital gains. There should be no distinction between a dollar

earned by someone who teaches elementary school and a
dollar earned by a speculator in pork bellies.

3. Institute withholding everywhere — on dividends, interest,
   and the sale of capital assets. The reason: Taxpayer compliance is in the 90 percent range wherever there is withholding.

4. Establish a dozen or more rates that rise as income goes up.
   With the elimination of all deductions, the rates could be
   arranged so those in the middle and near the bottom would
   not be hit with a tax increase. The bottom rate, now 15 percent, could begin in the single digits. As for the top rate, it
   would not come close to the 91 percent of earlier decades.

5. Cancel all existing tax code preferences — from the tax
   exemption for securities issued by state and local governments to tax-free fringe benefits provided to employees by
   corporations.

6. Remove tax offenses from the criminal code. Treat tax evasion and nonfiling as civil matters with draconian economic
   penalties that remove the profit motive.

While the information required for such a tax might not fit on
a postcard to be mailed on April 15, it could be confined to one side
of a single sheet of paper.

If you still have doubts, ponder this:

During the 1950s and 1960s, more Americans moved into the
middle class than at any time in the nation's history — this during
a period when the top tax rate was 91 percent and wealth concentration was at a much lower level.

And if we do nothing?

Then the United States will become a test case to determine
whether a democratic society can exist in a nation where wealth
and income are concentrated in a comparatively few hands, where
taxes fall most onerously on those least able to pay.

NOTES

NOTE ON STATISTICAL SOURCES: Most statistics used in this book came from government sources. They include the U.S. Internal Revenue Service, Annual Budget of the U.S. Government, the Economic Report of the President, the Bureau of Labor Statistics, the Bureau of Economic Analysis, the Census Bureau, and the Securities and Exchange Commission. In the case of IRS data, the statistics were drawn from the most recent year available.

PROLOGUE: AN AMERICAN ORIGINAL

1. *New York Times,* July 12, 1989, p. B2.
2. Annie S. Daniel, "The Wreck of the Home: How Wearing Apparel Is Fashioned in the Tenements," *Charities* 14, no. 1, (Apr. 1905), pp. 624–29.
3. *National Income Tax Magazine,* Oct. 1928, p. 370.

CHAPTER 1. THE TAX CHEAT NEXT DOOR

1. Docket no. 97N083535, Criminal Court of the City of New York, Part AP1, County of New York.
2. *Jocelyne Wildenstein vs. Alec Nathan Wildenstein et al.,* State Supreme Court, New York County, Index No. 350381/97.
3. *Jocelyne Wildenstein vs. 19 East 64th St. Corp.,* State Supreme Court, New York County, index no. 11793/97.
4. *New York Law Journal,* Mar. 16, 1998.
5. *Wildenstein vs. Wildenstein.*
6. Ibid.
7. Ibid.
8. *New York Law Journal,* Mar. 16, 1998.
9. Ibid.
10. *Wildenstein vs. Wildenstein.*
11. Ibid.
12. General Accounting Office (GAO), "Tax Administration: IRS Does Not Investigate Most High-Income Nonfilers," GGD-91-36, Mar. 1991.

13. Ibid.
14. Newspaper Enterprise Association, Cleveland, Ohio, authors' files.
15. *Congressional Record,* June 8, 1937, p. 5459.
16. *Philadelphia Inquirer,* Nov. 16, 1979.
17. *U.S. News & World Report,* Apr. 11, 1983, p. 54.
18. *Wall Street Journal,* Apr. 10, 1984.
19. *Chicago Tribune,* Oct. 23, 1986.
20. *Charleston Gazette,* Mar. 10, 1994.
21. M2 Presswire, Speech in Des Moines, Ia., July 20, 1999.
22. GAO, "IRS' Tax Year 1994 EIC Compliance Study," GAO/GGD-98-150, pp. 23–24.
23. GAO, "Earned Income Credit Noncompliance," GAO/t-GGD-97-105, p. 6.
24. Deposition of Stanley Schulman, *Winnick vs. Schulman,* Los Angeles County Superior Court, case no. BC-093090.
25. Deposition of Stanley Schulman, *Winnick vs. Schulman.*
26. Declaration of James J. Farrell, *Winnick vs. Albemarle Investments,* Los Angeles County Superior Court, case no. BC-138801.
27. Deposition of Stanley Schulman, *Winnick vs. Schulman.*
28. Ibid.
29. Examination of judgment debtor Stanley Schulman, *Winnick vs. Schulman.*
30. Ibid.
31. Ibid.
32. Ibid.
33. Ibid.
34. Deposition of Stanley Schulman, *Winnick vs. Schulman.*
35. Ibid.
36. Examination of judgment debtor Stanley Schulman, *Winnick vs. Schulman.*
37. Examination of Jean Schulman, *Winnick vs. Schulman.*
38. Deposition of Stanley Schulman, *Winnick vs. Schulman.*
39. Ibid.
40. Ibid.
41. *The Business Press,* Nov. 22, 1999.
42. *Red Herring* magazine, July 1998.
43. Deposition of Sujatha Subramanian, *Tata Consultancy Services vs. Syntel Inc.,* U.S. District Court, Detroit, Civil Action No. 90-CV-71155.
44. Deposition of Rengaswamy Mohan, *Tata Consultancy Services vs. Syntel Inc.*
45. Ibid.
46. Authors' files.
47. Authors' interview.
48. GAO, "Tax Administration: IRS Can Better Pursue Noncompliant Sole Proprietors," Aug. 2, 1994, GAO/GGD-94-175.

49. Authors' interview with anonymous source.
50. United Press International, Apr. 14, 1992.
51. *Dixon vs. Commissioner of Internal Revenue,* U.S. Tax Court, Docket No. 8767–98.

CHAPTER 2. TREASURE ISLANDS

1. *Saturday Evening Post,* Feb. 20, 1960, p. 26.
2. Authors' interview.
3. www.offshorebiz.com
4. www.arweb.com/cr/business/finance
5. www.stockscape.com
6. www.online.offshore.com.ai/publicity
7. www.fc99.ai
8. www.shorex.com, Conference Programme, Dec. 1997.
9. *Mondaq Business Briefing,* Apr. 4, 1997.
10. *Harmful Tax Competition: An Emerging Global Issue,* Organisation for Economic Cooperation and Development, Paris, 1998, p. 17.
11. Ibid., p. 22.
12. www.arweb.com.blz.magna
13. Ibid.
14. E-mail, Magna Charta Society to the authors, Apr. 3, 1998.
15. Authors' interview.
16. www.taxamnesty.com/GATE/Magna%20Charta/ronbio.htm
17. Authors' interview.
18. www.arweb.com.blz.magna
19. E-mail, Magna Charta Society to the authors, May 21, 1998.
20. Authors' interview.
21. E-mail, Magna Charta Society to the authors, May 21, 1998.
22. *New York Times,* Aug. 3, 1999, p. 1.
23. www. stockscape.com/newsletters/pugsley
24. *U.S. vs. Barry Trupin,* United States District Court for the Southern District of New York, case no. 97 CR 0097.
25. www. offshore-manual.com
26. *The Oxford Club Communiqué,* May 15, 1999, p. 7.
27. Ibid.
28. "The Unique Benefits You'll Receive as a 'Citizen' of the Sovereign Society," Oxford Club mailing, July 1999.
29. "The Desk of John Pugsley," July 1999, *Communiqué.*
30. *Washington Post,* Aug. 10, 1981.
31. Mailing, July 1998 *Communiqué,* "Meet the International Advisory Board of the Sovereign Society."

32. www.stockscape.com, excerpt from May 1996 issue (No. 76) of *John Pugsley's Journal.*
33. "The Unique Benefits."
34. Ibid.
35. Ibid.
36. www.domini-inc.com
37. Authors' interview.
38. General Accounting Office, "Private Banking: Raul Salinas, Citibank, and Alleged Money Laundering" (Letter Report, Oct. 30, 1998, GAO/OSI-99-1).
39. www.kpmgbelize.com
40. *New York Daily News,* Jan. 10, 1999.
41. *New York vs. William (Waldemar) Jezler et al.,* Indictment Nos. 3738/95, 3739/95, 3740/95, New York State Supreme Court, New York County.
42. *New York Daily News,* Jan. 10, 1999.
43. www.rpifs.com
44. www.nationalapi.com
45. Ibid.
46. www.ipc-offshore.com
47. Ibid.
48. www.offshore-outlook.com
49. www.vocal.net/offshore
50. www.adminconsult.com
51. www.mtlion.com/pill.html
52. *Tax Notes,* Jan. 25, 1999, p. 443.
53. Ibid.
54. *Congressional Record,* Sept. 19, 1995, E1804.
55. *U.S. vs. Ronald L. Chappell et al.,* U.S. District Court for the Eastern District of California, case no. CR-S-97-216.
56. Press release, United States Attorney, Eastern District of California, Aug. 20, 1998.
57. Ibid., Mar. 5, 1999.
58. Ibid.
59. www.ehmt.com/belize.htm
60. Ibid.
61. www.oxfordclub.com, *Pillars of Wealth*
62. Letter from the chairman, Oxford Club 1996 Annual Report, p. 1.
63. Oxford Club 1996 Annual Report, p. 4.
64. Oxford Club, "Pillars of Wealth" pamphlet, Pillar III.
65. www.oxfordclub.com
66. www.worth.com
67. Welcome letter from James Boxley Cooke, honorary chairman, Oxford Club.

68. Ibid.
69. Oxford Club 1996 Annual Report, p. 4.
70. Ibid.
71. *South Florida Business Journal,* Dec. 10, 1990.
72. *Sunday Times,* London, Nov. 17, 1991.
73. Ibid.
74. Oxford Club 1996 Annual Report, p. 20.
75. Ibid.
76. Ibid., p. 25.
77. Ibid., p. 22.
78. Ibid., p. 29.
79. *Washington Post,* Nov. 6, 1980.
80. *Communiqué,* May 1997, p. iii.
81. Ibid., p. iv.

CHAPTER 3. THE INTERNET: AVOIDANCE MADE EASY

1. Absolute Asset Trust Protection Services, www.arweb.com
2. www.offshoresecrets.com
3. Ibid.
4. Ibid.
5. www.go-offshore.com
6. Ibid.
7. Ibid.
8. www.ensynergy.com.shelfshop/
9. www.antiguaibc.com
10. www.global-money.com
11. *Selected Tax Policy Implications of Global Electronic Commerce,* U.S. Department of the Treasury, Office of Tax Policy, Nov. 1996, p. 20.
12. www.offshoretrust.nu
13. Ibid.
14. Ibid.
15. *Selected Tax Policy Implications,* p. 40.
16. James A. Dorn, ed., *The Future of Money in the Information Age,* Washington, D.C., Cato Institute, 1997.
17. *Tax Notes,* Mar. 18, 1996, p. 1591.
18. *Selected Tax Policy Implications,* p. 38.
19. Dorn, *The Future of Money.*
20. *Tax Notes,* Nov. 10, 1997, p. 664.
21. Simon Singh, *The Code Book* (New York: Doubleday, 1999), p. 293.
22. http://ul.net/~offshore
23. *PC/Computing,* Nov. 1, 1999, p. 159.

24. *Network Solutions,* July 1, 1999, p. 17.

25. Singh, *The Code Book,* p. 296.

26. *Washington Post,* Apr. 3, 1995.

27. *Network Solutions,* July 1, 1999, p. 17.

28. www.endtaxes.com

29. http://gpmt.com

30. www.privacyworld.com

31. www.offshoreglobe.com

32. www.seychelles.net/intatt/offshore_banking.html

33. Ibid.

34. *Private Banker International,* Oct. 11, 1999, p. 4.

35. www.SwissNetBanking.com

36. Ibid.

37. *USA Today,* Sept. 20, 1999.

38. www.SwissNetBanking.com

39. www.caribbank.com

40. Ibid.

41. Authors' interview.

42. Ibid.

43. Ibid.

44. www.caribbank.com

45. Ibid.

46. Authors' interview.

47. Ibid.

48. www.aftab.com/guestbook/guestbook.html

49. *First Fidelity Bank vs. Orka Associates Inc. et al.,* New Jersey Superior Court, Essex County, case no. L-15434-93.

50. Ibid.

51. Ibid.

52. In re Gregory Chusid, U.S. Bankruptcy Court, Philadelphia, case no. 96-16472.

53. *The Record,* Bergen County, July 2, 1997.

54. *First Fidelity Bank vs. Orka Associates.*

55. *First Fidelity Bank vs. Gregory Chusid et al.,* New Jersey Superior Court, Bergen County, case no. BER-L-10905-94.

56. Ibid.

57. Ibid.

58. Ibid.

59. Ibid.

60. Ibid.

61. Ibid.

62. In re Gregory Chusid.

63. Ibid.
64. 157 N.J.L.J. 1208.
65. Authors' interview.
66. www.cbcltd.com
67. Ibid.
68. Ibid.
69. Ibid.

CHAPTER 4. CONGRESS'S HIDDEN AGENDA

1. *Congressional Record,* May 5, 1998, S4223.
2. Ibid.
3. Associated Press, Apr. 29, 1998.
4. *Washington Post,* Apr. 30, 1998.
5. *Wall Street Journal,* Dec. 9, 1999.
6. *Congressional Record,* May 5, 1998, S4337.
7. Ibid., S4225.
8. Ibid., May 6, 1998, S4409.
9. Ibid., S4406.
10. *Tax Notes,* May 4, 1998.
11. *Los Angeles Times,* May 3, 1998.
12. *Memphis Commercial Appeal,* May 1, 1998.
13. *Tax Notes,* June 29, 1998, p. 1740.
14. *Congressional Record,* May 7, 1998, S4520.
15. Ibid.
16. Ibid., June 21, 1994, S7201.
17. Ibid.
18. *Tax Notes,* July 31, 1995, p. 510.
19. *Congressional Record,* Nov. 15, 1995, S17072.
20. *Tax Notes,* July 24, 1995, p. 382.
21. Ibid., Aug. 14, 1995, p. 850.
22. Ibid., May 1, 1995, p. 659.
23. Ibid.
24. Ibid., July 24, 1995, p. 381.
25. Ibid., Oct. 30, 1995, p. 521.
26. Ibid., May 25, 1998, p. 935.
27. www.house.gov/natcommirs/main.htm
28. Ibid.
29. Ibid.
30. www.house.gov/natcommirs/section3
31. *Tax Notes,* June 30, 1997, p. 1804.
32. Ibid.

33. Ibid., Dec. 13, 1999, p. 1360.
34. Ibid.
35. www.ustreas.gov/tigta
36. Ibid.
37. *New York Times,* Nov. 18, 1999, p. 1.
38. News release, Senator Dick Lugar, Jan. 20, 1999.
39. *Congressional Record,* Apr. 10, 1997, E633.
40. Ibid., Apr. 15, 1999, H2058.
41. *New York Daily News,* June 18, 1998.
42. *Washington Post,* Aug. 4, 1995.
43. *Tax Notes,* Feb. 16, 1998, p. 883.
44. *Philadelphia Inquirer,* Apr. 10, 1988.
45. *New York Times,* Sept. 28, 1986, p. 1.
46. *Congressional Record,* Sept. 27, 1986, S13922.
47. *New York Times,* June 9, 1986, p. 18.
48. www.opensecrets.org
49. *Tax Notes,* Oct. 26, 1998, p. 405.
50. Ibid., Sept. 29, 1997, p. 1780.
51. *Palm Beach Post,* Apr. 31, 1997.
52. *Mother Jones,* Nov. 1998, p. 56.
53. www.amway.com
54. *Forbes,* Oct. 16, 1995, p. 22.
55. *Congressional Record,* June 9, 1995, E1222.
56. *Tax Notes,* Apr. 3, 1995, p. 7.
57. Ibid.
58. *Forbes,* July 26, 1999, p. 110.
59. Ibid.
60. Seventh Annual Message of Theodore Roosevelt, Dec. 3, 1907, *A Compilation of the Messages and Papers of the Presidents,* vol. 16, New York, Bureau of National Literature, p. 7464.
61. *Congressional Record,* Feb. 25, 1999, E295.
62. Ibid., Mar. 25, 1999, E579.
63. Ibid., Jan. 6, 1999, H234.
64. Ibid., May 22, 1998, E974.
65. Ibid., Aug. 5, 1999, S10309.
66. Ibid., Mar. 25, 1999, E579.
67. "Today's National Polls," *National Journal,* July 30, 1999.
68. *Money,* Jan. 1997, p. 78.
69. *Congressional Record,* Apr. 16, 1996, H3456.
70. Ibid., Jan. 26, 1995, S1558.
71. Ibid., Apr. 16, 1996. H3458.
72. *Tax Notes,* June 9, 1997, p. 1294.

73. Ibid., Apr. 20, 1998, p. 348.
74. Ibid., Jan. 26, 1998, p. 376.
75. *Congressional Record,* July 31, 1997, S8415.
76. *Practical Accountant,* Oct. 1997.
77. *Tax Notes,* Dec. 21, 1998, p. 1567.
78. Ibid.
79. Ibid.
80. *Wall Street Journal,* Sept. 15, 1999, p. 1.

CHAPTER 5. PURSUING THE POWERLESS

1. *New York Times,* Feb. 24, 1999, p. B1.
2. Ibid.
3. Ibid.
4. *Morning Call,* Allentown, Pa., Feb. 27, 1997.
5. *U.S. News & World Report,* Aug. 1, 1983, p. 31.
6. GAO, "IRS Audits: Weaknesses in Selecting and Conducting Correspondence Audits," GGD-99-48, Mar. 31, 1999.
7. Ibid.
8. Ibid.
9. Ibid.
10. Ibid.
11. Ibid.
12. Ibid.
13. Ibid.
14. *Psychology Today,* Mar. 1982, p. 74.
15. *New York Times,* Feb. 13, 2000, p. 1.
16. Authors' interview.
17. "IRS Oversight," hearings before the Senate Finance Committee, Apr. 30, 1998, p. 159.
18. Ibid., pp. 133–34.
19. Ibid., pp. 134–35.
20. Ibid., p. 135.
21. Ibid.
22. Ibid., p. 139.
23. Ibid.
24. Ibid.
25. *New York Times,* Apr. 17, 1997, p. 1.
26. *Business Week,* Mar. 31, 1962, p. 86.
27. Ibid., Feb. 8, 1964, p. 96.
28. *Tax Notes,* Oct. 22, 1984, p. 369.
29. *Discover,* May 1986, p. 46.

30. *Philadelphia Inquirer,* June 23, 1985.

31. GAO, "Tax Administration: Information on IRS' Philadelphia Service Center," GAO/GGD-86-25FS, Nov. 22, 1985, p. 33.

32. Ibid., "Tax Systems Modernizations — IRS Needs to Resolve Certain Issues with Its Integrated Case Processing System," GAO/GGD/AIMD-97-31, Jan. 1997.

33. *CPA Journal,* Nov. 1990, p. 16.

34. *New York Times,* Feb. 10, 1997, p. D1.

35. Testimony of Gene L. Dodaro, assistant controller, General Accounting Office, before the Senate Governmental Affairs Committee, Mar. 26, 1996.

36. *Congressional Press Releases,* Mar. 14, 1996.

37. *New York Times,* Jan. 31, 1997, p. 1.

38. Ibid.

39. *Government Computer News,* Dec. 14, 1998.

40. *U.S. vs. Steven M. Javie,* U.S. District Court, Philadelphia, case no. 98-CR-328-1.

41. *U.S. vs. Jesse Ray Kersey,* U.S. District Court, Norfolk, Va., case no. 97-CR-27.

42. *U.S. vs. George T. Toliver,* U.S. District Court, Harrisonburg, Va., case no. 97-CR-10006.

43. Ibid.

44. *U.S. vs. Steven M. Javie.*

45. Ibid.

46. Ibid.

47. Ibid.

48. Ibid.

49. *Philadelphia Inquirer,* Jan. 16, 1999.

50. Correspondence with authors.

51. Ibid.

52. Ibid.

53. *Sports Illustrated,* Apr. 20, 1998, p. 92.

54. Correspondence with authors.

55. Authors' interview.

56. Ibid.

57. Authors' interview.

58. www.MopanRiverResort.com

59. *Tulsa World,* Aug. 8, 1986.

60. Ibid., Feb. 19, 1998.

61. *Vancouver Sun,* Feb. 8, 1997.

62. Ibid.

63. *Tulsa World,* Jan. 4, 1998.

64. www.belizereport.com

65. www.MopanRiverResort.com

66. Ibid.

67. Ibid.

68. *U.S. vs. Joseph R. Ross,* U.S. District Court, Northern District of Oklahoma, case no. 86-CR-91-C.

69. Dow Jones News Wire, Sept. 30, 1983.

70. Authors' files.

71. *New York,* Jan. 25, 1999, p. 37.

72. Final Report of the Committee on Governmental Affairs, U.S. Senate, 105th Cong., 2d sess., Report 105-167; Vol. 1, "Investigation of Illegal or Improper Activities in Connection with 1996 Federal Election Campaigns," Mar. 10, 1998, p. 524.

73. *New York Daily News,* Dec. 15, 1999.

74. Ibid., Jan. 3, 1999.

75. "Biz Buzz Show," CNNFN, Dec. 8, 1999.

76. *Denise Joy Rich vs. Alexander R. Hackel et al.,* New York State Supreme Court, New York County, case no. 100710-93.

77. Ibid.

78. Ibid.

CHAPTER 6. A CULTURE OF DECEIT

1. Hearing before the Subcommittee on Human Resources of the Committee on Ways and Means, House of Representatives,104th Congress, 1st sess., Part 1 of 2, p. 379.

2. *Who's Who Among American High School Students,* 29th Annual Survey of High Achievers, 1998.

3. The Center for Academic Integrity, www.academicintegrity.org

4. *Chicago Tribune,* Mar. 7, 1999.

5. *U.S. News & World Report,* Nov. 22, 1999, p. 55.

6. www.apluspaper.com

7. www.junglepage.com

8. www.schoolsucks.com

9. www.cyberessays.com

10. www.a1-termpaper.com

11. www.Lazystudents.com

12. http://members.xoom.com/downcrap/index.htm

13. www.inconnect.com/~rex/Cheats.html

14. Ibid.

15. Ibid.

16. *New York Times,* Dec. 13, 1999, p. B1.

17. *The American School Board Journal,* Dec. 1997, p. 28.

18. *New York Times,* Apr. 23, 1995; Sec. 4, p. 16.

19. Ibid., Feb. 18, 1998, p. 1.

20. *Bucknellian,* Feb. 16, 1995.

21. *New York Times,* July 7, 1995, p. 24.

22. Alvin Kernan, *In Plato's Cave* (New Haven and London: Yale University Press, 1999), pp. 278–79.

23. *New York Times,* Feb. 18, 1998, p. 1.

24. Authors' interview with confidential source.

25. *Insurance Information Institute Reports,* July 1997.

26. Ibid.

27. *U.S. vs. Louisa Lilawati Soman,* U.S. District Court, Sacramento, California, case no. CR-98-036.

28. General Accounting Office, "Debt Collection: Improved Reporting Needed on Billions of Dollars in Delinquent Debt and Agency Collection Performance," June 1997.

29. U.S. Department of Agriculture, Office of Inspector General, "Food and Nutrition Service Child and Adult Care Food Program: National Report on Program Abuses," audit report no. 27601-7-SF, Aug. 1999.

30. Deposition of Usha Balakrishnan Mohan, *Tata Consultancy Services vs. Syntel Inc.,* U.S. District Court, Detroit, civil action no. 90-CV-71155.

31. Federal Document Clearing House, Congressional testimony; Statement of William R. Yates before the Subcommittee on Immigration and Claims, House Judiciary Committee, May 5, 1999.

32. Ibid.

33. Ibid.

34. Ibid.

35. U.S. Department of Labor, Office of Inspector General, "The Department of Labor's Foreign Labor Certification Programs: The System Is Broken and Needs to Be Fixed," report no. 06-96-002-03-321, May 22, 1996.

36. Authors' interview with anonymous source.

37. Securities and Exchange Commission, Litigation Release no. 15680, Mar. 25, 1998.

38. Tape-recorded telephone conversation of March 25, 1996, presented to the House Government Reform and Oversight Committee.

39. *New York Times,* May 2, 1998, p. A15.

40. *Los Angeles Times,* July 11, 1999.

41. *Philadelphia Daily News,* July 14, 1999.

42. *Washington Post,* Jan. 27, 1998.

43. *New York Times,* Jan. 27, 1998.

44. *London Guardian,* Jan. 19, 1994.

45. 93 S. Ct. 595.

46. Ibid.

47. Ibid.

48. Ibid.

49. U.S. Congress: Hearings before the Committee on the Judiciary, U.S. Senate, 1st sess., "Nomination of Zoe E. Baird," Jan. 19 and 21, 1993, p. 73.

50. Senate Judiciary Committee hearing on Zoe E. Baird nomination, p. 98.
51. Ibid., p. 24.
52. Ibid., pp. 78–79.
53. Ibid., p. 138.
54. Ibid., p. 140.
55. *New York Times,* Jan. 15, 1993.
56. Ibid., Jan. 16, 1993.
57. Senate Judiciary Committee hearing on Zoe E. Baird nomination, p. 80.
58. Ibid., p. 81.
59. *Chicago Tribune,* June 13, 1993.
60. *Buffalo News,* Jan. 27, 1993.

CHAPTER 7. CONGRESS'S PLAN TO RAISE YOUR TAXES

1. Randolph E. Paul, *Taxation in the United States* (Boston: Little, Brown, 1954), p. 108.
2. Emil Lengyel, *1,000 Years of Hungary* (New York: John Day, 1958), p. 32.
3. *Congressional Record,* Mar. 8, 1999, p. S2381.
4. Ibid., Mar. 2, 1999, p. H872.
5. Ibid., June 15, 1999, p. H4229.
6. *USA Today,* June 19, 1998.
7. Andrew W. Mellon, *Taxation: The People's Business* (New York: Macmillan, 1924), p. 83.
8. *Congressional Record,* Mar. 22, 1939, p. 3136.
9. *Atlantic Monthly,* Aug. 1952, p. 76.
10. http://flattax.house.gov/
11. *Congressional Record,* Nov. 7, 1997, p. E2204.
12. Ibid., Apr. 15, 1997, p. S3195.
13. Ibid., Mar. 6, 1995, p. E522.
14. Ibid., Mar. 6, 1997, p. H783.
15. www.senate.gov/~jec/flatax.html
16. Flat-Rate Tax Hearings before the Senate Finance Committee, 97th Congress, Second Session, Sept. 28–29, 1982, Part 1 of 2, p. 86.
17. *St. Petersburg Times,* Dec. 13, 1987.
18. Ibid.
19. "Talkback Live," CNN, Aug. 24, 1999.
20. *Congressional Press Releases,* Apr. 16, 1999.
21. *Congressional Record,* Apr. 15, 1999, p. S3765.
22. *Orange County Register,* Oct. 20, 1999.
23. Associated Press, Aug. 31, 1999.
24. *Atlanta Journal and Constitution,* Sept. 7, 1999.
25. *Boston Globe,* Feb. 24, 1998.

26. Cox News Service, Oct. 22, 1997.

27. Citizens for a Sound Economy Educational Foundation Inc., Form 990, Internal Revenue Service, 1998, Schedule A, Statement 14.

28. www.cse.org

29. Ibid.

30. *Congressional Record,* Feb. 10, 1999, p. H542.

EPILOGUE: STARTING OVER

1. Authors' interview.

INDEX